INTERNATIONAL LAW: UNITED STATES FOREIGN RELATIONS LAW

by

PHILLIP R. TRIMBLE
Professor of Law Emeritus
University of California, Los Angeles

TURNING POINT SERIES®

New York, New York
FOUNDATION PRESS
2002

Mat #40040585

Turning Point Series is a registered trademark
used herein under license.

COPYRIGHT © 2002 By FOUNDATION PRESS
395 Hudson Street
New York, NY 10014
Phone Toll Free 1–877–888–1330
Fax (212) 367–6799
fdpress.com

ISBN 1–58778–406–8

 TEXT IS PRINTED ON 10% POST
CONSUMER RECYCLED PAPER

TURNING POINT SERIES

CIVIL PROCEDURE

Civil Procedure: Class Actions by Linda S. Mullenix, University of Texas (Available 2002)

Civil Procedure: Economics of Civil Procedure by Robert G. Bone, Boston University (Available 2002)

Civil Procedure: Preclusion in Civil Actions by DavidL. Shapiro, Harvard University (2001)

Civil Procedure: Jury Process by Nancy S. Marder, Illinois Institute of Technology (Available 2002)

Civil Procedure: Territorial Jurisdiction and Venue by Kevin M. Clermont, Cornell (1999)

CONSTITUTIONAL LAW

Constitutional Law: Equal Protection by Louis M. Seidman, Georgetown University (Available 2002)

Constitutional Law: Religion Clause by Daniel O. Conkle, Indiana University, Bloomington (Available 2002)

CRIMINAL LAW

Criminal Law: Model Penal Code by Markus D. Dubber, State University of New York, Buffalo

INTERNATIONAL LAW

International Law: United States Foreign Relations Law by Phillip R. Trimble, UCLA

LEGISLATION

Legislation: Statutory Interpretation: Twenty Questions by Kent R. Greenawalt, Columbia University (1999)

PROPERTY

Property: Takings by David Dana, Northwestern University and Thomas Merrill, Northwestern University (Available 2002)

CORPORATE/SECURITIES

Securities Law: Insider Trading by Stephen Bainbridge, UCLA (1999)

TORTS

Torts: Proximate Cause by Joseph A. Page, Georgetown University (Available 2002)

Dedicated to
Ellis Green, John Wilson and Stella Ong
and
All the UCLA Law School Staff who helped
sustain my career at the Law School

*

PREFACE

As the impact of globalism accelerates, virtually all Americans are involved, directly or indirectly, in international transactions, and their communities are regularly affected by developments abroad. These developments will inevitably stimulate reactions by governments, and accordingly will increase the prominence of foreign policy, international law and international institutions. As a result American lawyers and everyone who must deal with them need to understand the framework in which American foreign policy and international law is made.

This book explains the legal structure and process under which the United States makes international law and more generally participates in international relations. The most perplexing aspect of this subject, especially to foreign observers, is the uncertain allocation of decision-making authority between the President and Congress. The President obviously dominates the making of American foreign policy, but his role has been deeply controversial throughout our history and remains contested in important aspects today. In addition to providing a comprehensive survey of the law governing American foreign relations and international law-making by the United States, this book explains the power that the President has exercised for two hundred years in

terms of a hitherto denigrated clause of the Costi-
tution, the Vesting Clause,[1] whose meaning I will defend in light of the eighteenth century context of the
drafting of the Constitution. In the process I bring
together in a synergistic way three theories of constitutional interpretation—Original Intent, Historical Practice and Functionalism—that have in the
past been presented as independent and unconnected.

My audience includes (1) American students
and scholars of international law, constitutional law,
foreign policy, and political science and economy; (2)
foreign students, lawyers, officials and diplomats
who are interested in—and who are often perplexed
by—how the U.S. government makes decisions relating to its foreign policy, and (3) general practitioners
of law everywhere who have a professional concern
with these subjects. This book can usefully serve as
a text or supplement in courses dealing with national security law, foreign relations law, international
law, and U.S. foreign policy.

In preparing this book I have benefitted from
teaching courses and seminars in the field at the
UCLA, Stanford and Michigan law schools, and from
my experience in practicing some aspects of this law
as a lawyer for the U.S. Department of State, as the
American Ambassador to Nepal, and as a consultant
to the U.S. Arms Control and Disarmament Agency.
I have drawn on my publications in the American

---

1. "The executive Power shall be vested in a President of
the United States...." Art II. Sec. 1, U.S. Const. In the famous
Steel Seizure case, Justice Jackson peremptorily—and careless-
ly—dismissed this source of authority. See *infra* Chap. 1.

Journal of International Law, the Columbia, Harvard, Michigan, Pennsylvania, Northwestern, Iowa and UCLA Law Reviews, The Yale, Chicago, Berkeley, and Davis Journals of International Law, the Encyclopedia of the American Constitution, the Encyclopedia of the American Presidency, and the Encyclopedia of Arms Control.

Most fundamentally I have inherited the pioneering scholarship of Lou Henkin, whose 1972 Foreign Affairs and the United States Constitution established the field of foreign relations law as a distinct area of scholarly study and thereby set the foundation for all our efforts in this area of law. I have also especially profited from the subsequent enrichment of the field reflected in Mike Glennon's Constitutional Diplomacy (1990), Harold Koh's The National Security Constitution (1990), John Ely's War and Responsibility (1993), Tom Franck's Foreign Policy by Congress (1979, coauthored with Edward Wiesband), John Jackson's books and articles on international economic law, and, since the first drafts of this manuscript were prepared, the refreshing new scholarship of Curtis Bradley, Jack Goldsmith and John Yoo. In this book I have generally eschewed footnotes to sources other than statutes, judicial decisions and quoted material. At the end of each Chapter I have appended a Bibliographic Note that will acknowledge my sources and introduce the reader to a selection of writing, especially recent writing, that will enable her/him to explore the particular areas more deeply.

Beyond their scholarly work several colleagues have been especially important to my career. I owe special debts of gratitude to Lou Henkin and Mike Glennon for their support, counsel and advice over the past 20 years since I entered the Academy. Harold Koh and Tom Frank have been equally supportive colleagues in my ventures into this field and, like Lou and Mike, have offered their perspectives from which I have benefitted even in dissent. Our dialogues have extended my thinking and without them this book would not have been written.

I also thank my UCLA Colleague, Kal Raustiala, for his review and perceptive comments on the manuscript, Cheryl L. Kelly, UCLA Law School Class of 2003, for checking the quotations and citations, and my meticulous editors at Foundation Press for forging at least a semblance of consistent usage from an unruly manuscript.

Finally, I want to acknowledge the infinite wisdom and compassion of Valeria Vasilevski which she has expressed throughout the preparation of this manuscript and before.

About the Author

Phillip R. Trimble has been a Professor of Law at UCLA since 1981, teaching in the fields of international law, national security, and international human rights. During 1999-2001 he served as UCLA's Vice Provost for International Studies in the College of Letters & Science.

In the 1960's, Professor Trimble practiced tax and corporate finance law at Cravath, Swaine & Moore. His subsequent government career included service on the staff of the Senate Foreign Relations Committee under Senator Fulbright; Assistant Legal Advisor for Economic and Business Affairs in the Department of State during the Nixon, Ford, and Carter administrations; Counsel to the Mayor and then Deputy Mayor of New York City under Ed Koch; and American Ambassador to Nepal during the Carter Administration.

During his academic career Professor Trimble also was a consultant to the U.S. Arms Control and Disarmament Agency (and counsel to the U.S. delegation to the Nuclear Test Talks), and served on an arbitral panel under the U.S.-Canada Free Trade Agreement. He has been a visiting professor of law at the Stanford and Michigan Law Schools.

His publications have appeared in the Harvard, Stanford, Columbia, Michigan, Pennsylvania, and

UCLA law reviews, the Tax Law Review, the American Alpine Journal, the Himalayan Journal, the Linnean Society Newsletter, Birding, the American Journal of International Law, Comparative Labor Law, and the Yale, Stanford, Chicago, Berkeley, and U.C. Davis international law journals. He is the co-author of one of the leading casebooks on International Law (by Aspen Law and Business).

TABLE OF CONTENTS

PREFACE -- VII

ABOUT THE AUTHOR ------------------------------------ XI

Introduction -- 1

CHAPTER ONE. THE BASIS OF THE PRESIDENT'S
FOREIGN RELATIONS POWER—THE EIGH-
TEENTH CENTURY CONTEXT AND METHODS OF
CONSTITUTIONAL INTERPRETATION ------------ 10

A. **The Eighteenth Century Context** ------- 13

B. **Theories of Interpretation** ----------------- 27

Bibliographic Note----------------------------- 45

CHAPTER TWO. THE PRESIDENT'S FOREIGN RELA-
TIONS POWER—THE SUBSTANTIVE CONTENT 47

Bibliographic Note----------------------------- 78

CHAPTER THREE. CONGRESS ----------------------------- 79

A. **Limitations on Congressional Power** -- 85

B. **Congress' Investigative and Oversight
Powers—Informal Influences As-
serted by Congress**-------------------------- 104

Bibliographic Note----------------------------- 107

CHAPTER FOUR. FORMAL INTERNATIONAL LAWMAK-
ING—THE CONCLUSION OF INTERNATIONAL
AGREEMENTS BY THE UNITED STATES---------- 109

A. **The Conclusion of International
Agreements by the United States—
the Choices Available to the Presi-
dent.** --- 113

TABLE OF CONTENTS

B. Treaty Interpretation and Termination _____ 140

C. The Multiple Domestic Effects of a Treaty _____ 152

D. Formal International Law Making Through the Creation of Customary International Law _____ 177

   Bibliographic Note _____ 189

CHAPTER FIVE. MILITARY FORCE AND INTELLIGENCE OPERATIONS _____ 192

A. Background _____ 195

B. Minor Wars _____ 208

C. Major Wars _____ 216

D. The War Powers Resolution _____ 231

E. U.N. Peacekeeping _____ 243

F. Intelligence Operations _____ 247

   Bibliographic Note _____ 257

CHAPTER SIX. THE SEPTEMBER 11 ATTACKS _____ 260

   Bibliographic Note _____ 283

TABLE OF CASES _____ 285

INDEX _____ 289

INTERNATIONAL LAW:
UNITED STATES
FOREIGN
RELATIONS LAW

*

Introduction

Foreign relations covers a vast spectrum of activities, ranging from the mundane exchange of diplomatic courtesies to waging general war and issuing threats of nuclear annihilation. The following list, drawn from the popular press in the past few years, illustrates the disparate nature of the acts involved: bombing Afghanistan, Belgrade and Iraq; sending troops to Bosnia and the Navy to the Taiwan straits; dispatching covert intelligence agents and special forces to help destroy the Taliban and Al Qaeda; helping prosecute war criminals in the Hague; establishing an American military tribunal to try terrorists; creating international institutions to foster trade in goods and services and to protect intellectual property; imposing economic sanctions on trade with Cuba, Iraq, Iran and Libya; protesting human rights abuses in China, the Middle East and Africa; settling disputes over imported tuna from Mexico and exported beef and bananas to Europe; agreeing to provide oil to North Korea in order to encourage a commitment to nuclear non-proliferation; agreeing to stop nuclear testing; expanding NATO; promulgating new strategic military doctrine and adjusting or withdrawing from arms control treaties; and collecting intelligence information on terrorists and money laundering. The list could be expanded endlessly in both variety and magnitude. In legal terminology, the acts involved in foreign relations include all the steps taken by the United States Government in the conduct of foreign policy and the formation of international law, starting with the formal recognition of statehood and governments, the conduct of diplomatic relations, international negotiations, the conclusion and termination of treaties, joining and voting in international organizations, and the formation of customary international law, in addition to the many activities structured or regulated by international law, such as economic sanctions, military intervention and foreign economic assistance.

Across this entire spectrum of activity the President dominates American participation in foreign relations. Yet much of what the President does requires the support, formally or informally, of Congress; and Congress not infrequently forces the President to act in ways inconsistent with executive policy—often to the consternation or even disbelief of our trading partners and foreign observers. The roles of the President and Congress in directing U.S. foreign policy are often blurred and confusing, especially to those outside the United States who are affected by their decisions. Some of the confusion can be dispelled by understanding the legal structure that underpins the conduct of U.S. foreign relations. The purpose of this book is to explicate that structure. The dominant role of the executive branch will be explained in terms of the Vesting Clause of the U.S. Constitution that vests "the executive Power ... in a President of the United

States,"[1] an authority that has often been shunned in political/legal discourse. My analysis will employ a mix of theories of constitutional interpretation that have often been considered independent of, and even at odds with, one another, but which in my view can also be understood in combination as confirming the language of the constitution and Original Intent of the Founders.

Like all acts of government, the conduct of foreign relations is based on legal authority. The source of that authority is the Constitution. Consequently the focus of this book is on constitutional law, primarily that subfield dealing with the "separation of powers." Foreign relations law refers to the rules, principles, practices and procedures which structure the formation and execution of U.S. foreign policy, including its participation in international law and institutions. Foreign relations law is concerned primarily with allocating decision-making authority—first, between the levels of government, federal and state; and second, among the branches of the federal government, Congress, the President, the Senate and President acting as Treatymakers, and the courts. In this book I deal primarily with who is entitled to make foreign relations decisions, and not so much with the substantive legal consequences of those decisions—i.e. who can recognize the Beijing authorities as the Government of China, who can declare an embargo on trade with Iran, or who can authorize deploying troops in Bosnia; not with the resulting substantive law or legal conse-

1. U.S. Const. Art II sec. 1.

quences of the decision once it is made. Hence my focus is primarily on procedure and process rather than on substantive law.

Most of the disputes over foreign relations authority are between Congress and the President, so this book deals primarily with the principles and rules of law allocating authority between Congress and the President. Because the Constitution as interpreted today gives Congress broad authority (subject to the Bill of Rights) that covers any subject that materially touches foreign policy, as a practical matter we are concerned with defining the scope of presidential power. Presidential power includes areas of exclusive authority into which Congress may not intrude (e.g. appointing officials). Nevertheless, even a power that is exclusive in principle may not always translate into an exclusive power in practice. Foreign relations law is formed in a political context, and is often based on political compromise. The political actors involved are usually more interested in result than in constitutional principle, so it is important to understand that neither branch exercises power, even an exclusive power, in a vacuum. As a result a Senator may very well, as a practical matter, influence the appointment of an official, just as the executive branch may, as a practical matter, draft and induce passage of a law.

In addition to constitutional law, this book covers other sources of law, such as acts of Congress, executive orders and foreign relations common law, which supplement the constitutionally-based structure. For example, I call attention to major delegations of authority by Congress to the President, as in the International Emergency Economic Powers Act and the National Security Act of 1949, legislation governing the courts, such as the Foreign Sovereign Immunities Act of 1976, and federal common law, such as the Act of State doctrine. Because foreign relations are almost exclusively carried out by the federal government, I focus on federal law. The constitutional law of federalism, and the role of the 50 states in foreign relations, is explored only briefly in light of the revival of judicially enforced limits on federal power by the Supreme Court. The main story is of conflict between Congress and the President, and the resulting constitutional common law distributing authority among the political branches.

Foreign relations law is a rather specialized and unusual subfield of law. There are three aspects of this subfield that make it seem anomalous to lawyers trained to think of constitutional law as being made by the courts and found primarily in Supreme Court decisions. First, the legal disputes are usually between political actors, such as the Senate, Congress or a congressional committee, and the President, rather than between private parties. Second, the disputes are normally resolved in a political forum, not the courts. Thus the President may veto legislation because it invades his constitutional prerogatives, or he may sign legislation and state that he will not comply with an objectionable provision. Congress may respond by overriding the veto, passing a resolution or taking other action that indicates its disagreement with the President's legal position, or it may do nothing and thereby seem to acquiesce to the President's assertions. In this context both the President and Congress regard their statements and actions as declaring and making constitutional law, outside the normal law-making process. It may seem anomalous to think of the President as an independent law-making authority, and to regard political compromise between the President and Congress as a kind of common law-making, especially since the politicians in the process are usually acting for transparently "political," rather than "legal," reasons. Furthermore, the resolution of a given dispute may depend on who is politically stronger. President Reagan may have prevailed in a situation where President Clinton would have had to compromise. The triumph of the politically strong may seem antithetical to the rule of law, so foreign relations law may look more like a kind of structured "high politics." On the other hand, all law is grounded in politics and, notwithstanding the political bickering over significant issues, the great body of foreign relations law has proved to be stable over the years, thereby bolstering this field's claim to be properly classified as law.

A third unusual aspect of foreign relations law is that the political branches not only *make* the law in unusual ways, they also assert the right to *interpret* the law that they make. Indeed, the processes of making and interpreting constitutional law are often mixed together in the same acts. For example, when Presidents have declared on signing a bill into law that the executive branch will not apply a particular provision that the President considers to be unconstitutional, the President's statement, and especially any supporting legal memoranda, may outline the legal reasoning supporting the decision in the same way that a court would explain its result in a judicial opinion. Congress may similarly address the constitutional issues in hearings, resolutions and legislative reports.

The political branches have regularly claimed equal authority with the Supreme Court to interpret the Constitution on these matters. For example, President Jackson remarked:

> The opinion of the judges [of the Supreme Court] has no more authority over Congress than the opinion of Congress has over the judges, and on that point the President is independent of both. The authority of the Supreme Court must not, therefore, be permitted to control the Congress or the Executive ... but to have only such influence as the force of their reasoning may deserve.[2]

In any event, most of the issues raised must, as a practical matter, be first resolved internally by Congress—by passing a law Congress implicitly asserts the constitutional authority to do so—and then by

2. Quoted in Louis Fisher, Separation of Powers: Interpretation Outside the Courts, 18 Pepperdine L. Rev. 57, 64 (1990). See generally Louis Fisher, Constitutional Dialogues 233–74 (1988); and Louis Fisher, The Curious Belief in Judicial Supremacy, 25 Suffolk Univ. L. Rev. 85 (1991).

the President—whether to take a given action or comply with a given law—and Congress may in turn respond. The two political branches thus necessarily make at least implicit interpretations of their authority. The issues that arise have thus normally been resolved by political compromise. The courts have been reluctant to decide cases of this type, and the political branches have not been inclined to seek their help anyway. Foreign relations law has accordingly been developed by the political branches, with only occasional comment from the Supreme Court. Consequently, the resulting constitutional law cannot be found in the usual place, Supreme Court decisions, but must be discerned from other, sometimes unconventional, authoritative sources. These sources are found principally in statements of the President, opinions of the Departments of Justice and State, statements of officials and members of Congress, resolutions of Congress, legislative history, historical practice, and the abundant historical lore explicating the Original Intent of the Framers of the Constitution. Collectively they produce a constitutional common law of foreign relations.

Chapter One of this book describes the eighteenth century context in which the Constitution was framed, as background for understanding the structure and text of the document, and the principal methods of constitutional interpretation that we employ to fill out the meaning of the ambiguous constitutional text. Chapters Two and Three cover the powers of the two dominant institutions, the President and Congress, and shows how their powers overlap, conflict and are reconciled. Chapter Four presents the constitutional law applicable to the making of international law by the United States, primarily through the treaty power and by other international agreements, but also through the development of customary international law. Chapter Five deals with the contentious issues of war-making and the conduct of intelligence operations. I do not treat the role of the courts in a separate chapter because the courts play a lesser role in the making and application of U.S. foreign relations law. Instead, I refer to the relevant decisions as they relate to my substantive discussion of executive power, war, treaties, etc. Similarly, I deal with issues of federalism in the chapters on Congress and on international agreements. Chapter Six examines the foreign relations law dimensions of the September 11 attacks.

CHAPTER ONE

THE BASIS OF THE PRESIDENT'S FOREIGN RELATIONS POWER—THE EIGHTEENTH CENTURY CONTEXT AND METHODS OF CONSTITUTIONAL INTERPRETATION

The President dominates American foreign policy and is the principal force shaping the constitutional law governing foreign relations. The starting point for understanding the allocation of foreign relations authority, and specifically the source of presidential foreign affairs power, is the text of the Constitution itself. For some, especially critics of executive policies, much has been made of the fact that the text seems lacking in guidance. Articles I and II catalog specific congressional and executive authorities, but there is no provision expressly stating that the President (or anyone else) has the authority to conduct foreign relations. To the contrary, if one were simply to read the text, it might seem that Congress would have most of the relevant authority because it has most of the enumerated powers. Congress has specifically enumerated powers to regulate foreign commerce; to raise armies and navies and make rules for their regulation; to declare war; to define offenses against the law of nations and piracy; to grant letters of marque and reprisal (a kind of eighteenth century private war-making); to appropriate funds; and to enact all laws necessary and proper to execute *any* power, including presidential powers, of the federal government.

The President, on the other hand, has relatively few express powers specifically relating to foreign relations, and several of those are shared with the Senate or Congress. The President has the power to make treaties and appoint ambassadors, but only with the participation of the Senate. His Commander-in-Chief power is countered by the congressional war, legislative and appropriation powers. The President has the power to receive ambassadors and the duty (and implicitly the power) to take care that laws (including treaties and customary international law) be faithfully executed. But these sparse specific grants in the text hardly cover or explain the vast powers in fact exercised today by the Executive branch of government.

Much ink has been spilled attempting to explain the general phenomenon of presidential dominance—in terms of "inherent" authority, extra-constitutional authority derived from sovereignty, functional justifications, and historic practice that reflects an increasingly powerful executive, especially since World War II. Scholars have debated these theoretical approaches, often, it seems, on the assumption that the text of the Constitution is silent on the location of the foreign relations power because such a power is not specifically mentioned. Much of the debate can be short-circuited, however, and the persistence of presidential dominance explained, by drawing on the flat statement in the first clause of Article II: "[t]he executive Power shall be vested in a President of the United States."[1] This broad, open-ended provision (the Vesting Clause) could literally encompass the power to conduct foreign relations, but, at least in recent decades, a pall over use of the Vesting Clause to explain the President's power has been cast by an often repeated dictum from Justice Jackson in the *Steel Seizure* case:

> The example of . . . unlimited executive power that must have most impressed the forefathers was the prerogative exercised by George III, and the description of its evils in the Declaration of Independence leads me to doubt that they were creating their new Executive in his image. Continental European examples were no more appealing. And if we seek instruction from our own times, we can match it only from the executive powers in those governments we disparagingly describe as totalitarian. I cannot accept the view that this clause is a grant in bulk of all conceivable executive power but regard it as an allocation to the presidential office of the generic powers thereafter stated.[2]

1.   U.S. Const. Art. II sec. 1. This approach is not new. It was defended by Alexander Hamilton in his "Pacificus–Helvidius debate" with James Madison over President Washington's Neutrality Proclamation of 1798.

2.   Youngstown Sheet & Tube Co. v. Sawyer, 343 U.S. 579, 641 (1952) (concurring op.).

One can readily agree with Justice Jackson that the Vesting Clause did not confer the British monarchical prerogative on the President. Indeed, the Framers expressly altered the most important elements of royal prerogative in crafting executive power. They removed at least some part of the War Power from the executive, in addition to removing the royal powers to raise armies, impose taxes and regulate commerce. In addition, they qualified the new President's exercise of the Treaty and Appointment Powers.

At the same time, Justice Jackson's limitation of the scope of Article II to the specifically enumerated functions is simply too narrow to explain all the authority that the President has always exercised. The powers specifically granted to the executive in Article II, like the duty to receive Ambassadors and the Commander in Chief Power, cover only a small part of both traditional and modern executive practice. It is implausible—indeed inconceivable—that the Framers would have overlooked or not had an understanding of the allocation of authority to deal with foreign affairs, given its importance to the new nation at the time. The Vesting Clause's "executive power" is the most plausible repository of that authority.

A. The Eighteenth Century Context

In fact the concept of "executive power" had an established meaning in eighteenth century British usage and writing well known to the Framers, and in state constitutions established after independence. Equally important, the Framers were reacting to the failures of the Articles of Confederation that were especially deficient in the management of foreign relations. They clearly understood that the new unitary executive branch would remedy these defects. Both these contextual elements suggest that the Vesting Clause was understood by the Framers to embody a residual foreign relations power not otherwise specifically allocated to Congress or the Senate.

British Practice and Writers. The prevailing political culture and the philosophers who explained it undoubtedly had a major influence on the Framers' thinking about the system of government they were creating. The formal and practical roles of Crown and Parliament comprised an unwritten British constitution which by the eighteenth century was, at least in general terms, relatively stable. The Framers of the American Constitution well understood British practice, even as they reacted against it in revolutionary ways. Consequently it is important to consider the allocations of power under the British constitution and the writers who theorized about it.

In Great Britain the Crown monopolized the conduct of foreign relations unchallenged until the tumult of the seventeenth century. The watershed events of that century—the English Civil Wars of 1642–48, the Restoration of the Stuart monarchy in 1660, and the Glorious Revolution of 1688—primarily concerned religion, political power, and the struggles between King and Parliament, and not foreign affairs prerogatives. However, Stuart Kings had raised funds and armies without Parliament's assent to fight wars in Scotland, and part of the resolution of the Glorious Revolution firmly barred such practices.[3] The 1689 Declaration of Rights confirmed that taxation and raising an army could only be done with parliamentary approval. Still, in the eighteenth century, the King appointed ambassadors, negotiated with foreign powers, concluded treaties, dispatched secret agents and established rules concerning foreign commerce.

The Framers of the American Constitution allocated the parliamentary powers to raise armies and levy taxes to Congress, thus carrying forward the principles of the Declaration of Rights, but they also gave Congress the power to regulate foreign commerce and other royal powers. Furthermore, the Crown's powers to appoint ambassadors and conclude treaties were to be shared between the President and the Senate, while the power to make war was divided ambiguously between the President and Congress. At the same time the general Royal Prerogative to conduct other aspects of foreign relations was not specifically reallocated. In light of the attention to detail regarding important powers excluded from executive prerogative in the new Constitution, ordinary conventions of textual

3. I am indebted to the UCLA seminar paper by Brian K. Elder, An Evolution of Executive Power in Anglo–American Legal Culture: From the English Civil War to the American Constitution (1998), for assistance with this part.

interpretation suggest that the executive power in the Vesting Clause was a residual—and meaningful—category of authority.

This conclusion is reinforced by the writings of the major political theorists of the period who advanced explanations of "executive power" that were known to the Framers and would naturally have informed their thinking. Blackstone and Montesquieu were referred to most frequently, but they also relied heavily on John Locke.[4]

Locke held that

> "the legislative is the supreme power; for what [institution] can give laws to another [e.g. the Executive] must needs be superior to him...."[5]

Nevertheless, because in Locke's view laws once made "have a constant and lasting force," they must be carried out (or executed) by a separate Executive. In addition, Locke posited a "federative power," which covered foreign relations. The federative power included the power to make war and peace, the power to join alliances, and the power over "all the transactions with all persons and communities without the commonwealth."[6] This corresponds with a general foreign relations power of government. As noted above, the American Constitution divided some parts of these specific feder-

---

4.   Donald S. Lutz, The Relative Influence of European Writers on Late Eighteenth–Century American Political Thought, 78 Am. Pol. Sci. Rev. 189 (1984).

5.   John Locke, Second Treatise of Civil Government § 150, at 125 (Gateway Edition 1955).

6.   Id. § 146, at 121.

ative powers, such as making war, concluding treaties, and appointing and receiving foreign ambassadors, among Congress, the Senate and the President, but the text of the Constitution did not refer directly to a general "federative" power. Although in Locke's thinking executive power was conceptually distinct from federative or general foreign relations power, he added that

These two powers, executive and federative, though they be really distinct in themselves, yet one comprehending the execution of the municipal laws of the society within itself ... the other the management of the security and interest of the public without, ... yet they are always almost united. ... this federative power ... is much less capable to be directed by antecedent, standing, positive laws, than the executive; and so must necessarily be left to the prudence and wisdom of those whose hands it is in to be managed for the public good. For the laws that concern subjects one amongst another, being to direct their actions, may well enough precede them. But what is to be done in reference to foreigners, depending much upon their actions and the variation of designs and interest, must be left in great part to the prudence of those who have this power committed to them, to be managed by the best of their skill for the advantage of the commonwealth.

... the executive and federative power of every community ... are hardly to be separated and placed at the same time in the hands of distinct persons ... it is almost impracticable ... that the executive and federative power should be placed in persons that might act separately, which would be apt some time or other to cause disorder and ruin.[7]

Following Locke's reasoning, because the federative and executive powers cannot realistically be separated, and because the executive power (albeit qualified) was given to the President, it follows that the President has, in the Vesting Clause, a textually based general foreign affairs power, at least if the Lockean framework is applied to the American Constitution. Locke's writings also foreshadow the twentieth century functional justifications for plenary executive power over foreign relations.[8]

The Framers' thinking, of course, was not limited to Locke. Blackstone and his Commentaries on Law were especially influential. Blackstone could draw on a century of actual experience of executive power in British practice after the Glorious Revolution, and his Commentaries were written in 1765–69. It was the most influential law book in England and America. Among the executive powers detailed by Blackstone are

7. Id. § 147–48, at 121–23.

8. Locke also opined that the executive had an inherent emergency power which was necessary because the legislature was too slow and could not anticipate future developments, and only the Crown could act on behalf of all the members of the political community. Assertions of such an emergency power by President Lincoln at the outset of the Civil War were rejected by Justice Taney. See Ex parte Merryman, 17 F. Cas. 144 (Cir.Ct. D.Md.1861).

— sending embassadors to foreign states, and receiving embassadors at home,

— make treaties, leagues and alliances with foreign states,

— the sole perogative of making war and peace,

— power to grant letters of marque and reprisal,

— power to grant safe-conducts,

— *generalissimo*, or first in military command,

— sole power of raising and regulating fleets and armies,

— prohibit the export of arms and ammunition, and the right of subjects to travel abroad,

— regulate commerce,

— grant letters of patent,

— establish currency and coin money.

"The supreme executive power of these kingdoms is vested by our laws in a single person, the king or queen."[9] It is surely no coincidence that Blackstone's detailed specification of the contents of executive power are replicated virtually verbatim in the American Constitution, with the obvious qualification that many of the most important executive powers were allocated to or shared with another branch.

9. See William Blackstone, 1 Commentaries on the Laws of England, Book I, Chapter 3, page 183; the list of executive powers is culled from *Id.*, Book I, Chapter 7, pp. 245–68. (Chicago Press 1979).

Others, including Whig theorists and Montesquieu, supplemented the idea of separated powers with theories of mixed government, in which different institutions of government reflecting different social or economic classes would operate together in a system that provided internal checks and balances to assure that no single branch or faction would itself prevail. Montesquieu contributed the idea that a separate judiciary should participate in the execution of laws to forestall a tyrannical executive. Both Blackstone and Montesquieu emphasized that the crown or executive had the foreign relations power in part because only that branch could speak for the entire political community. They also emphasized the functional advantages of speed and unity of purpose held by the executive.

The ideas of Locke, Montesquieu and Blackstone were clearly reflected in the American Constitution's basic separation of powers between the President, Congress and the Judiciary; the separate compositions and constituencies of the House of Representatives, the Senate and the President; and the system of checks and balances among the different branches of government reflected throughout the Constitution. Of course, the Framers had just fought a revolutionary war against Great Britain, and the British models were obviously not transplanted without change. For example, a fundamentally important ideological influence on colonial thinking—unknown to the British constitution—was the idea of "popular sovereignty." However, as to the structure of government, as opposed to its political foundation, the shadows of eighteenth century thinkers, like Locke, Montesquieu and especially Blackstone, seem uncannily reflected in the 1789 Constitution. The lesson from Blackstone is that the Framers well understood the concept of executive power in British practice, that they carefully and literally parcelled out its components to different branches of the new government, but they retained the residual executive power in the President. Unless the Vesting Clause is meaningless it incorporates the unallocated parts of Royal Prerogative.

The Articles of Confederation and the Revolution. The Framers were above all practical men who had immediate experiences in actual government, including the state constitutions created during and after the Revolution and the difficulties experienced under the Articles of Confederation. The crises that precipitated the Revolution and ensuing Declaration of Independence were created by King George's stubborn insistence on upholding parliamentary authority over the colonies. The colonies convened a Continental Congress in 1774 to petition the King to redress their grievances, but the King spurned the colonists' pacific overtures, and instead he dispatched more troops to America. The Revolution started at Lexington and Concord in April 1775, and continued at Bunker Hill in July 1775. In response King George solicited and enforced the parliamentary Declaration of Rebellion of August 23, 1775, and on this basis London pressed a trade embargo and capture of American vessels. By 1776 the King had become the focus of American grievances, even though those grievances concerned parliamentary overreaching, and independence was formally declared on July 4, 1776.

In the period surrounding the Declaration of Independence, almost all the state governments adopted new constitutions providing for legislative primacy over the executive. Governors were elected by the legislatures in all but one state. Executives were also subject to strict limits on the time and on the number of terms they could serve. Pennsylvania's executive was collective, consisting of 12 persons rather than one, and many states further limited executive power by requiring approval or advice on major actions by a council appointed by the legislature. The new states plainly rejected a Crown-like dominant executive, but efforts to prevent executive tyranny did not take the form of taking away Crown powers and giving them to the legislature, but rather took the form of assuring that the executive would exercise its powers in accordance with legislative wishes. The nature and scope of executive power under the British constitution continued in the new state governors, although, as a practical matter, those governors had to exercise their powers according to legislative will.

The Articles of Confederation were drafted in the Continental Congress in 1776 and 1777. They were ratified in 1781, and remained in effect as the instrument establishing the national government through 1788. Under the Articles of Confederation, the states granted the Continental Congress a limited number of governmental powers. There was no idea of separation of powers. All the legislative, executive, and judicial powers of the national government, which were sparingly granted, were vested in the Continental Congress. Those powers included the power to carry on foreign relations and to "determine" on questions of war and peace. They notably did not include the power to tax. The Continental Congress waged the Revolutionary War and controlled the negotiations for peace. Congressional control of the war effort quickly proved impractical, so Congress delegated broad powers to committees and to General Washington. That too proved to be inefficient. Troop morale suffered because Congress delayed authorizing supplies. Its inability to tax contributed significantly to its ineffectiveness. Its conduct of diplomacy similarly suffered from a lack of focused direction, breaches of secrecy, and inflexible negotiating positions that were cumbersome to change. For example, it took Congress seven months to come to agreement on the terms for peace with Great Britain. State courts then failed to enforce the resulting Jay Treaty provisions protecting Loyalists and British debt, which in turn gave Britain justification to refuse to vacate, as promised, its forts in the Ohio country. The Government was also unable to threaten retaliation when Britain closed ports in the West Indies to American vessels because it lacked power to regulate foreign commerce. Finally, in the face of regional differences over matters like protection of New England commercial and fisheries interests and freedom of navigation up the Mississippi River (important to the South), Congress was unable to forge a unified national policy for purposes of negotiating with foreign powers. For example, negotiation with Spain was frustrated because Southern states feared that the Government would subordinate attempts to open New Orleans and secure free navigation up the Mississippi River, in order to gain commercial advantages for New England. All these shortcomings of Congress formed the context of the 1787 convention in Philadelphia.

The 1787 Philadelphia Constitutional Convention. In general, the major issues that dominated the Convention did not involve foreign affairs. The most pressing issues concerned the political foundation of the new government (popular sovereignty or agent of the states), the distribution of power between the states and the federal government, voting rights, composition and constituencies of the legislature, and territorial expansion. The result was a government made up of three separate branches, with separate powers, and a system of governance incorporating checks and balances among those branches. The federal government would possess only limited powers which were specifically enumerated in the Constitution. All other powers were reserved to the states and to the people. Congress was bicameral. The House was composed of representatives elected directly by the people, from districts equal in population so that the more populated states had more voting power. The Senate consisted of two Senators per state, regardless of its size. Legislation was subject to approval by both houses of Congress and to a presidential veto which could, however, be overridden by 2/3 vote of both houses of Congress.

As to foreign relations, the first order of business at Philadelphia was to make that domain a matter of federal concern. Accordingly, the states were denied the powers to impose tariffs, to enter into any "Treaty, Alliance, or Confederation," to grant letters of marque and reprisal, to keep troops or warships in time of peace without the consent of Congress, to enter into any "Agreement or Compact" with a foreign power, and to "engage in" war unless actually invaded or threatened. Article VI of the new Constitution (the Supremacy Clause) provided for the supremacy of national treaties over state law and required state judges to enforce them. To make foreign relations a federal concern, the Framers also delegated to the Congress a variety of powers relating to foreign relations: to regulate foreign commerce, to raise armies and navies, to define offenses against the law of nations, to punish piracy and felonies on the high seas, and to declare war. By assuring these powers to Congress, the federal government could deal with problems like Spanish threats to navigation on the Mississippi and British closure of foreign ports to American commerce.[10] Under

10. The legal basis for federal control of foreign relations may best be inferred from the text of the Constitution and its apparent structure, especially given the context of its drafting. There are, nevertheless, other theoretical explanations, based on reasoning external to the text, that have been advanced to explain why the federal government controls foreign relations.

the resulting constitutional structure, the federal government controls all significant aspects of the nation's foreign relations. The major issues today, as explained in the Introduction, concern how the federal government conducts those foreign relations. The states may promote their commerce abroad, conduct informal negotiations to deal with local problems, and adopt non-binding resolutions inconsistent with national policy (e.g. on trade with China), but foreign policy is firmly the domain of the federal government.

One of the most dramatic changes in practice from the Articles of Confederation and the state constitutions was the decision to create a unitary

Justice Sutherland in the *Curtiss-Wright* case opined that sovereignty was transferred from Great Britain to the federal government (never passing through the 13 states), and the power to conduct foreign relations is inherent in sovereignty. United States v. Curtiss–Wright Export Corp., 299 U.S. 304 (1936). See also Chinese Exclusion Case, 130 U.S. 581 (1889). Expanding upon this explanation, the federal foreign relations power could also be said to derive from international law (which reflects the idea of sovereignty). Such an "extra-constitutional" explanation is not especially persuasive. Sutherland's history is controversial: the 13 states did exercise many attributes of sovereignty. As to international law, under modern conceptions the United States makes international law, not vice versa. Although sovereignty and statehood are fundamental international law concepts, and international law confirms the "existence" of the United States as a person in the international system of nation-states, that function is not connected with the allocation of domestic authority within the state. A more plausible approach would regard foreign relations as within the domain of the federal government because that result is implied from the structure of the Constitution as a whole in the context of its creation, and from the many specific foreign relations-related powers, including the Vesting Clause, delegated to the new federal government.

executive. In Article II the Framers created a separate executive branch of government headed by a single President. The President would be independently elected, albeit indirectly, by the people, and would therefore be independent of Congress. These steps would assure that the executive would have the ability to define a unified national interest, and could act quickly and decisively, thereby rectifying a major defect of the Confederacy.

In addition to inferences drawn from the eighteenth century context, the meaning of the "executive power" vested in the President can be elucidated by the "intent" or probable understanding of the Constitution's Framers ("Original Intent"). This kind of analysis is a major staple of argument concerning foreign relations powers. Whether by a lawyer crafting a legal argument in court, or a politician asserting a prerogative in a political forum, or an academic writing about the meaning of the Constitution, the invocation of Original Intent is normally a major part of the brief.

B. Theories of Interpretation

Original Intent. Original Intent includes statements of participants in the Philadelphia convention or the ratifying conventions held in individual states, and contemporaneous statements by these "Framers," such as the Federalist papers. Original Intent also can be found in speeches, judicial decisions and other writings by the Framers in the early years of the Republic, and actions of the early Presidents and Congresses who were well aware of the Framers' intent. Thus, at the Philadelphia convention, Madison explained that a proposed amendment—later adopted—would make it clear that the "President could repel sudden attacks." From this it has generally been agreed that the President may use military force to defend the country in the event of invasion (and perhaps in other situations as well), even though nothing in the text states or implies such an authority.

There are, nevertheless, several problems with finding and using Original Intent as a definitive source of constitutional interpretation. First, it is difficult to impute a unified intent to any deliberative body, where different participants may have had different intentions and understandings (not to mention motives). Second, the product of deliberation inevitably includes compromises that may mask inconsistent intentions of the different participants or may simply defer arguments over matters that could not be resolved. Third, it is inevitably hazardous to impute a collective purpose based on an isolated statement by one individual. Fourth, there were 14 deliberative bodies involved in the drafting and ratification of the Constitution and some of these deliberations were secret. Fifth, the surviving evidence of what happened is quite fragmentary. As Justice Jackson remarked:

> Just what our forefathers did envision, or would have envisioned had they foreseen modern conditions, must be divined from materials almost

as enigmatic as the dreams Joseph was called upon to interpret for Pharaoh. A century and a half of partisan debate and scholarly speculation yields no net result but only supplies more or less apt quotations from respected sources on each side of any question.[11]

Sixth, the surviving evidence may not be wholly reliable. One of the best sources consists of Madison's notes on the deliberations in Philadelphia which were revised 30 years after the fact. Seventh, the materials are often contradictory.

Justice Jackson was wrong to brush aside the Vesting Clause as an important source of presidential authority, but he was correct to note that the quotations of the Framers employed by advocates of particular political outcomes "largely cancel each other .... A Hamilton may be matched against a Madison."[12] Indeed a Hamilton may be matched against a Hamilton, and a Madison against a Madison. Hamilton defended the Vesting Clause in his Publius article referred to above, but he later argued that Senate consent was required for removal of a (Federalist) official. Madison, who as Helvidius argued for restriction of presidential authority and who disparaged the Vesting Clause, took the opposite position on the removal issue. The point is that individual statements are unreliable guides to un-

11. *Supra* note 2 at 634–35.

12. Id. at 635, 635 nl. See Alex Kozinski and Harry Susman, Original Mean[der]ings, 49 Stan. L. Rev. 1583 (1997) (use of Original Intent for political purposes).

derstanding the original meaning of the Constitution.

Another kind of problem with using Original Intent is that any statement or point made can be expressed at different levels of generality to support different conclusions. For example, Madison's statement about presidential authority to "repel sudden attack" could be taken to justify responding to an invasion of the United States, or more generally, to any unanticipated emergency situation thrust upon the nation. Finally, perhaps the Framers themselves did not intend that their intent be conclusive in resolving issues in the future. Original Intent thus may tell us that Original Intent should not govern!

The many problems with persuasively demonstrating an Original Intent reinforce the need to refer to language, structure and context as preferable guides in constitutional interpretation. Indeed it seems more realistic to attempt to fathom an *original understanding* of constitutional text, based on general contextual analysis as opposed to specific statements of particular Framers. Original Intent in this sense provides a more secure foundation for interpreting the ambiguous constitutional text, but it would be unrealistic to ignore the fact that isolated statements of Framers and the other contextual components of Original Intent identified above form an important component of legal rhetoric in this field, whether in a legal brief, an academic article, or a political forum. Original Intent is also frequently supplemented with other approaches to constitutional interpretation.

Historical Practice. The Historical Practice of the political branches with respect to a particular issue may show their understanding of the meaning of the text which, in the absence of judicial decisions, seems entitled to significant weight. Members of Congress and the executive branch take an oath to uphold the Constitution, and no doubt take that oath seriously. The balance thus struck between the branches can be said to reflect their implicit agreement on the requirements of the Constitution. As Justice Frankfurter remarked:

The Constitution is a framework for Government. Therefore the way the framework has consistently operated fairly establishes that it has operated according to its true nature. Deeply-embedded traditional ways of conducting government cannot supplant the Constitution or legislation, but they give meaning to the words of a text or supply them. It is an inadmissibly narrow conception of American constitutional law to confine it to the words of the Constitution and to disregard the gloss which life has written upon them. In short, a systematic unbroken, executive practice, long pursued to the knowledge of the Congress and never before questioned, engaged in by Presidents who have also sworn to uphold the Constitution, making as it were such exercise of power part of the structure of our government, may be treated as a gloss on 'executive Power' vested in the President by § 1 of Art. II....[13]

In addition, Senators and Presidents have regularly expressed the view that their actions and opinions are entitled to equal weight to Supreme Court opinions as a matter of con stitutional law. Looking at the precedents embodied in historical practice then can be seen as equivalent to looking at Supreme Court opinions for evidence as to what the law requires. The interaction of the branches creates a kind of constitutional common law in which the rules can be inferred from the pattern of compromises reached over time. As a method of constitutional interpretation Historical Practice nevertheless has some flaws.

First, it may seem anomalous to take the politically motivated actions of Congress and the President, leading to unprincipled political compromise, and call it law. Even when a Senator is defending a constitutional principle, such as the Senate's role in approving treaties, she more often than not is acting for fairly obvious, partisan, political motives. For example, when a Senator insists that the Senate review an arms control treaty because of its constitutional role under Article II, she may not coincidentally oppose the substance of the treaty. Democrats routinely attack presidential prerogative when a Republican is President, and vice versa. Such partisan shifting of positions undercuts the claim of the process to be called legal, as does the absence of a formal principle of stare decisis and a

13. Id. at 610–11.

discreet set of volumes, like the U.S. Reports, where the law can be found.

In addition, the President has often taken initiatives that Congress may simply not have bothered to oppose, because of the limited time available and other politically more important priorities. Accordingly, this method of interpretation often favors executive power. Members of Congress are practical politicians who are especially goal, and reelection, oriented. They get little credit with their constituents for defending constitutional principle per se. Consequently separation of powers issues are usually raised only when there are significant underlying disagreements about the policy involved. There is even an institutional imbalance in that the executive branch has numerous lawyers who consider it part of their job to defend executive prerogative, while Congress has no real counterparts.

Finally, by saying that whatever happens is law, this method of interpretation collapses law and behavior. It just doesn't sound like law. It seems especially anomalous to say that the President and Congress, through political compromise, can amend the Constitution. On the other hand, major shifts in constitutional understanding have occurred through the political process without formal amendments, for example the shift in understanding of federal-state relations, growing out of the Depression and the New Deal, which led to a great expansion of federal, congressional and presidential power. Clearly the general understanding of the Constitution in our political culture has undergone revolutionary changes from time to time throughout history, and there is no reason why distribution of foreign relations authority should not change too, in evolutionary if not revolutionary ways. Moreover, despite their political birth, inter-branch compromises have shown considerable consistency over time. In addition, despite the practical and political disadvantages, politicians have been known to defend constitutional principles even in the absence of policy disagreement or partisan advantage.

That is not to say that Historical Practice stands alone as a method of interpretation. The constitutional text is always the starting point for analysis. Historical Practice must be connected to that text. In that regard the Vesting Clause is a plausible, sometimes the only plausible, textual source to which such practice relates. In fact Historical Practice and the other principal approach to constitutional interpretation in this area—Functionalism—need not be considered to be independent of each other, or opposed to textualism. Practical decision-makers, including the Supreme Court, do not invariably follow a single method of interpretation, but use them synergistically and according to context.[14]

Functionalism. A third general approach to constitutional interpretation—loosely described as "Functionalism"—has been especially prominent in the contemporary separation of powers context. Functionalism is a rather vague and open-ended concept that seems to cover several different analyt-

14. Cf. Brian F. Havel, Forensic Constitutional Interpretation, 41 Wm. & Mary L. Rev. 1247 (2000).

ical methods. Under this approach the interpreter examines the nature of the functions involved, i.e., executive, legislative, or foreign affairs—and allocates power accordingly. Functional approaches can also involve balancing the interests of competing branches and taking account of the practical, political consequences of allocating power to one branch or another.

The 1936 *Curtiss-Wright* case is one of the most prominent examples of functionalist reasoning in the foreign relations law area. In that case Justice Sutherland justified presidential authority by reference to the executive branch's institutional advantages in foreign affairs. He explained:

> ... we are here dealing ... with ... the very delicate, plenary and exclusive power of the President as the sole organ of the federal government in the field of international relations.... It is quite apparent that if, in the maintenance of our international relations, embarrassment—perhaps serious embarrassment—is to be avoided and success for our aims achieved ... the President [must have] a degree of discretion and freedom from statutory restriction which would not be admissible were domestic affairs alone involved. Moreover, he, not Congress, has the better opportunity of knowing the conditions which prevail in foreign countries, and especially is this true in time of war. He has his confidential sources of information. He has his agents in the form of diplomatic, consular and other officials. Secrecy in respect of information gathered by them may

be highly necessary, and the premature disclosure of it productive of harmful results.... [15]

For these reasons the Court concluded that the President must have the general power to conduct the nation's foreign relations.[16] The Court reasoned that the President must have a general foreign relations power because the executive branch can most effectively and efficiently perform that function in the overall national interest. *Curtiss-Wright* identified the executive's access to information, including confidential information, and its ability to maintain secrecy as elements of its functional advantage. The executive also can act expeditiously and can uniquely speak authoritatively for the nation with one voice. In fact the Framers created a unitary executive for precisely these reasons, so it is not unreasonable to impute to the Vesting Clause powers implied by a functional analysis. The Framers were well aware of the functional advantages of executive control of foreign affairs, and early Congresses were generous in accepting executive prerogative.

15. 299 U.S. 304, 319–20 (1936).

16. This statement was dictum because the case actually involved authority delegated to the President by Congress. Moreover, Justice Sutherland's opinion was framed within historical analysis that has been sharply criticized—he argued that the foreign affairs power of government was inherent in national sovereignty and, without explanation, Sutherland opined that this power came to reside in the executive branch without being delegated by the states. Despite its weak historical foundation and excessive breadth the *Curtiss-Wright* case, and especially the above-quoted dictum shorn of its context, is a staple of constitutional argument by executive branch lawyers and officials.

The functional approach has been especially prominent since World War II. With the advent of the Cold War, a permanent standing army, and a Soviet threat to national security, the dominant political belief in the American political culture was that the President needed to be able to act quickly, secretly, and decisively to counter the Soviet threat. Even after the end of the Cold War, the threats of terrorism and the demands of globalization may offer a similar environment to justify presidential power. As problems become more complex and more global in scope, the executive's expertise, its access to foreign sources of information, and the need for quick and decisive action reinforce the case for a powerful executive.

On the other hand, there are functional weaknesses potentially buried in the executive's strengths. Speedy action may not be wise action; the value of deliberation is sacrificed. And the unitary nature of the executive branch, ultimately depending on the decision of one person, can lead to arbitrary, even tyrannical, action. The President can also favor certain regions and interests at the expense of others whose views would be more effectively represented in Congress. The functional strengths of Congress lie in its deliberative character. Decisions are usually considered thoroughly, often in public, so that all the affected interests have an opportunity to be heard. Compromise, which is a hallmark of the legislative process, assures a fair result for all regions and interests. The public nature of legislation also gives it more legitimacy.

Nevertheless, Congress has functional weaknesses. It tends to be influenced by short-term interests, and often concentrates on narrow or immediate issues. Sometimes it deals with broad problems, like relations with China, as if a single factor, like human rights, should be of determinative significance. Additionally, Congress acts through the blunt instrument of legislation. Once a policy has been legislatively directed, it remains in force until someone can overcome the inertia preventing new legislative action. When a problem vacates the headlines, it may not be easy for the legislature to react to changed circumstances.

Although there has been much academic and media criticism of the trend toward increased presidential power, at the expense of Congress, this trend can be explained by reference to institutional or functional considerations rooted in practical politics. The roles of the President and Congress can also be grounded deeply in American democratic principles. Congress is above all a political body. Its members are practical politicians who see themselves as responsible for the effective functioning of the government, in addition to being accountable to their particular constituencies. Because of their role as national statesmen, they recognize that many foreign policy problems are truly national in scope and require that the nation speak with "one voice," which a legislative body cannot provide. Being practical politicians they also understand that foreign policy decisions require compromises of competing interests, and, often, trade-offs between regional or factional constituencies are needed to promote the overall national interest. Most fundamentally, the strictly political interests of Congress lead it to expect, and eventually defer to, presidential leadership. Those political interests include, most obviously, the desire to be reelected. To that end, a member must sometimes advance special interests and thereby maintain a favorable public posture before her constituents as an effective legislator and politician. Those interests may dictate a position, for example, on trade or military programs, or on foreign aid to Greece or Israel. But, at the same time, a member may well understand that it would not be good for the nation as a whole for her position to be adopted. In our democratic system it serves her interest simply to have the opportunity to be seen vigorously advocating it.

In addition, most foreign policy is far removed from immediate political concerns. Politically, there is almost no advantage to a member of Congress in having to take a position, through a recorded vote, on pressing foreign policy questions with no immediate implication for local constituencies and with uncertain long-term consequences. To the contrary, it may be preferable to accept presidential leadership and preserve the ability to criticize policy decisions when they become politically unpopular. Acquiescence here enables congressmembers to take credit for popular decisions and to criticize, while gathering helpful publicity and stature, those that go awry. Thus, a member may see no advantage, for example, in taking a position on Cambodia. Stopping communism may be popular, but if victory results in advancing the fortunes of Pol Pot, it may not be so desirable. As Professor Koh points out, voting for a policy necessarily entails taking responsibility for its failure.

> In many cases, a critical mass of congressional members has simply been unwilling to take responsibility for setting foreign policy, preferring to leave the decision—and the blame—with the president. As Senator Fulbright recalled, long before the mid–1970s, "[a] majority [of Congress] may have wished to end the war [in Indochina], but less than a majority of the two Houses were willing to take the responsibility for ending it."[17]

It may serve a member's political interest to let the President take the heat for decisions that may be desirable in the overall national interest but are unpopular in certain sectors. For example, voting for or against retaliatory tariffs, like those imposed in response to the European Community's ban on hormone-treated beef, may be politically awkward for congressmen. Such tariffs will hurt some importers while helping some farmers, but will also risk a general trade war that would hurt everyone.

The functional advantages of the executive described above are complemented by the President's

17.   Harold Hongju Koh, The National Security Constitution 132 (1990). My critique is elaborated in Phillip R. Trimble, The Acquiescent Congress and Foreign Affairs, 15 Yale J. Intl. L. 345 (1990).

control of the bureaucracy and his command of a major political party, both with the concomitant power to dispense government and privately raised funds. The contemporary political culture also contains features that reinforce the practical power of the President. The President and the media, especially television, form a symbiotic relationship. Television thrives on captivating images and sound bites. The White House, the Oval Office, the Great Seal, visiting kings and powerful foreign leaders enable the President to command instant attention of the media. The President's activities are also easier to cover and more pleasant to watch than a typical legislative debate.

Another method of reasoning that is often classified as "functionalist" holds that each branch must have the power to do whatever is necessary to enable it to carry out its core functions, e.g., those expressed in the text, and, conversely, another branch may not "encroach upon" that power. Thus Congress may not limit the President's ability to remove officials because that would undercut his ability to make sure that his subordinates were faithfully executing the laws, a core executive branch function. Recently a plurality of the Court opined that Congress could not require public disclosure of certain aspects of the manner in which the President received advice regarding judicial appointments, because that would interfere with his appointments power.[18] This kind of argument fre-

18. Public Citizen v. United States Department of Justice, 491 U.S. 440 (1989) (Kennedy, J. concurring).

quently appears in the foreign relations law context. Executive branch lawyers in particular often argue, for example, that Congress has encroached upon the President's authority to conduct foreign affairs.

Functionalism also sometimes blends into balancing the institutional interests of one branch versus another, i.e., deciding whose functions would be more impaired in a given context. In *U.S. v. Nixon*[19] the Court found that the President's interest in assuring a free flow of confidential advice, which was important to his executive power, did not outweigh the judiciary's interest in assuring a fair trial. Functionalism can even be expressed, in a game-theoretical context, as the optimal result of implicit bargaining among the branches to advance their respective interests.[20]

Yet another form of analysis that is often labeled "functional" is reflected in Justice Jackson's concurring opinion in the 1952 *Youngstown* case. In that opinion he offered the following methodology for interpreting Presidential powers:

> The actual art of governing under our Constitution does not and cannot conform to judicial definitions of the power of any of its branches based on isolated causes or even single Articles torn from context. While the Constitution diffuses power the better to secure liberty, it also contemplates that practice will integrate the dispersed

19.   418 U.S. 683 (1974).

20.   See McGinnis, Constitutional Review by the Executive In Foreign Affairs and War Powers, 56 Law and Contemp. Probs. 293 (No. 4 1993).

powers into a workable government. It enjoins upon its branches separateness but interdependence, autonomy but reciprocity. Presidential powers are not fixed but fluctuate, depending upon their disjunction or conjunction with those of Congress. We may well begin by a somewhat oversimplified grouping of practical situations in which a President may doubt, or others may challenge, his powers, and by distinguishing roughly the legal consequences of this factor of relativity.

1. When the President acts pursuant to an express or implied authorization of Congress, his authority is at its maximum, for it includes all that he possesses in his own right plus all that Congress can delegate. In these circumstances, and in these only, he may be said (for what it may be worth) to personify the federal sovereignty. If his act is held unconstitutional under these circumstances, it usually means that the Federal Government as an undivided whole lacks power. . . .

2. When the President acts in absence of either a congressional grant or denial of authority, he can only rely upon his own independent powers, but there is a zone of twilight in which he and Congress may have concurrent authority, or in which its distribution is uncertain. Therefore, congressional inertia, indifference or quiescence may sometimes, at least as a practical matter, enable, if not invite, measures on independent presidential responsibility. In this area, any actu-

al test of power is likely to depend on the impera-
tives of events and contemporary imponderables
rather than on abstract theories of law.

3.   When the President takes measures incompatible with the expressed or implied will of Congress, his power is at its lowest ebb, for then he
can rely only upon his own constitutional powers
minus any constitutional powers of Congress over
the matter. Courts can sustain exclusive presidential control in such a case only by disabling the
Congress from acting upon the subject....[21]

Jackson's second category suggests that the institutional or functional advantages of the executive
branch "invite" it to fill a vacuum left by congressional inaction (which itself may reflect its institutional or functional weakness), and Jackson seems
to regard such presidential initiatives as constitutionally legitimate. Jackson's analysis may also be
seen as acknowledging that the President and Congress, through their actions and omissions, are implicitly interpreting the constitutional balance, and
the courts will credit these interpretations.

All these manifestations of a "functional" approach are informal, pragmatic, flexible and open-
ended. Critics argue that such approaches are hope-
lessly indeterminate, enabling a judge or an advo-
cate to justify practically any preferred result. Two
justices in the *Youngstown* case employed "functionalist" reasoning but reached opposite conclusions. Functionalism obviously favors the accretion

21.   Supra note 2 at 635–38.

of executive power, but it seems to do so for reasons rooted in considerations well known to the Framers. Functional analysis comfortably fills out the content of the Vesting Clause in accordance with Original Intent.

Bibliographic Note

The basic legal scholarship on which this Chapter rests includes Louis Henkin, Foreign Affairs and the United States Constitution (2d ed. 1996); the books by Harold Hongju Koh and Michael J. Glennon referred to in the Preface; and Foreign Affairs and the U.S. Constitution (Henkin, Glennon and Rogers ed. 1990).

My account of the eighteenth century context and the Constitutional Convention draws on J.R. Jones, The Revolution of 1688 in England (1972); G.C. Gibbs, The Revolution in Foreign Policy, in Geoffrey Holmes (ed.), Britain After the Glorious Revolution 1689–1714 (1969); Jerrilyn Greene Martson, King and Congress: The Transfer of Political Legitimacy, 1774–1776 (1987); Merrill Jensen, The Articles of Confederation (1940); Gordon S. Wood, The Creation of the American Republic (1969); Bernard Bailyn, The Ideological Origins of the American Revolution (1967); Jack N. Rakove, Original Meanings: Politics and Ideas in the Making of the Constitution (1996); Gordon S. Wood, The Radicalism of the American Revolution (1991).

Impressive recent scholarship has substantially enriched our contextual understanding of the Framers' intent. See, e.g., John C. Yoo, The Continuation of Politics by Other Means: The Original Understanding of War Powers, 84 Cal. L. Rev. 167 (1996); Michael D. Ramsey, The Myth of Extra–Constitutional Foreign Affairs Power, 42 Wm. & Mary L. Rev. 379 (2000); and Saikrishna B. Prakash and Michael D. Ramsey, The Executive Power over Foreign Affairs, 111 Yale L.J. 231 (2001).

For early practice I have drawn on David P. Currie, The Constitution in Congress: The Federalist Period, 1789–1801 (1997); and David P. Currie, The Constitution in Congress: The Jeffersonians, 1801–1829 (2000).

Professor Philip Bobbitt presents a typology of various kinds of constitutional argument made in a judicial forum in Constitutional Fate: Theory of the Constitution 3–119 (1982). Recent anthologies with sections dealing with theories of constitutional interpretation include A Constitutional Law Anthology (Glennon, Lively, Haddon, Roberts, and Weaver eds., 2d ed. 1997) at 46–87; and Modern Constitutional Theory: A Reader (Garvey and Aleinikoff eds., 2d ed. 1991) at 26–113. Both anthologies also contain sections containing material dealing with theoretical approaches to separation of powers issues. Almost all this writing focuses on the judiciary. A volume dedicated to the debate over "original intent" is Interpreting the Constitution (Jack N. Rakove ed. 1990). See also Samuel W. Cooper, Considering "Power" in Separation of Powers, 46 Stan. L. Rev. 361 (1994).

Chapter Two

The President's Foreign Relations Power—The Substantive Content

The specific functions encompassed by the President's foreign relations power include the authority to appoint (with Senate approval) and remove ambassadors, appoint and remove other envoys, recognize foreign states and governments, establish diplomatic relations with them, communicate official positions of the United States (including its views on treaties and customary international law), conduct negotiations, conclude international agreements, dispatch agents on international missions including intelligence missions, and protect the secrecy of diplomatic and intelligence documents. It includes domestic law-making authority with respect to several matters involving the borders of the country, such as excluding aliens and authorizing international bridges, as well as the applicability of customary international law in U.S. courts and other matters affecting diplomats and foreign governments. None of these functions is specifically authorized by the text of the Constitution, but they can readily—and persuasively—be grounded in the Vesting Clause. They were all exercised by the British monarch, and therefore were within the

47

generally understood notion of executive power in the eighteenth century. With only episodic exceptions, the Framers and subsequent Presidents and Congresses have treated them as presidential functions.

Additional foreign affairs powers which are in some way or another shared with or regulated by Congress—treaty and international agreement-making, use of military force, and covert intelligence operations—will be treated in Chapters Four and Five.

Appointment and Removal of Officials and Diplomats. The President has express power to appoint Ambassadors, although that power can only be exercised with the approval of a majority of the Senate. Because of the Senate's role this appointment power is sometimes said to be "shared" with the Senate, but conceptually it is an exclusive presidential power that may simply be checked by the Senate. Presidents starting with Washington have even asserted that the Senate should not reject a nominee without good reason, but there are many examples of the Senate using its check to achieve its own unrelated, political ends. Recently, for example, Senator Helms blocked all new ambassadorial appointments until the Clinton Administration agreed to subordinate the Arms Control and Disarmament Agency, a hitherto independent agency, by merging it into the Department of State. The practical power of the Senate, and the entire Congress for that matter, gives members ample informal opportunities to assure that on occasion their own candidates receive a presidential appointment. As a matter of formal law, however, it is clear that the President has the exclusive power to appoint Ambassadors and other "officers of the United States." In *Buckley v. Valeo*,[1] the Supreme Court struck down a law permitting Congress to appoint members of the Federal Election Commission, and in *Bowsher v. Synar*,[2] the court held that a congressional officer (the Comptroller–General) could not exercise executive functions.

In foreign relations Congress has sometimes tried directly to appoint members of U.S. delegations negotiating international matters. Such attempts unconstitutionally invade the President's exclusive foreign relations power to control international negotiations. Congressional intrusions of this sort represent a practical burden on the executive branch's discharge of its foreign affairs functions. Congressional-appointed members may have narrow agendas (not necessarily even reflecting the views of "Congress"), and are themselves political actors with separate constituencies who may even have a constitutional guarantee of immunity from penalties for premature disclosure of sensitive information. Although there are undoubted advantages to congressional participation in a negotiation—it may even be a prerequisite to getting approval of the results—the cost is significant and hence the principle of exclusive executive power is important. President George Bush, Sr. declared that he would not

1. 424 U.S. 1 (1976).
2. 478 U.S. 714 (1986).

honor Congress' appointment of its staff members as delegates to an international conference. He simply ignored that part of the law and Congress did not pursue the matter.[3] On the other hand, in the Trade Act of 1974 Congress provided that its staff would serve as "observers" to trade negotiations under the Act and that they were entitled to current information concerning the negotiations. In practice those provisions were honored.[4] Indeed, the executive often encourages congressional participation as "observers" or "advisors," rather than as "members," of important negotiating delegations, thereby maintaining the formal exclusivity of executive power, but accommodating the practical influence of the legislature on the process.

The appointment power also serves as the basis of certain implied powers of the President. The power to appoint implies the power to remove, although the Constitution is silent on the matter. The First Congress debated this constitutional issue, with inconclusive results, and Congress ended up giving the President statutory authority to remove officials. The matter is now clearly settled in favor of the President, who can remove Ambassadors and other officials with impunity. The Supreme Court has held that the removal power was exclusively executive so that Congress may not limit the ability

3. McGinnis, *supra* note 20 Chap. One, at 309–14. For the legal analysis see 14 Op. of Legal Counsel 38 (1990).

4. Trade Act of 1974 § 161, Pub.L.No. 93–618, 88 Stat. 2008 (1975)(codified at 19 USC § 2211). The author participated in the early practice under this statute.

of the President to fire an official, even one appointed with the approval of the Senate.[5]

Another contentious issue is presidential authority to appoint special representatives and envoys without approval of the Senate. These envoys may even be called "ambassadors." This practice too dates from the Washington Administration, and has in fact been used to carry out some very important, diplomatic negotiations. Washington dispatched Jay to negotiate peace with Great Britain; Nixon used White House aide Kissinger to establish relations with China; and Clinton employed Carter, Nunn and Powell to negotiate the return of democracy to Haiti.

The power to appoint ambassadors can also be taken to imply the following additional powers relating to diplomacy and foreign relations. These powers also have important legal consequences, both domestically and as a matter of international law.

Recognition of Statehood. Foreign relations start when a government formally "recognizes" that a discrete part of the globe—a country or nation in popular terminology—will be officially regarded as a "state" in the sense understood in international law. Thus in 1971 the United States recognized the former land of East Pakistan as the new state of Bangladesh. In 1990, the formerly distinct states of North Yemen and South Yemen combined, and the United States recognized Yemen as a new state.

5. Myers v. United States, 272 U.S. 52 (1926).

Upon the dissolution of the Soviet Union and of Yugoslavia, the former components were recognized as new states. The President has exclusive authority to exercise this power on behalf of the United States.

In order to qualify under international law as a state the entity must have: (1) a permanent population, (2) a defined territory, (3) a government that exercises governmental functions over the population of that territory, and (4) the "capacity" to engage in international relations with other states.[6] The first three are mostly objective matters of fact, but the last qualification involves a more subjective determination. That determination is made by the existing states in the international community, acting unilaterally and by voting for admission of a new state into the United Nations. As a practical matter, a state becomes such only when recognized by other states. For example, Palestine, Chechnya, and Tibet would seem (in 2002) to satisfy all four tests. Yet their full admission to the international community in a legal sense depends on the essentially political act of recognition. Under United States law and practice the President has the exclusive authority to perform this act, reflecting the functional advantages of the executive branch, although Congress has not been shy about attempting to influence the President.

Tibet provides a recent demonstration of tension between the branches on this issue. Historically

6. See Restatement (Third) of Foreign Relations Law (1987) § 201.

Tibet was an independent kingdom with varying and ambiguous relationships to the Chinese Empire.[7] After the collapse of that empire in 1911, Tibet was effectively independent until the Chinese Communists consolidated power in 1950. Since 1911 China has maintained that Tibet is part of China. No government in modern times has recognized Tibet as a state. Since 1950 Tibet has sought but failed to obtain agreement with Beijing on political and cultural autonomy. After riots in 1959 the Tibetan leadership went into exile and it then launched an international campaign for support. The United States was sympathetic to the Tibetan cause from time to time, even providing covert military assistance. However, the U.S. Government had meticulously acknowledged Beijing's claim that Tibet is an integral part of China. Members of Congress were not so reticent. In 1987 Congress invited the Dalai Lama to meet with its Human Rights Caucus. The Dalai Lama stated that Tibet is "an independent state under illegal occupation." Since then Congress has passed non-binding "sense of the Congress" resolutions expressing support for the Tibetan people and urging the executive to take account of Tibet in its dealings with China. In 1991 Congress declared "the sense of the Congress that ... Tibet ... is an occupied country under the established principles of international law."[8] In

7. See generally Melvyn C. Goldstein, The Snow Lion and the Dragon: China, Tibet and the Dalai Lama (1997); A. Tom Grunfeld, The Making of Modern Tibet (1996).

8. Foreign Relations Authorization Act, Fiscal Years 1992 and 1993, Pub.L. 102–138, 105 Stat. 647, 714. For a sympathetic

1997 some members of Congress proposed the establishment of a U.S. ambassador to Tibet. In response the Clinton Administration promised to name a "special coordinator" in charge of policy toward Tibet. It was a mild symbolic victory for Congress, and added a voice for Tibet within executive branch deliberations. Nevertheless, the congressional initiative did not undermine the proposition that recognition is an executive prerogative. Tibet has still not received recognition as an independent state.

The legal consequences of being recognized as a state are that, under international law, the new state acquires a legal personality (much as a corporation becomes a recognized legal person upon filing of incorporation papers), with capacity, *inter alia*, to own property, make contracts, and create a currency. The new legal person is entitled to rights and obligations under international law, such as the right to have its territorial sovereignty respected, the right to grant nationality to persons, corporations, vessels and aircraft, the right to regulate all matters within its territory, as well as regulating its nationals and protecting them abroad, and the duty to respect human and property rights of aliens in its territory. It may join international organizations like the UN, conclude treaties, and have its laws respected abroad.

legal argument, see Hiliary K. Josephs, Denise J. Harvey, and Mary E. Landergan, Independence for Tibet: An International Legal Analysis, 8 China L. Rptr. 21 (1994).

Recognition of Governments. The next step after recognition of an entity's statehood is the recognition of its government. This amounts to a formal acknowledgment that a particular regime is effectively governing the recognized state, i.e., that it controls the territory and the machinery of government of the recognized state. The two kinds of recognition are conceptually distinct. A state may recognize another state, but withhold recognition of its government. For years the United States recognized China as a state but withheld recognition of the government in Beijing, recognizing instead the government in Taiwan as the government of China. Similarly, for more than a decade the United States recognized Angola as a state but declined to recognize its government. The act of recognition is frequently effected through an exchange of diplomats, although, as explained below, the establishment of diplomatic relations is itself conceptually distinct from the recognition of a government. The President has the exclusive authority to recognize foreign governments. That authority may be inferred from the President's power to appoint ambassadors, and it is also within the eighteenth century understanding of executive power codified in the Vesting Clause. Its legitimacy is confirmed by early Historical Practice and Supreme Court decisions, such as the *Pink* and *Belmont* cases discussed in Chapter Four.

Recognition of a government has legal consequences under international law and within the United States. A recognized government may sue in

U.S. courts, control the foreign state's property in the United States, assert claims on behalf of its nationals and exercise all the other rights of foreign states under international law.

In the past the United States sometimes took the view that a government must have the consent of the governed, in addition to being in de facto control, in order to be recognized as a government. Non-recognition was used to apply political pressure against disfavored regimes, such as those coming to power through coups d'etat, especially in Latin America. Latin American states responded with the Estrada Doctrine, which held that once a state is recognized, the recognition of its government—no matter how it came to power—automatically follows. It rejected the use of recognition to make political judgments about governments. Most states now seem to follow the Estrada approach. In recent decades U.S. practice, i.e. executive branch practice, has become more in line with the rest of the world by not making an issue of recognition when a government changes, and by focusing instead on the issue of whether to have diplomatic relations with the new government. Nevertheless, there have been exceptions to this development. In the past two decades non-recognition has been used as a political tool against the Noriega government of Panama, the Vietnam-backed regime in Cambodia, the Soviet-backed government of Afghanistan, and subsequently the Taliban regime in that country.

Establishment of Diplomatic Relations. The third step along the road of foreign relations, after recognition of a state and of its government, is the establishment of diplomatic relations. This too is a separate and independent step. A state may recognize another state and its government, but not have diplomatic relations with it. For example, the United States recognizes Cuba as a state and the Castro government as its representative, but does not have formal diplomatic relations with Cuba.

As with recognition of statehood and governments, the President has exclusive authority to decide to open (or terminate) diplomatic relations with another government. Nevertheless, perhaps unlike the simpler cases involving recognition of statehood and government, the President needs the support of Congress to carry on diplomatic relations effectively. Congress must authorize and fund the Department of State, officials and diplomats, and U.S. embassies and consulates abroad.

When nations establish diplomatic relations they usually exchange diplomatic missions and establish embassies in each other's capitals. The diplomatic missions are normally headed by an ambassador plenipotentiary (which means that she can speak with unquestionable full authority for her country), although in cases where relations are not so good or important the chief of mission may be a lower ranking "chargé d' affaires." The diplomats and embassy are entitled to diplomatic immunity under international and U.S. law. This immunity provides virtually absolute protection against criminal prosecution and other assertions of legal jurisdiction. However, the most significant legal consequences flow from recognition, not from establishing diplomatic relations. For example, a recognized government like Cuba can bring lawsuits in the United States and can claim state property in the United States, even though the two governments do not maintain diplomatic relations. Furthermore, even governments without formal diplomatic relations can maintain representatives in each other's capital through "interest sections" in a friendly state's embassy. Thus Cuba has an interest section in the Czech Embassy in Washington, staffed with Cuban diplomats. Finally, states often establish consulates outside the capital for the purpose of promoting commerce and looking after the welfare of their nationals. Consular officials and premises are also entitled to immunity from local legal jurisdiction, although to a lesser extent than diplomats.

The source of authority for this power, like that for the recognition powers discussed above, could be inferred from specific grants of power in the text of the Constitution: The President has the power to appoint ambassadors (albeit with the consent of the Senate) and the power or duty to receive ambassadors, under Article II. In addition, given the executive practice before and after 1789, it may also be comfortably grounded in the Vesting Clause. The President's claims to exclusive power in this domain have been repeatedly endorsed by the Supreme Court.[9]

9. See Restatement (Third) of Foreign Relations Law § 204, reporters note 1(1987).

Although Presidents have always claimed this power to be exclusive, i.e., a power which may not be encroached upon by Congress, there have been occasional examples of congressional interference, such as Congress' attempts to restrict official contacts with the PLO, to require the recognition of Jerusalem as the capital of Israel, and to close consulates.[10] Those legislative acts clearly invaded core executive functions, and hence were arguably unconstitutional, but the pressure for practical cooperation between the branches seems to have led Presidents in some cases to comply. Typically the executive branch lawyers will maintain that the act of Congress is "precatory" or advisory only, thereby maintaining the formal proposition that the President's power is exclusive, even when the President decides to act consistently with the act of Congress in question.

Communicating with Foreign Governments—The Essence of Foreign Policy-Making. The obvious next step along the road of foreign relations is communicating with foreign governments, once they have been recognized and diplomatic relations have been established. Here matters become more controversial. The President claims exclusivity in the exercise and control of this function, including the power to decide the substantive content of U.S. foreign policy, but Congress has not always agreed. Everyone concedes that the President monopolizes control over the channels of communication, but there is

10. See Louis Henkin, Foreign Affairs and the United States Constitution 112–13 (2d ed. 1996).

more controversy over who can tell him what to say. In the Reagan years the President declared U.S. policy to be in favor of supporting the rebels or "Contras" in the Nicaraguan civil war. He executed that policy through secret intelligence and paramilitary operations, and he urged other governments to likewise support the Contras. Congress declared a different policy and sought to bar funds (even salaries) to the executive for carrying out its pro-Contra Nicaragua policy. The resulting constitutional (and policy) conflict became known as the Iran–Contra affair, and was never definitively resolved.[11] In the aftermath of the Iran Contra investigation Congress sought to involve itself more deeply into the substance of foreign policy execution by regulating "requests" to foreign governments to conduct covert actions in support of U.S. foreign policy, such as asking Saudi Arabia to fund the Contras. Congress dropped that attempt after President Bush vetoed the legislation.

Despite occasional rhetorical objections from Congress, as a practical matter the executive takes the initiative in formulating and announcing foreign policy on almost all matters. At the same time Congress can have significant, even decisive, influence on executive decision-making because most policies cannot be effectively executed without legislative authorization and funding from Congress. With that support may come advice or even policy direction so that in practice the exclu-

11. See generally Harold Hongju Koh, The National Security Constitution (1990).

sivity of the President's power to declare foreign policy may be blurred. Congress has ample opportunity to make its preferences known. In the first place, Congress creates all the executive branch agencies that carry out executive functions. It authorizes and pays for the Department of State and other foreign relations-oriented agencies, as well as the Foreign Service and other officials. It funds government operations, such as acquiring embassies abroad and attending meetings of international organizations. Through authorization and appropriations legislation, coupled with congressional oversight of these operations, Congress can deny funds for specified activities and thereby effectively force termination of those activities (like supporting international organizations to provide abortions, closing of embassies and consulates, and even withdrawal from an international organization). In all these cases Congress may be theoretically encroaching upon an exclusive presidential power. Sometimes Presidents object, and even proceed in defiance of Congress, but most of the time the two branches compromise. Consequently, even where the President defends his exclusive authority, and even when he is backed by impeccable legal authority, in fact Congress can wield determinative influence in those relatively rare cases in which it chooses to do so.

Current examples of important presidential policy requiring formal congressional support include such matters as foreign assistance loans to Russia, economic sanctions against states that support terrorism and those committing massive human rights violations (like Burma), and all the military, intelligence and other initiatives taken in response to the September 11 attacks. Congress has even taken the initiative in forcing new policies on a reluctant executive, as with promoting human rights in the mid 1970s, and harsh sanctions against Cuba and Iran in the 1990s.

Despite the practical congressional influence, the President's formal claims to monopolize authority to enunciate foreign policy has a strong pedigree. Although not spelled out in the text or discussed by the Framers, the President's claim is supported by eighteenth century practice informing the Vesting Clause, coupled with the functionalist advantages sought by the Framers for the new executive. Early pronouncements of some of the Framers confirm this interpretation. On the floor of the House of Representatives in 1800 John Marshall stated that "[t]he President is the sole organ of the nation in its external relations, and its sole representative with foreign nations."[12] Even Jefferson once delivered an effusive endorsement of presidential authority: "The transaction of business with foreign nations is executive altogether."[13] Early Congresses

12. Annuals, 6th Cong., col. 613. This statement, like the dictum from *Curtiss-Wright*, is often quoted out of context. Marshall was defending the right of the President to execute a treaty obligation by extraditing a person against a claim that extradition was a judicial function. Even literally the statement can be read to mean only that the President communicates policy, and not to mean that the President also has authority to make policy.

13. Opinion on the Powers of the Senate (April 24, 1790) in 5 The Writings of Thomas Jefferson 161 (Paul Leicester Ford ed., 1895).

also assumed or conceded that the President alone had authority under the new Constitution to speak for the nation and to carry on diplomatic relations. The third Congress passed the Logan Act which makes it a crime for a private citizen to communicate U.S. policy to a foreign government.[14] The purpose of the legislation was to assure executive control of official communications to foreign governments. Presidents since Washington have claimed that monopoly. President Monroe's doctrine was an early example. President Grant even declined to honor a law requesting the Secretary of State to thank Argentina for a recent congratulatory message, on the grounds that Congress may not direct the executive to communicate to foreign governments views dictated by Congress. All the major foreign policy initiatives of at least the past 100 years have proceeded from the initiative of the executive branch.

The Supreme Court also has endorsed the general proposition that the President has the exclusive authority to determine the content of foreign policy. In *U.S. v. Pink*, the Court declared with reference to foreign affairs that the President has the power to determine the "public policy of the United States."[15] In *Curtiss-Wright* Justice Sutherland described the Court's view of the content of the President's foreign relations power:

In this vast external realm, ... the President alone has the power to speak or listen as a

14. 18 USC § 953.
15. 315 U.S. 203, 229 (1942).

representative of the nation. He makes treaties with the advice and consent of the Senate; but he alone negotiates. Into the field of negotiation the Senate cannot intrude; and Congress itself is powerless to invade it.... The Senate Committee on Foreign Relations at a very early day in our history (February 15, 1816), reported to the Senate, among other things, as follows:

> The President is the constitutional representative of the United States with regard to foreign nations. He manages our concerns with foreign nations and must necessarily be most competent to determine when, how, and upon what subjects negotiation may be urged with the greatest prospect of success. For his conduct he is responsible to the Constitution. The committee considers this responsibility the surest pledge for the faithful discharge of his duty. They think the interference of the Senate in the direction of foreign negotiations calculated to diminish that responsibility and thereby to impair the best security for the national safety [16] ...

Negotiations. Establishing diplomatic relations with a foreign government blends into communicating with it and then into negotiating with it. As the dictum quoted above from *Curtiss-Wright* indicates, negotiation too is an exclusive presidential prerogative. Historical Practice confirms the general accuracy of Justice Sutherland's dictum. Washington

16. United States v. Curtiss–Wright Export Corp., 299 U.S. 304, 319 (1936).

established the precedent of exclusive executive control of the negotiation process not only by actually dispatching envoys, which has never been controversial, but also by defending their work from intrusive congressional investigation and control, as discussed more fully under Executive Privilege below. Jefferson rebuked France's representative, Citizen Genet, for going to Congress in 1793 with a complaint, and early Congresses conceded that negotiation was exclusively presidential. Subsequent Congresses have from time to time tried to restrict the executive's negotiation prerogative, but without success. For example, Wilson went to Versailles despite an act of Congress that prohibited attendance at a conference without specific congressional authorization. In the wake of the Iran–Contra scandal Congress attempted to restrict the ability of the President to make certain requests to foreign governments, but President Bush vetoed the legislation of which that restriction was a part, and in the subsequent negotiation Congress agreed to drop the restriction. Bush also stated that he would ignore a restriction on negotiating with the PLO.[17] In signing the 1997 Defense Authorization Act, President Clinton stated:

> Provisions purporting to require the President to enter into or report on specified negotiations with foreign governments, as well as a provision that limits the information that could be revealed in negotiations, intrude on the President's constitutional authority to conduct the Nation's diplo-

17. 26 Weekly Comp. Pres. Docs. 266 (Feb. 16, 1990).

macy and the President's role as Commander in Chief. I will interpret these provisions as precatory.[18]

Negotiation includes many stages involving numerous decisions along the way. The executive branch decides what to negotiate about, when to start a negotiation, with whom to negotiate, the tactics to be pursued and the compromises to be made. Throughout this process, however, Congress can and often does influence the executive branch's decisions. The congressional role may be formal or informal. Since Wilson's failure to secure Senate approval of the Versailles treaty after World War I, Presidents have often appointed Senators to important negotiating delegations, and have often consulted members of Congress regarding negotiating positions.[19] In addition, in the case of trade agreements, members of Congress have been part of the negotiating delegation and have followed the course of the negotiations carefully, especially in those subject to a "fast-track" procedure for approval of such agreements.[20] As noted above, the President has resisted congressional attempts to appoint or designate negotiators, but Presidents have often complied in practice, while stating that they treat a

18. William J. Clinton, Statement on Signing the National Defense Authorization Act for Fiscal Year 1997, Sept. 23, 1996, 32 Weekly Comp. Pres. Docs. Sept. 24, 1996, pp. 1842–43.

19. See Louis Fisher, Congressional Participation in the Treaty Process, 137 U.Pa.L.Rev. 1511 (1989).

20. Louis Fisher, The Politics of Shared Power—Congress and the Executive 151 (3d ed. 1993).

congressional direction as "advisory" rather than mandatory.

Congress has also sought to force negotiations on subjects in which it is interested, as when the Senate directed the President to try to negotiate an arms control treaty dealing with modifications of the environment or a treaty dealing with specified fishing problems. To the latter President Clinton responded:

Section 105(b)(2) directs the Secretary of State, in cooperation with the Secretary of Commerce, to seek to secure international agreements on the subject of bycatch reduction. Under our Constitution, it is the President who articulates the Nation's foreign policy and who determines the timing and subject matter of our negotiations with foreign nations. Accordingly, in keeping with past practice, I shall treat this provision as advisory, not mandatory.[21]

The executive branch in fact sought such agreements.

The President has likewise objected to congressional direction as to how to organize decision-making authority within the executive branch, such as congressional selection of particular officials to discharge specified functions. For example, the 1996 Intelligence Authorization Act Congress required the establishment of two new sub–committees of

21. Statement on Signing the Sustainable Fisheries Act, October 11, 1996 32 Weekly Comp. of Pres. Docs. No. 40, p. 2040, 2041.

the NSC. President Clinton "noted" that he had already started to examine these reforms on his own, and the President added that the congressional provisions "unduly intrude upon Executive prerogatives and responsibilities."[22] In the Trade Act of 1974 Congress directed that the U.S. Trade Representative, not the Secretary of State, conduct trade negotiations, a direction that has been honored. In legislation dealing with intelligence Congress provided that covert intelligence activities be carried out by the CIA unless the President specifically decided that another entity should do it in accordance with a legislatively prescribed standard. This command too seems to have been followed.

The record thus shows that even when Congress acts in a precatory or advisory manner, through "sense" of the Congress resolutions or by requesting the executive to consider a particular course of action, the executive often accedes. Indeed the language of these resolutions and other congressional acts are themselves frequently worked out between the branches. The President may win the formal legal battle, preserving executive authority, by conceding the practical result to congressional desires.

Members of Congress sometimes negotiate directly with foreign governments. Normally they inform the State Department of their plans and discussions. The President may even encourage such missions, as with President Clinton's use of Representative Bill Richardson (who visited and negotiated

---

22. Statement on signing the Intelligence Authorization Act Fiscal Year 1997, id. at 2039.

with North Korea, Burma and Nigeria). Occasionally members of Congress proceed on their own. House Speaker Wright conducted his own diplomacy to end the Nicaraguan Civil War. Senators recently negotiated for the release of hostages in Kashmir, human rights in Nigeria, and economic prospects in Afghanistan. Although these emissaries may have some impact, especially if their mission is encouraged by the President, they still do not speak "officially" for the United States. These examples nevertheless show again how exclusive presidential power is in practice blurred, influenced, and even shared with Congress.

Even when Congress is not directly connected to a negotiation, its influence may be expressed in other ways. For example, it is not uncommon for Congress to specify negotiating objectives (e.g. more effective dispute-settlement in trade agreements). In addition, the Senate may influence prospective negotiations through pressure on an ambassador during the confirmation process. Furthermore, the executive branch frequently briefs congressional committees during the course of a negotiation, hears their views and prudently tries to accommodate them. Sometimes Congress formalizes this process. For example, the "Derwinski amendment" purports to require the President to report proposals and counter-proposals made during arms control negotiations.[23] Congress can also constrain the executive's flexibility by legislation with respect to the substance of the negotiations. The "Jackson amend-

23. 22 U.S.C. § 2577.

ment" (named after the conservative Democratic Senator from Washington) urges that no arms control agreement limit the United States to levels of strategic forces inferior to the limits imposed on the then Soviet Union.[24] These laws seem to trespass on the executive function, but the executive reaction has normally been accommodation rather than defiance.

Other Manifestations of the President's Foreign Relations Power. The product of a negotiation is often an international agreement. The President formally controls all aspects of the negotiation process leading to the conclusion of an agreement, although Congress can influence that process as well as a practical matter. Once the agreement is negotiated, the President may then bring it into force by "ratifying" it. The law governing the authorization, ratification, and effect of international treaties is covered in Chapter Four.

The foreign relations power has supported a variety of mostly uncontroversial domestic activities, such as authorizing transborder bridges, pipelines and cables. The President has claimed more controversial powers at the border, including excluding aliens not covered by an act of Congress,[25] and excluding foreign vessels.[26] He has asserted U.S.

24. H.R.J. Res. 1227 § 3, Pub. L.No. 92–448 (1972), reprinted in John Norton Moore et. al., National Security Law 610 (1990).

25. Garcia–Mir v. Meese, 788 F.2d 1446 (11th Cir.1986).

26. The executive branch unilaterally acted to exclude, and then to regulate, access to U.S. ports in the early 1970s.

jurisdiction and control over the oceans.[27] In all these examples the President acted without congressional authorization, relying on the foreign relations power embodied in the Vesting Clause.

The President also makes domestic law based on the foreign affairs power that is applied by the courts in the context of certain narrow areas of litigation involving foreign states and officials. The executive branch determines whether or not a person qualifies for diplomatic immunity. In the past the President also determined whether a government was entitled to sovereign immunity in American courts and whether the Act of State doctrine applied in a given case. These were the most conspicuous examples of domestic law-making by the President. In the past two decades, in reaction to the excesses of presidential power culminating in Watergate, presidential law-making has been in disfavor. The current Supreme Court seems to have definitively rejected executive branch authority to permit or deny application of the Act of State doctrine,[28] and Congress removed foreign sovereign immunity decisions from the executive branch when it enacted the Foreign Sovereign Immunities Act of 1976 (FSIA).[29] Nevertheless, even in these two areas, the President can still appear in court and

27. See President Reagan, U.S. Ocean Policy, 19 Weekly Comp. Pres. Doc. 383 (Mar. 10, 1983) and Proclamation by President Truman, 13 Dept. of State Bul. 485 (July–Dec 1945).

28. W.S. Kirkpatrick & Co. v. Environmental Tectonics Corp., 493 U.S. 400 (1990).

29. Pub.L.No. 94–583, 90 Stat. 2891 (1976)(codified at 28 U.S.C. §§ 1330, 1603–11).

"suggest" that the act of state doctrine apply or not apply, or "suggest" how the FSIA should be interpreted, just as the President advises the court on how to interpret treaties and other aspects of international law. Although the courts have the final say, as a practical matter they almost always follow executive advice. These examples of domestic lawmaking by the President can also be revived in an urgent situation, as the *Dames & Moore* case arising out of the Iran Hostage crisis well illustrates.[30]

Finally, the foreign relations power may combine synergistically with other powers, like the Commander in Chief power, or be joined with the Take Care clause, to support military action and intelligence missions, which are the subjects of Chapter Five.

Executive Privilege. From the beginning Presidents have invoked the constitutional doctrine known as "executive privilege" in order to withhold documents from the public and from Congress on grounds of foreign policy and national security. Such documents typically include diplomatic correspondence with foreign nations, instructions to American negotiators, their reports of foreign government views, reports of diplomatic incidents that may become subject to negotiation, information concerning current foreign policy initiatives, as well as intelligence reports and documents relating to military plans and programs. Executive privilege also extends to documents describing pre-decision deliberations, such as recommendations to the President,

30. Supra Chapter Four.

minutes of policy-setting meetings, and other records of the views of persons involved in the policy-making process. Executive privilege covers matters beyond foreign policy (e.g. on-going criminal investigations, personnel matters, and domestically focused pre-decision deliberations).

Information requested by the media and other members of the public is now governed by the Freedom of Information Act. Because this Act protects defense and foreign policy sensitive information from disclosure, there is no need for the Executive to invoke the Constitution in this context. Constitutional disputes arise when sensitive information is requested by a member of Congress or a congressional committee. In fact these disputes are rare. For example, between 1964 and 1973, the executive branch denied only 30 requests for information out of a total of over 200,000 demands from Congress.[31] When a congressional committee demands information that executive officials do not wish to provide, normally there is an extensive negotiation.[32] Attempts may be made to narrow the scope of the request, or to substitute redacted documents or summaries of requested documents instead of the documents themselves, or to limit access, e.g. to members of Congress and not their staffs. In almost all cases the political branches compromise. When the matter is sufficiently impor-

[31]. See 6 Op. Off. Legal Counsel 751,782.

[32]. See Joel D. Bush, Note, Congressional–Executive Access Disputes: Legal Standards and Political Settlements, 9 J.L. and Pol. 719 (1993).

tant or politically hot, it may be taken to court, but the courts have been reluctant to decide the merits. There are two recent examples where the court simply ordered the parties to compromise the issues and supervised the process to assure that it was done.[33] On several occasions in recent decades Presidents have even abandoned the privilege in the face of negative media comment and public reaction, which may associate the invocation of the privilege with crimes, cover-up, corruption, and Watergate-like wrongdoing.[34]

The President's authority to invoke executive privilege is not expressly specified in the text of the Constitution, but it is well entrenched constitutional doctrine that can be grounded in the Vesting Clause. Early Historical Practice, including decisions taken by officials who were also Framers, confirmed the legitimacy of the privilege. President Washington refused to provide the House of Representatives with diplomatic correspondence relating to the Jay treaty negotiation concluding the Revolutionary War. That decision could be explained on the grounds that the treaty was only of concern to the Senate, the Framers having deliberately excluded the House from the treaty process. Nevertheless, in a separate incident, Washington also claimed the

33. See U.S. v. American Tel. & Tel. Co., 551 F.2d 384 (D.C.Cir.1976); U.S. v. American Tel. & Tel. Co., 567 F.2d 121 (D.C.Cir.1977); U.S. v. House of Representatives, 556 F.Supp. 150 (D.D.C.1983).

34. See Randall K. Miller, Congressional Inquests: Suffocating the Constitutional Prerogative of Executive Privilege, 81 Minn. L. Rev. 631 (1997).

right to refuse to provide the Senate with diplomatic correspondence from his representative in France dealing with French politics, personalities and military affairs.[35] In addition, following a disastrous military defeat in 1791—the St. Clair expedition against Indians in the Ohio country—the Washington Cabinet (including Jefferson) affirmed the principle of executive privilege in connection with its review of documents sought by Congress, although in the end the documents were all released. The privilege has regularly been invoked by subsequent Presidents and respected by Congress and the Supreme Court.

United States v. Nixon[36] declined to permit the President to invoke the privilege in a domestic criminal proceeding (where the Court said that the executive's need to protect the confidentiality of its deliberative process had to be balanced against the judiciary's duty to do justice in criminal trials). In its opinion, the Court suggested that the result might be different if the matter involved "military, diplomatic, or sensitive national security secrets."[37] Some recent Supreme Court opinions have adopted a functional balancing test in resolving separation of powers disputes between the political branches, but this approach seems inappropriate for cases involving foreign affairs. Applying such an approach in those cases would require determining whether

35. Gordon B. Baldwin, The Foreign Affairs Advice Privilege, 1976 Wisc. L. Rev. 16, 33–4.

36. 418 U.S. 683 (1974).

37. Id. at 706.

handing over the documents in question would impair the executive's ability to conduct foreign relations more than secrecy impairs Congress's ability to legislate. Such a balancing could lead a court into assessments of the likely foreign government reaction and consequences for foreign policy, tasks which courts have regularly shied away from. Indeed, in such a case, a President would be justified in declining to permit the courts even to see the secret documents or to decide what secret information need be revealed. Extra-judicial compromise is the appropriate course of action.[38]

Under the foreign affairs power the President operates a vast program to "classify" information as secret, and prevent its disclosure by government employees. The program applies to documents and data generated or received by officials, such as cables to and from embassies abroad, and memoranda dealing with foreign policy, defense or intelligence matters. A presidential Executive Order establishes criteria for classifying information as "confidential," "secret" or "top secret" and provides procedures for access to the information, and its handling, storage and review. Violations such as

---

38. In non-foreign policy cases President Clinton, like Nixon before him, sought judicial support for an executive privilege claim, but lost the balancing test. Professor Yoo criticizes Nixon's and Clinton's failure to emulate Jefferson in the Burr trial by asserting privilege and compromising so as to avoid a judicial decision that might define presidential power but which in the end could restrict presidential flexibility. Jefferson maintained the sole right to determine what information was privileged. John C. Yoo, The First Claim: The Burr Trial, *United States v. Nixon*, and Presidential Power, 83 Minn. L. Rev. 1435 (1999).

unauthorized disclosure carry administrative penalties, including possible dismissal from government service. The classification program is functionally related to conducting diplomacy, and hence is implied by or grows out of the foreign relations power that encompasses executive privilege. Congress has recognized and implicitly approved the program.

Executive Privilege is related to the common law State Secrets Privilege, under which the executive may block the production of evidence in court on foreign policy and national security grounds. That privilege is absolute, and may be invoked by the head of the executive department holding the information (unlike Executive Privilege which must be invoked by the President himself).[39] The State Secrets Privilege is not available in criminal cases. In those cases the Government must utilize the procedures of the Classified Information Procedures Act,[40] which provides for a confidential examination of secret evidence to determine its relevance. Then, if any secret evidence is relevant, the Government must either permit its disclosure at the trial or abandon the prosecution.

The President may assert common law based privileges, like the attorney-client and matrimonial privileges, and has a right of privacy that shields personal letters and the like from disclosure. He also has an official immunity from being sued for

39. U.S. v. Reynolds, 345 U.S. 1 (1953).

40. See Jeff Jarvis, Protecting the Nation's National Security: The Classified Information Procedures Act, 20 Thur. Marshall L. Rev. 319 (1995).

actions taken within the scope (broadly conceived) of his office,[41] but that privilege does not extend to acts outside the scope of his office, such as acts taken before being elected.[42]

Bibliographic Note

The literature on executive power is vast. The classic text is Edward Samuel Corbin, The President: Office and Powers 1789–1984 (5th ed. 1984). The most comprehensive and detailed recent treatment is Louis Henkin, Foreign Affairs and the United States Constitution (2d ed. 1996). See also the Restatement (Third) of Foreign Relations Law and the works cited in the first and third paragraphs of the Bibliographic Note to Chapter One.

Peter M. Shane and Harold H. Bruff, Separation of Powers Law (1996), presents a comprehensive collection of materials on presidential power, domestic as well as foreign policy related, in the context of American separation of powers doctrine. Recent scholarship includes H. Jefferson Powell, The President's Authority over Foreign Affairs: An Executive Branch Perspective, 67 Geo. Wash. L. Rev. 527 (1999) (including extensive discussion of Executive Branch legal memoranda).

41. Nixon v. Fitzgerald, 457 U.S. 731 (1982).

42. Clinton v. Jones, 520 U.S. 681 (1997).

CHAPTER THREE

CONGRESS

Congress has comprehensive authority to legislate with respect to foreign relations. Although its powers are formally limited to those powers that are specifically enumerated in Article I of the Constitution, the enumerated powers in practice cover all aspects of the subject. The most important non-military powers relating to foreign relations include the powers to regulate foreign commerce, levy taxes and tariffs, borrow money, and regulate the value of the dollar. In the military area Congress has the power to raise an army and navy, to make rules for their government and regulation, and to declare war, as well as having various powers relating to the state militias (or national guard as they are now called) and the now obsolete powers to grant Letters of Marque and Reprisal (a kind of private war power) and to make rules regarding the law of prize. With respect to international law Congress has the power to define and punish piracy and other offenses on the high seas.

The broadest power, and one of the most important in the context of foreign relations, is the power to make any law "necessary and proper" to "carry into execution" any power of the Government (the

"Necessary and Proper Clause"[1]), including powers, such as the foreign relations power, exercised by the President under the Constitution. Finally, of equal importance, no money can be spent by the Government unless the funds have been appropriated by Congress. This appropriations power gives Congress the ability to check the President by refusing to fund any program that it opposes.

Employing these powers Congress legislates with respect to all aspects of foreign affairs, and has clear constitutional authority under the Necessary and Proper Clause to do so. The most striking aspect of congressional foreign relations power is not its breadth, but the restraint with which it has been exercised. Congress occasionally legislates in minute detail with respect to foreign policy, but more often it delegates vast parts of its legislative authority to the executive. For example, Congress has delegated law-making power to regulate foreign commerce to the President under the International Emergency Economic Powers Act (IEEPA) and the Export Administration Act (EAA). Congress has also delegated power to the President to carry out decisions of the UN Security Council under the UN Participation Act. Under these and similar acts Presidents have imposed economic sanctions against many countries, human right-based sanctions against South Africa, Rhodesia and Burma, and more selective regulation affecting dozens of countries.

1.   U.S. Const. Art. I, sec. 8.

In addition to passing laws, Congress establishes federal offices and provides for the appointment of officials. Congress therefore creates and defines the missions of all the executive branch departments. Congress has normally been content to authorize and fund executive branch agencies, leaving them free to pursue general mandates without much restriction or oversight. After establishing the agencies of government Congress then authorizes and funds their activities. There are two separate stages in this legislative process—authorization and appropriation. Congress first authorizes the expenditure of funds for activities of the programs and agencies it has established, and then in a separate process it appropriates those funds (often a lesser amount than originally authorized). Both the authorization process and the appropriations process are regular legislative processes, i.e. the bills are passed by both Houses of Congress and presented to the President, so an appropriation bill can regulate substantive matters just as effectively as an authorization bill. Some commentators have argued that "mere" appropriations measures cannot regulate substantive matters, but that position is not supported in legal doctrine or practice.

There are separate committees for each department's authorizations and appropriations. For example, in the Senate the defense authorization bills are drafted and initially approved by the Armed Services Committee, the State Department authorization bills by the Foreign Relations Committee, and trade authorization legislation by the Finance

Committee, while appropriations for all those authorized programs are under the jurisdiction of the Appropriations Committee. Using its legislative powers Congress has frequently endorsed general foreign policy objectives, e.g., human rights, and Congress can attach conditions to expenditures that effectively determine an applicable course of action.

The appropriations process gives Congress its principal leverage over foreign policy. Policy implementation costs money, and unless Congress has appropriated funds the executive cannot effectively execute the foreign policy that it has the constitutional prerogative to announce. The practical effect of congressional prerogative, however, is diluted by virtue of the large amount of discretion that Congress habitually gives the President in the legislative process. In part because of the inevitability of unanticipated foreign policy developments, Congress permits the President to transfer funds from one account or agency (e.g. the CIA) to another (e.g. AID) and to reprogram appropriated funds (e.g. aid to Cambodia to Bosnia). In addition, the President may use general, lump-sum accounts, such as the Defense Department's Operations and Maintenance account, to meet unexpected contingencies. Congress has also explicitly provided contingency funds and emergency legislation to permit the commitment of emergency funds even in the absence of an appropriation.

Another significant source of congressional power over foreign policy comes through its power to *expressly deny funds* for specified purposes. In recent years Congress has used its Appropriations power to influence a broad range of foreign policy matters, from matters of critical concern to the nation as a whole to items of interest to particular constituencies or even a single member. For example, Congress has used the power of the purse to restrict and formally terminate the war in Southeast Asia, to end covert support for insurgents in Angola, and to limit presidential assistance to the Contras in Nicaragua. It has also assured the funding of specific projects of interest to particular members of Congress in Israel, Armenia and the Ukraine. Through the appropriations process Congress has also limited aid to international organizations that support abortion, and has denied funding for the salaries of executive branch officials in specified contexts.

In almost all cases Congress does not unilaterally foist its positions unannounced on the executive. Instead the annual appropriations process sets the stage for an elaborate negotiation in which the branches trade off programs and priorities. For example, in 1996 Congress conceded increased funding for North Korea and a new Middle East development bank in deference to executive priorities, and it dropped a proposal to deny funding to organizations that provided abortions, but it then sharply limited overall funds for family planning programs to the point that the Clinton Administration said it would be forced to close some birth control programs abroad. Dealing with the same bill the President agreed to adopt some sanctions against Burma in exchange for the Senate's abandoning a more stringent approach. The lesson is that political compromise pervades the exercise of independent constitutional powers. Even though Congress has the exclusive power to determine funding priorities, it recognizes the importance of an effective foreign policy and the need to honor some measure of presidential discretion.

The power of the purse is an especially powerful tool, especially in light of the Anti–Deficiency Act,[2] which makes it a crime to spend or authorize the expenditure of funds unless there is a corresponding appropriation. Regardless of the likelihood of actual criminal prosecution, it is fair to say that no responsible executive official will risk being branded a criminal by knowingly authorizing the expenditure of funds without an appropriation. This prospect also enhances the role of lawyers in agency decision-making. For example, before an international agreement may be concluded, the State Department's Office of the Legal Advisor issues an opinion regarding its legality, including not only the constitutional authority of the executive branch to conclude the agreement but also the availability of adequate funds to carry it out.

Congress also has non-legislative powers. Ever since the First Congress it has exercised a right to investigate just about anything it wants. Correct practice requires that the subject be related to a legitimate legislative purpose, but since Congress can legislate comprehensively regarding foreign af-

2.   31 U.S.C. § 1341(a)(1)(A), 33 Stat. 1213.

fairs, little would seem to be excluded in this area. The Senate has its own right to investigate and demand information regarding treaties.

A. Limitations on Congressional Power

Specific Prohibitions. The Constitution contains a number of specific prohibitions affecting Congress. It cannot impose an export tax, nor may it discriminate among U.S. ports. Taxes and tariffs must be uniform throughout the country. These express limitations do not raise significant contemporary issues.

Enumerated Powers. The second formal limitation on congressional power stems from the fact that when the states created the federal government under the 1789 Constitution, they delegated only the specific powers enumerated in Article I, section 8 to the new Congress. In contrast to vesting "the" executive power in the President, they did not delegate a general legislative power. The Tenth Amendment reinforced the limited nature of the delegation to Congress by specifying that the "powers not delegated to the United States by the Constitution, nor prohibited by it to the States, are reserved to the States respectively, or to the people."

The actual force of the Tenth Amendment, however, seemed to evaporate after the New Deal Supreme Court interpreted the enumerated powers, especially the Commerce Clause, so broadly that virtually all subjects of national interest were within Congress' power. Federal spending also became so expansive that the Spending Power became an important practical source of congressional influence. Furthermore, in the foreign policy arena, the Treaty Power set forth in Article II and the foreign affairs power, embodied in the Vesting Clause, clearly were powers of the federal government which Congress could implement under the Necessary and Proper Clause. The Tenth Amendment did not seem to be an impediment to federal or congressional power over foreign affairs. Nevertheless, some recent Supreme Court decisions have limited Congress' powers under the Commerce Clause and the Fourteenth Amendment, and the Court has judicially enforced principles of federalism. These decisions, if expanded to cover foreign relations matters like human rights, could restrict the executive's conduct of foreign policy.

The Tenth Amendment and the Bill of Rights. The extent to which congressional implementation of the Treaty Power under the Necessary and Proper Clause could trump states' rights protected by the Tenth Amendment, and even the Bill of Rights, was sharply contested for much of the twentieth century. The literal language of Article VI suggests that treaties, unlike statutes, are law of the land even if they violate the Bill of Rights (including the Tenth Amendment). Article VI says that laws made "in Pursuance" of the Constitution are law of the land, while treaties made "under the Authority of the United States" have that status. Thus it could be argued that a treaty would be law of the land even if not made pursuant to, or in accordance with, the Constitution so long as it is made under the authority of the country. The difference in language, however, seems best explained by referring to the historical context of its drafting. The different language regarding treaties seems intended simply to assure that treaties made by the Government under the Articles of Confederation would be honored under the new 1789 Constitution, not that it was intended to give treaties superior status as law.

The issue reached the Supreme Court in *Missouri v. Holland*.[3] In that case, to counteract an alarming decline in migrating ducks and geese, Congress had passed a law to regulate the hunting of migratory birds. However, the law was vigorously attacked on the grounds that it invaded states' rights protected by the Tenth Amendment to the Constitution. Some lower courts in fact had declared the act of Congress to be unconstitutional. The federal Government concluded a treaty with Canada calling for such regulation by both parties, and Congress passed legislation to implement the treaty obligations. Consequently the Government defended the implementing legislation under the Necessary and Proper Clause. Conservative states' rights advocates, however, argued that the Tenth Amendment overrode the federal Government's treaty power with respect to matters within the historical prerogatives of state governments. Later on, in the 1940s and 1950s, these same arguments were made to

3. 252 U.S. 416 (1920).

challenge the ability of the federal Government to conclude treaties dealing with labor matters and civil rights, which then were still considered to be exclusively state prerogatives.

In *Missouri v. Holland* the Supreme Court rejected the states' rights argument. Justice Holmes said:

It is said that a treaty cannot be valid if it infringes the Constitution, that there are limits, therefore, to the treatymaking power, and that one such limit is that what an act of Congress could not do unaided, in derogation of the powers reserved to the States, a treaty cannot do. An earlier act of Congress that attempted by itself and not in pursuance of a treaty to regulate the killing of migratory birds within the States had been held bad in the District Court. Those decisions were supported by arguments that migratory birds were owned by the States in their sovereign capacity for the benefit of their people, and that ... this control was one that Congress had no power to displace. The same argument is supposed to apply now with equal force.

Whether the two cases cited were decided rightly or not they cannot be accepted as a test of the treaty power....

We do not mean to imply that there are no qualifications to the treatymaking power; but they must be ascertained in a different way. It is obvious that there may be matters of the sharpest exigency for the national well being that an act of Congress could not deal with but that a treaty

followed by such an act could, and it is not lightly
to be assumed that, in matters requiring national
action, "a power which must belong to and some-
where reside in every civilized government" is
not to be found. . . . We are not yet discussing the
particular case before us but only are considering
the validity of the test proposed. With regard to
that we may add that when we are dealing with
words that also are a constituent act, like the
Constitution of the United States, we must realize that they have called into life a being the
development of which could not have been fore-
seen completely by the most gifted of its beget-
ters. It was enough for them to realize or to hope
that they had created an organism; it has taken a
century and has cost their successors much sweat
and blood to prove that they created a nation.
The case before us must be considered in the light
of our whole experience and not merely in that of
what was said a hundred years ago. The treaty in
question does not contravene any prohibitory
words to be found in the Constitution. The only
question is whether it is forbidden by some invisi-
ble radiation from the general terms of the Tenth
Amendment. We must consider what this country
has become in deciding what that Amendment
has reserved.

The State as we have intimated founds its
claim of exclusive authority upon an assertion of
title to migratory birds, an assertion that is embodied in statute. No doubt it is true that as
between a State and its inhabitants the State may

regulate the killing and sale of such birds, but it does not follow that its authority is exclusive of paramount powers....

As most of the laws of the United States are carried out within the states and as many of them deal with matters which in the silence of such laws the State might regulate, such general grounds are not enough to support Missouri's claim.... No doubt the great body of private relations usually fall within the control of the State, but a treaty may override its power....[4]

The decision was very unpopular with states' rights advocates. Senator Bricker, a conservative Republican from Ohio, led a campaign to amend the Constitution to overturn the decision (and to make all treaties non-self-executing as well), but that effort (known as the Bricker Amendment) was finally defeated in 1955. It seems likely that one effect of international interdependence will be more treaties dealing with matters traditionally regulated by the states. For example, in recent years the United States has become actively involved in negotiating agreements on human rights, criminal law, family law, and "private international law" matters, designed to provide a uniform law for "private" transactions that cross national borders, such as contracts, judicial process, arbitral awards, child adoption and custody, wills of persons with assets in more than one state, etc. These agreements deal with matters normally dealt with by state legislatures and raise again the issues re-

4.   252 U.S. 416, 432–34 (1920)

solved by *Missouri v. Holland.* Under *Holland* Congress could acquire the ability to legislate in areas traditionally left to the states (e.g. family law, education and local police practice) as a result of these new treaties unless the Supreme Court were to extend the federalism limits developed in the last decade in domestic affairs to the Treaty Power.[5] In the meantime the Senate has established a practice of attaching Understandings to its Resolutions of Ratification of human rights treaties negating any additional federal legislative power by virtue of the treaty. Such a practice effectively overrules *Holland* for purposes of that treaty's effect, and it could be used selectively for treaties that deal with core state functions.

Conservatives also raised the spectre of the Treaty Power's overriding individual liberties enshrined in the Bill of Rights. In 1957, however, the Supreme Court squarely held that legislation pursuant to treaties must comply with the Bill of Rights.[6] The matter is not controversial today. Thus Congress could not pass a law prohibiting all hate speech, even if the United States were obligated to do so by a treaty binding on it under international law.

The requirements of the Bill of Rights are nevertheless not necessarily the same when the Government operates abroad or when the activity in question directly affects foreign policy. Thus, in *Reid v. Covert* Justice Harlan suggested in a concurring

5. See Curtis A. Bradley, The Treaty Power and American Federalism, 97 Mich. L. Rev. 390 (1998).

6. Reid v. Covert, 354 U.S. 1 (1957).

opinion that the Bill of Rights could operate differently when the government acts abroad so that some practices constitutionally required at home would be relaxed abroad, e.g., the right to a jury trial. Recently the Court held that the Fourth Amendment requirement of a judicial warrant before searching a residence does not apply abroad.[7] The Court also held that Congress may deny the right to travel abroad in circumstances where the First Amendment might dictate a different result at home.[8] The very existence of constitutional rights abroad for non-citizens is open to question.[9] In the wake of the September 11 attacks, the rights of aliens have been especially scrutinized and controversially restricted.

Structural Limitation—The Legislative Veto. The *Chadha* case[10] established another limit on congressional power by striking down its use of the "legislative veto." As the size and complexity of government multiplied, especially in the last seventy-five years, Congress struggled with the problem of how to supervise and control executive branch operations. Efficiency required broad delegations of authority, but Congress had difficulty carrying out effective oversight. Executive branch action could be taken before Congress knew about it, and the episodic subsequent review provided by oversight

7. U.S. v. Verdugo–Urquidez, 494 U.S. 259 (1990).

8. Haig v. Agee, 453 U.S. 280 (1981).

9. See Louis Henkin, Foreign Affairs and the United States Constitution 307 (2d ed. 1996).

10. 462 U.S. 919 (1983).

hearings left very wide discretion with the executive as a practical matter. To meet these problems Congress devised the legislative veto, under which whenever the Executive or an administrative agency took a specified action, like imposing a special tariff on Brazil or deciding to sell arms to Jordan, that action would be reported to Congress. Thereupon, depending on the statute, a specified committee, or one House of Congress, or Congress as a whole, could veto the action, thereby terminating its legal effectiveness. The Supreme Court struck down the procedure in broad terms, holding that when Congress takes action that is "essentially legislative in purpose," i.e., having the "purpose and effect of altering the legal rights, duties and relations of persons ... outside the legislative branch,"[11] it must act in the normal law-making fashion, i.e., both Houses of Congress must approve the bill and present it to the President for approval, in which case the President may veto the legislation and Congress may override that veto only by a 2/3 vote of each House. As a result Congress can only act formally in that prescribed procedure.

The *Chadha* decision invalidated many legislative vetoes affecting foreign relations legislation. The subjects affected included foreign aid, defense contracts, sales of military equipment abroad, exports of nuclear material, and presidentially imposed trade sanctions and economic embargoes. One of the most prominent legislative vetoes was in the War Powers Resolution, discussed in Chapter Five

11. Id. at 952.

below, that permitted Congress to terminate U.S. military operations at any time by concurrent resolution.

In many cases Congress reacted to the *Chadha* decision by repealing one-House and concurrent resolution vetoes and substituting *joint* resolutions of disapproval. In these cases executive action would thus be subject to override only if Congress were able to pass a joint resolution, presumably over the President's veto. Thus a 2/3 majority of both houses would be necessary to reverse an executive decision, instead of one House or both Houses acting by majority vote. Congress has formally abandoned the legislative veto over arms sales, trade actions and export controls including those dealing with nuclear cooperation agreements. Nevertheless, some legislative vetoes are still on the books, and as a practical matter they may be respected. According to a congressional observer, Congress has enacted over 200 laws containing new legislative vetoes, mostly committee vetoes,[12] since the *Chadha* decision. Although Presidents have objected and said they will consider such measures inoperative, in fact agencies seem often to have complied in practice. For example, transfers of funds from one account to another, or from one program to another, are subject to informal committee approval. The threat that Congress could withdraw executive flexibility, or even reduce funding, induces executive deference to congressional com-

12. See Louis Fisher, The Legislative Veto: Invalidated, It Survives, 56 Law and Contemp. Probs. 273, 288–91 (No. 4 1993).

mittees, no matter what the Supreme Court says the law requires. In an especially controversial compromise Secretary of State Baker in the Reagan Administration informally agreed not to spend specified funds for the Contras without prior committee approval. Although the lawyers objected, the politicians complied. The practical need for future support from Congress favored political compromise over constitutional principle.

Invasion of Executive Power. Congress may not pass legislation that encroaches upon the powers of a coordinate branch of government, including the President's foreign relations power. The rule is clear when an express executive power is invaded. Although there is less judicial authority when the encroachment is upon a non-express executive power, such as the foreign relations power, there is no reason why Congress should be able more readily to encroach upon the President's foreign policy making than, say, on the appointment of ambassadors.

The case for debarring Congress from legislating in a manner that encroaches upon another branch's prerogative starts with the structure of the Constitution and its basic separation of powers. It is obvious that Congress could not encroach upon the judiciary's powers under Article III by deciding a case before the courts (although of course it may always change the law applicable to a case, even while the case is pending). Nor can Congress diminish the compensation of judges,[13] which is expressly protected by the Compensation Clause, nor may it

13. United States v. Will, 449 U.S. 200 (1980).

single out a named individual for punishment in violation of the Bill of Attainder Clause.[14] Similarly Congress cannot formally appoint an official or an ambassador, or require the removal of a named official, because that legislation would invade the President's appointment power. In *Myers v. U.S.*,[15] the Supreme Court held that Congress may not require its consent to the removal of postmasters who are executive officials. The power to remove officials (unlike the power to appoint them) is not expressly mentioned in the text, but the Court nevertheless invalidated the congressional attempt to encroach upon the executive function. It held that the President must have the power to remove officials in order to protect his power under the Take Care clause; i.e., he needs to be able to fire a subordinate who is not faithfully executing the laws. A plurality of the Supreme Court also recently opined that Congress could not encroach upon the President's exercise of the appointment power by making public the deliberations of an American Bar Association committee giving advice on judicial appointments.[16] These cases involved congressional encroachment on powers expressly mentioned in the text of the Constitution, but the same rule should prevail in the case of powers not expressly mentioned. Non-specified powers can be as important, or more so, than express powers. And the

14. United States v. Lovett, 328 U.S. 303 (1946).

15. 272 U.S. 52 (1926).

16. Public Citizen v. U.S. Department of Justice, 491 U.S. 440 (1989).

political branches do not seem to treat the two
categories differently. Indeed, the foreign relations
power should be considered to be an express power
for this purpose. The Vesting Clause may not be
specific, but it is certainly "express."

In recent years, Congress has tried to appoint
delegates to international conferences, to dictate the
conduct of negotiations, to prohibit negotiation with
the PLO, to insist that the U.S. embassy in Israel
be relocated to Jerusalem, and to close consulates in
France and elsewhere. Earlier, Congress tried to
prevent Presidents from attending international
conferences, to denounce specified treaties and to
recognize the government of Cuba. Presidents have
generally ignored these incursions into their domain
and Congress has acquiesced.

Outside the foreign relations law field, the Supreme Court has sometimes employed a "balancing
test" in cases where Congress burdened a non-
express power of another branch. Under this kind
of analysis the task is to weigh the degree to which
the measure hinders the executive in accomplishing
constitutionally assigned functions, as compared
with the need to accomplish other legitimate congressional objectives. However, such an approach
seems inappropriate in foreign affairs. Assessing the
relative importance of vindicating the foreign relations power in a given case, e.g., negotiating with
the PLO, would require inquiries that the courts
traditionally avoid and making judgments beyond
their functional competence. In addition, the Court
does not seem committed to balancing as an exclu-

sive approach to constitutional interpretation. In other separation of powers cases it has been eclectic. In any event, the courts would likely lean toward favoring executive power in any balance because they traditionally defer to the executive in matters touching foreign affairs.

Some commentators have argued that when Congress acts under its appropriations powers the result, or at least the analysis, should be different.[17] For example, if a balancing test is employed, Congress should get special weight in the balance because the power of the purse is so fundamental to the system of government. It is Congress's ultimate check on executive authority. This check was a key element of Parliament's control of the King, and it was regarded as especially important by the Framers. Although the Appropriations Clause is unquestionably fundamentally important, the apparent constitutional impetus toward compromise of competing claims for authority, coupled with the common law of actual practice, refute claims for a special congressional priority. There are many examples of Presidents' ignoring particular directions in appropriations measures.

Another academic issue raised by commentators concerns the manner in which the President may be required to protest when Congress attempts to legislate foreign policy through its appropriations pow-

17. Peter Raven–Hansen and William C. Banks, From Vietnam to Desert Shield: The Commander in Chief's Spending Power, 81 Iowa L. Rev. 79, 117 n.263 (1995).

er.[18] Congress often asserts its power through riders containing an objectionable policy direction in a general appropriations bill. Because it is usually not practical for a President to veto the general appropriations bill, Presidents have instead exercised the right to interpret the Constitution independently and to simply ignore the offensive provision. In this way the President and his lawyers engage in acts of constitutional interpretation and, over time, in the making of constitutional common law. Some argue, however, that the congressional power of the purse is absolute, so the President must comply with any restriction imposed through the appropriations process.[19] Others say that the President is obligated to veto the entire bill if he thinks a part of it is unconstitutional, and if he does not veto the bill he must obey it because of his duty to take care that the laws are faithfully executed.[20] Alternatively, other commentators argue, the President should be obligated to seek a judicial determination that the offensive measure is unconstitutional before he refuses to obey it.[21]

The better view is that the President is not obligated to execute an unconstitutional provision of a bill even if he has signed it into law, and he is

18. The issue is treated comprehensively id. at 115–26.

19. Raoul Berger, Executive Privilege: A Constitutional Myth 306 (1974).

20. See Arthur S. Miller, The President and Faithful Execution of the Laws, 40 Vand. L. Rev. 389, 397–98 (1987).

21. Panel Discussion, The Appropriations Power and the Necessary and Proper Clause, 68 Wash. U. L. 623, 649 (1990) (Prof. Kate Stith).

not obliged to seek judicial support which probably would not be available anyway. True, the President is obligated to take care that the laws are faithfully executed. However, he also takes an oath to uphold the Constitution (including upholding his executive powers under the Constitution properly interpreted). Article VI states that acts of Congress are law of the land only if made in pursuance of the Constitution. Consequently, the Take Care clause refers only to laws that are constitutional. These issues arise only rarely and episodically. The President has not used the practice of refusing to comply with unconstitutional directives as a kind of line-item veto.[22] On the contrary, congressional restrictions are common and have for the most part been honored by the executive.

At the same time, another practice in the appropriations field undercuts Congress' role. The executive has much flexibility through reprogramming, transfer, draw-down, contingency funds, etc. Under these practices the executive can legally employ a variety of devices to use funds appropriated for one purpose to carry out a different activity. For example, President Bush, Sr. funded the initial deployment of troops in preparation for the Gulf War using reprogrammed funds. Congress then was effectively forced to appropriate more funds to make up the accounts from which the President had borrowed. And of course the appropriations power can

22. A formal Line Item Veto conferred by Congress on the President was invalidated in Clinton v. New York, 524 U.S. 417 (1998).

as a practical, political matter be preempted by presidential action. Once a President has deployed troops in harms way the Congress could hardly decline to provide funds for their sustenance.

Finally, there may be a legal issue in the converse situation, viz. where Congress refuses to appropriate funds. Washington took the position that Congress was obligated to appropriate funds to implement a treaty, even if the House of Representatives disagreed with the policy underlying the treaty. Professor Henkin has asserted more broadly that Congress is required to appropriate funds to cover the activities of the other branches that are within their "independent constitutional authority."[23] Other commentators have even asserted that if Congress does not appropriate such funds, the President may spend them anyway.[24] Such positions do not seem to be reflected in practice, as Congress' recent refusal to appropriate funds for U.S. dues to the United Nations, legally required by the UN Charter, well demonstrated. If Congress refuses to fund an activity, the executive must either find the funds elsewhere—which is usually not difficult to do, e.g. by reprogramming other funds or using discretionary, contingency funds—or force Congress to act politically. It seems especially improbable

23. Louis Henkin, Foreign Affairs and the United States Constitution 115 (2d ed. 1996).

24. E.g. J. Gregory Sidak, The President's Power of the Purse, 1989 Duke L. J. 1162; Don Wallace, Jr., The President's Exclusive Foreign Affairs Powers Over Foreign Aid, 1970 Duke L. J. 293, 453.

that the courts would attempt to compel Congress to appropriate funds.

International Law. Some commentators have suggested that Congress' power should be limited by international law, in addition to the limitations imposed by the Constitution. The Supreme Court has never agreed. Although the Court has referred to the law of nations as a source of power, it has consistently endorsed the right of Congress to pass laws that violate a treaty or customary international law. The general rule applicable to statutes applies in this context as well, notably an act of Congress will supersede—as U.S. domestic law—an earlier inconsistent statute, treaty or rule of customary international law. The courts nevertheless attempt to avoid construing a statute to violate international law unless Congress' intent is clear or no other interpretation is possible. Such a rule of statutory construction is based on the recognition that if a statute violating international law is given effect in U.S. courts, the United States will still be violating international law in the eyes of the rest of the world and could therefore face retaliation or other negative consequences as a result of the domestic judicial decision.

Delegation of Legislative Power. A fundamental corollary of constitutional government and the rule of law is that the respective institutions of government should perform their assigned functions. Since the Constitution vests specified legislative powers in Congress, Congress should exercise them, not the President or the Secretary of Agriculture. However, the growth of government in size and complexity, as well as its vastly expanded mandate, requires more attention than Congress can give. Congress accordingly has delegated its authority to executive and administrative agencies. This transfer of power from Congress is an old one. For example, before the Civil War Congress decided the merits of individual, private contract claims against the government, but the burden became too much so Congress created the Court of Claims. Notwithstanding the obvious need and common practice of delegation, the courts have maintained in principle that there are limits on the power of Congress to delegate.

Nevertheless, the general principle limiting delegations has been observed almost entirely in the breach. The Supreme Court has only twice invalidated acts of Congress on the grounds that they impermissibly delegated legislative authority, and those decisions were unpopular verdicts by a conservative Court fighting a losing battle in 1935 against the New Deal. Now the standard formulation of the law is that delegation is permissible if Congress prescribes standards to govern the application of the delegated authority. Nevertheless, the vaguest standards satisfy the test (e.g. action "in the interests of national security," or "to deal with any unusual and extraordinary threat to the national security, foreign policy or economy," or action to deal with "burdens on U.S. commerce"). In addition, in the *Curtiss-Wright* case, the Supreme Court said that even the toothless limits applicable to domestic affairs do not apply to foreign relations cases. Consequently, the delegation doctrine is not a practical limit on congressional power.

Some delegations have required the President to find that certain facts exist, e.g. a "national emergency," a "threat to foreign policy" or a "burden on U.S. commerce," as a prerequisite for exercising the delegated authority. When challenged, however, the courts have regularly declined to examine whether the facts justify the President's invocation of the standard. Presidential authority under legislative delegations in foreign affairs has thus not been legally problematic.

B. Congress' Investigative and Oversight Powers—Informal Influences Asserted by Congress

---

We have seen that Congress has extensive foreign relations powers with few significant limitations, but it does not exploit the full measure of foreign policy control that it could constitutionally exercise. Instead Congress has delegated vast realms of authority to the President, and has acquiesced in presidential assertions of sweeping foreign relations power. It would nevertheless be misleading to picture the Congress as totally passive or uninfluential. In addition to its occasional, independent legislative prescriptions, Congress plays an important role in shaping policy and exposing problems through its powers of investigation and oversight, with the attendant media attention that can also influence policy and chasten executive power just as effectively as finely crafted laws.

Congress' oversight powers are not expressly granted in the Constitution, but rather are implied as part of Congress' legislative powers.[25] The British Parliament, state legislatures, and the early Congresses all asserted a power to investigate matters of interest to them, and to that end to compel the testimony of officials and other persons and the production of documents. For example, Congress appointed a special committee to investigate the disastrous St. Clair expedition attacking Indians in the Ohio country. Several Framers, including Madison, voted for the measure, and the Washington cabinet, including Jefferson, accepted the role of the committee, thereby confirming their implicit understanding of legitimate legislative power. Since the Founding, Congress has regularly investigated the operations of government. Presidents have agreed that this function is legitimate, and the Supreme Court endorsed the power as well.[26]

Although theoretically any investigation or oversight hearing must be exercised in pursuit of a valid legislative purpose, this is not a significant limitation in foreign affairs because of Congress' virtual plenary authority in that field. Congressional committees have regularly sent staff members on mis-

25. Eastland v. United States Servicemen's Fund, 421 U.S. 491, 504 (1975) ("the power to investigate is inherent in the power to make laws"); McGrain v. Daugherty, 273 U.S. 135 (1927).

26. Id.

sions abroad, interviewed officials, and combed through executive branch documents, diplomatic cables and files (subject to the rarely invoked executive privilege). Oversight hearings have also provided an opportunity to make congressional views known and to induce executive branch compromise on policy differences. For example, Congress required by law that the executive branch report to Congress every arms control proposal to a foreign government, together with an assessment of its verifiability. The mere reporting requirement undoubtedly induced caution in developing negotiating positions, and an actual report could generate a hostile reaction which the executive branch would feel politically compelled to accommodate. Although often informal, this type of oversight serves as a significant source of congressional influence on an otherwise exclusive executive prerogative. Finally, individual members of Congress may also use their formal and informal powers over appointments, scheduling hearings and even votes in unrelated matters to advance their views. Senator Helms, for example, as Chair of the Senate Foreign Relations Committee, was conspicuously aggressive in attempting to force the executive branch to accept unwelcome changes. To force a reorganization of the State Department he blocked appointments by simply not scheduling hearings. He delayed consideration of treaties which he opposed, and successfully forced policy changes with respect to economic sanctions against Cuba, Iran and Libya. He even forced reorganization of the UN. Every executive branch official knows that Congress has the vast legislative powers described above and, more importantly, it pays the bills. Accordingly, deference and solicitude—not confrontation—characterize the normal official's attitude toward Congress.

The oversight process still is haphazard. Often congressional committees are captured by the executive agencies they are supposed to be monitoring. Special interests may dominate both. Congress is driven by publicity, the media, and short-term problems that excite public attention. Congress does not have complete information or vision. A member's attention is usually aroused only when there is a scandal or immediate problem that brings attention and reelection assistance. Accordingly, Congress for the most part is content to let the bureaucracy run by itself, but when Congress acts, even informally or casually, it can have an immediate and effective impact.

Bibliographic Note

On the issues growing out of the appropriations process, see William C. Banks and Peter Raven–Hansen, National Security Law and the Power of the Purse (1994); Peter Raven–Hansen and William C. Banks, Pulling the Purse Strings of the Commander in Chief, 80 Va. L. Rev. 833, 838–45 (1994); Louis Fisher, Presidential Spending Power (1975); Louis Fisher, Presidential Independence and the Power of the Purse, 3 U.C. Davis J. Int'l L. & Pol'y.

107 (1997); and Louis Henkin, Foreign Affairs and the United States Constitution (2d ed. 1996).

On Congress and foreign policy, see James M. Lindsay, Congress and the Politics of U.S. Foreign Policy (1994); Barbara Hinckley, Less Than Meets the Eye: Foreign Policy Making and the Myth of the Assertive Congress (1994); Thomas M. Frank and Edward Weisband, Foreign Policy By Congress (1979). The early Congresses are covered comprehensively in David P. Currie's The Constitution in Congress: The Federalist Period, 1789–1801 (1997), and his The Constitution in Congress: The Jeffersonians, 1801–1829 (2000).

On *Missouri v. Holland* and the potential limits imposed by the Tenth Amendment on the Treaty Power and the Necessary and Proper Clause, see Curtis A. Bradley, The Treaty Power and American Federalism, 97 Mich. L. Rev. 390 (1998); David M. Galove, Treatymaking and the Nation: The Historical Foundations of the Nationalist Conception of the Treaty Power, 98 Mich. L. Rev. 1075 (2000); and Professor Bradley's reply, The Treaty Power and American Federalism, Part II, 99 Mich. L. Rev. 98 (2000). See also Thomas Healy, Is *Missouri v. Holland* Still Good Law? Federalism and the Treaty Power, 98 Colum. L. Rev. 1726 (1998).

The impact of globalization and law-making by international organizations is treated in Julian G. Ku, The Delegation of Federal Power to International Organizations: New Problems with Old Solutions, 85 Minn. L. Rev. 71 (2000).

CHAPTER FOUR

FORMAL INTERNATIONAL LAWMAKING— THE CONCLUSION OF INTERNATIONAL AGREEMENTS BY THE UNITED STATES

International law provides the structure and means by which foreign relations are carried out. International law recognizes and reinforces the principle of territorial sovereignty, the authority of governments over territory and nationals, and governments' authority to regulate activities on the high seas and in the atmosphere and outer space. International law also provides the means for cooperation in foreign relations. The principal source of international law, and the principal means of international cooperation and interaction, is found in treaties. This Chapter explains how the United States Government participates in international lawmaking through the conclusion and implementation of treaties, and, in Subchapter D, through the creation of customary international law.

A treaty may create legally binding obligations under both international law and under domestic law. Under international law the United States is bound to perform whatever obligations it has assumed under the treaty. In the event of default the other treaty party or parties may retaliate or at least suspend or terminate further operation of the treaty. There is no international court of general jurisdiction over all treaty disputes. However, the parties to a treaty may agree to submit disputes under it to the International Court of Justice (ICJ) or to another tribunal of their choice. Members of the World Trade Organization are bound to submit all disputes within the scope of that organization to a judicial-like procedure. Because of the absence of ICJ or other general compulsory judicial process, most international law issues are settled by negotiation.

The structure of the Constitution allocates the power to conclude treaties to the federal government, and denies that power to the states.[1] Within the federal government, as indicated in Chapter Two, the President has exclusive constitutional authority to open a treaty negotiation and to control the process of the negotiation itself. Congress, the Senate or individual members may well have an impact as a practical matter on those decisions, but

1. See Article II sec. 2 and Article I sec. 10. The latter provides that "[n]o state shall enter into any Treaty, Alliance, or Confederation ... [or] without the Consent of Congress ... any Agreement or Compact with another State, or with a foreign Power ...." The text of the Constitution thus suggests that a "treaty" is only one type of international agreement, different from an "agreement or compact." In international practice all international agreements are "treaties," but in United States practice, as explained in Subchapter A, there are several distinct types of international agreement, of which the "treaty" is one form. Regardless of the terminology, however, the structure of the Constitution and historical practice confirm that all international agreement-making is exclusively controlled by the federal government.

as a matter of formal law the President has the exclusive power to negotiate international agreements on behalf of the United States. The first major legal issue arises when the President has finished the negotiation and wishes to bring the resulting treaty into force as a legally binding obligation of the United States. Upon successful conclusion of a negotiation the President must decide which constitutional procedure to use to secure the necessary domestic law authority to support the decision to bring the treaty into force as an obligation of the United States under international law. Subchapter A sets forth the four alternatives available to the President. Normally the choice is between submitting the agreement to the Senate for its approval in accordance with Article II of the Constitution, relying for approval on an act of the whole Congress, or, on some occasions, relying on the President's foreign relations power.

Following the Senate's approval or any required congressional action, the President makes an independent decision as to whether to "ratify" the treaty, thereby bringing it into force as an international obligation of the United States, subject to any conditions or "reservations" imposed by the Senate or Congress. Ratification of a treaty is a formal act that is entirely separate from the acts of signing the treaty and of getting the requisite legislative approval. Ratification is accomplished by depositing or exchanging an instrument, sometimes called the instrument of ratification, with the other party or parties to the treaty or with an agreed depository.

Following ratification of a treaty the President administers or executes its implementation. In this connection the President interprets its terms, follows the operation of the agreement, determines if another party is violating the treaty, and may declare such a violation to be a "material breach," in which case the President determines the appropriate response by the United States, including suspension or termination of the treaty. The President also has authority to make minor amendments to a treaty and to terminate a treaty in accordance with its terms. On some occasions the President's authority to interpret treaties unilaterally and to terminate them without the participation of the Senate or Congress has been challenged. These issues will be explored in Subchapter B below.

A treaty also has status as domestic law. Under Article VI of the Constitution a treaty is "law of the land," and in some circumstances may be enforced in a U.S. domestic court like a federal statute. These matters will be explored in Subchapter C.

At the outset it is important to understand the differences in terminology used to describe international agreements in international law as opposed to U.S. constitutional law. The Vienna Convention on Treaties uses the term "treaty" to refer to all written international agreements between states that are governed by international law. Thus in the vocabulary of international law and practice all international agreements are referred to as "treaties." In U.S. domestic practice, however, the term "treaty" refers to only one relatively small category of international agreement, viz. those agreements concluded under Article II. As we shall see below, there are additional categories of international agreement concluded by the United States (on the basis of congressional legislation or the President's foreign relations power), known as "executive agreements," that fall outside Article II. These executive agreements are "treaties" within the meaning of the Vienna Convention, but are not "treaties" within the meaning of the U.S. Constitution.

A. The Conclusion of International Agreements by the United States—the Choices Available to the President.

There are four distinct sources of authority for presidential conclusion of an international agreement on behalf of the United States. The President makes the choice as to which procedure to use. First, the President may submit the agreement as an Article II treaty to the Senate for its advice and consent to ratification by a vote of 2/3 of the Senators present. Article II is the only provision in the text of the Constitution that expressly provides authority for the conclusion of international agreements by the United States. Nevertheless, the President is not constitutionally required to use Article II. Alternatively the President may seek congressional authorization of an international agreement by joint resolution or act of Congress (which simply requires a *majority* vote of both houses), or he may use existing legislation as a basis for ratification of the agreement. These agreements are called congressional-executive agreements. This alternative procedure has become accepted as constitutionally equivalent to the Article II procedure. Subchapter B examines the type of agreement appropriate for Article II treatment as opposed to being approved as a congressional-executive agreement. Any international agreement so authorized is binding on the United States as a matter of international law, and both congressional-executive agreements and "self-executing" Article II treaties supersede earlier inconsistent federal statutes as a matter of domestic law. The effect of international agreements in U.S. domestic law, including the concept of "self-executing" treaties, will be addressed in Subchapter C.

Third, an international agreement may be contemplated by an earlier Article II treaty and derive its authority from the earlier treaty. Typical examples of this type of international agreement are agreements that allocate criminal jurisdiction over U.S. forces and bases contemplated by previously ratified Article II Mutual Defense Treaties. Such an agreement has the same legal force internationally and domestically as an Article II treaty. These executive agreements are relatively unusual and do not seem to have been controversial. Fourth, an international agreement may be concluded on the basis of the President's foreign relations power. These agreements are called presidential–executive agreements. An international agreement concluded pursuant to the President's foreign relations power has the same effect internationally as an Article II treaty, but the President does not normally use a presidential–executive agreement if it would be inconsistent with domestic law (for an exception, however, see *Dames & Moore* discussed infra at page 138. Presidential–Executive agreements have been the most controversial because they exclude any Senate or congressional participation in the agreement-making process. This type of agreement has been rare. They are used mostly for routine matters, like holding periodic consultations or meetings, exchanging information, and promoting or facilitating specified forms of cooperation. Almost all important international agreements are authorized by the Senate under Article II or by Congress as congressional-executive agreements.

Article II Treaties. Article II of the Constitution authorizes the President to "make" treaties with the "advice and consent" of the Senate, provided two-thirds of the Senators present concur. The treaty power accordingly is a presidential power which nevertheless must be exercised with the participation of the Senate. The precise role of the Senate in the various aspects of "making" a treaty is not entirely clear, and some aspects of the question have been quite controversial in recent years.

In the eighteenth century treaties were a major component of foreign relations, and the Framers discussed several aspects of the treaty power. Until nearly the end of the Constitutional Convention the draft text gave the power to make treaties, as well as the power to appoint ambassadors, to the Senate.

Most of the treaty-related debate centered on the exclusion from the process of the House of Representatives, the required vote for Senate action, the question of territorial expansion, and the power to be given to the smaller states. The Framers excluded the House on the grounds of its short-term perspective, its vulnerability to capture by "factions" and its responsiveness to swings in public opinion. The Senate, on the other hand, was considered better able to reflect the long-term national interest and it could operate with secrecy.

Near the end of the deliberations the Framers gave both the treaty power and the ambassadorial appointment power to the President, to be exercised with the participation of the Senate. It seems probable that the Framers envisioned an active role for the Senate in the entire treaty process, especially given the common use of the term "advice and consent" in state constitutions to describe an interactive relationship at all stages of the activity in question. Accordingly, it is fair to say that the original understanding of the Treaty Power envisioned Senate participation prior to the negotiation and conclusion of treaties.

However, this understanding was quickly reinterpreted in an informal manner. In 1789, in connection with an upcoming negotiation, President Washington personally appeared before the Senate and asked its advice on a series of specific negotiating questions. The Senate postponed consideration of all but one such question to a second session. This procedure was unsatisfactory to both the President and the Senate, and was immediately abandoned. Even the practice initiated by President Washington of seeking written advice on particular issues in a negotiation was abandoned by Washington before the end of his first Administration. A congressional study reported that "[b]y 1816 the practice had become established that the Senate's formal participation in treatymaking was to approve, approve with conditions, or disapprove treaties after they had been negotiated by the President or his representative."[2] An attempt in 1973 by Senator Hartke to affirm the "historic" role of the Senate in treatymaking by constituting it as a council of advice for that purpose came to naught in the face of executive branch constitutional objections.[3] The Senate and individual Senators may nevertheless influence the course of negotiations informally through expressions of views at hearings, participation as advisers to the U.S. delegation to a negotiation, and other formal and informal methods.

The Senate may also influence the conclusion of treaties formally, or in a legally binding manner, by attaching conditions to its consent to ratification of a treaty. Although not explicit in the text of the Constitution, the Senate has exercised its authority to attach conditions to its consent to ratification starting with the first treaty concluded under the

2. Congressional Research Service, Treaties and Other International Agreements: The Role of the United States Senate, 31–36 (1984).

3. S. 99, 93rd Cong., 1st Sess. (1973), 119 Cong. Rec. 7274–75 (1973); Arthur W. Rovine, Digest of United States Practice in International Law 172–76 (1973).

Constitution. Those conditions bind the President if he chooses to ratify the treaty, and may force the President to attach a reservation to United States adherence to the treaty or to amend the treaty by agreement with the other treaty party or parties. Senate-imposed conditions may also require the President to make a specified declaration to the other treaty party or parties in connection with ratification, or a Senate-imposed condition may state an understanding that the Senate seeks to impose on the President or on the U.S. courts (as opposed to the other parties to the treaty), for example an understanding regarding the interpretation of a term of the treaty or the treaty's more general domestic effect. The President normally includes Senate-imposed conditions requiring agreement by, or communication to, the other treaty party or parties in the instrument of ratification exchanged with the treaty partner or deposited in connection with ratification. However, the President has claimed the constitutional power to comply with Senate-imposed conditions outside the formal ratification process. In the ratification of the 1976 Treaty of Friendship and Cooperation with Spain, the Senate required a condition that could have appeared inappropriate to the Spanish parliament and thereby created more public controversy in a matter already plagued with problems. The President decided not to include the Senate's condition in the public instrument of ratification, but instead informed the Spanish government confidentially. As indicated by this precedent, the President may therefore determine the appropriate manner of communicating U.S. reservations to a treaty. The President also has exercised the power to accept or reject proposed reservations by other parties to a treaty, without the participation of the Senate.

It would seem reasonable that a Senate condition should relate to the treaty to which the condition was attached. However, in its 1997 acceptance of an arms control treaty dealing with Conventional Forces in Europe, the Senate attached a condition dealing with another arms control treaty and the politically weak President Clinton was forced to accept it. The President's acceptance was without conceding the constitutionality of the condition, but he accepted it nonetheless, perhaps at least potentially starting a constitutional precedent.[4] This condition was one of several steps taken by the Senate during the Clinton Presidency to assert or reassert Article II prerogatives.

A Senate-imposed condition may not infringe other provisions of the Constitution, such as the Bill of Rights or the President's foreign relations power.[5]

4. Professor Henkin stated in 1996 that "[t]he Senate has never attempted to do so, but one may ask, hypothetically, whether it can tell the President that it will consent to some treaty only if he dismisses his Secretary of State." Foreign Affairs and the United States Constitution 182 (2d ed. 1996). He concludes that if the condition is "proper" the President must comply or not ratify the treaty. For a critique of the Clinton conclusions, see Trimble and Koff, All Fall Down: The Treaty Power in the Clinton Administration, 16 Berkeley J. Int'l L. 55 (1998).

5. In 1997 the Senate asserted its prerogative to consent (or not consent) to treaty adjustments occasioned by state succes-

In addition to those limitations, it has been argued that principles of separation of powers and of federalism impose limits on the scope of the Treatymakers' authority under Article II. For example, in *Edwards v. Carter*,[6] plaintiffs asserted that the Article IV power of Congress to dispose of territory and property of the United States precluded the transfer of the Canal Zone to Panama under the Article II Panama Canal Treaty. The Court rejected this principle and pointed out that the existence of a congressional power does not mean that the power is exclusive. In fact many treaties deal with matters that are within Congress' powers. The normal way to accommodate the interests of the House or Congress as a whole during the exercise of the Treaty Power should be to make the treaty non-self-executing. Hence it is frequently said that treaties to spend monies, create crimes, or declare war must be non-self-executing, not that they are beyond the scope of Article II.

A similar constitutional argument is also presented in the context of treaties dealing with matters traditionally regulated by the states. It has been argued that such matters are outside the scope of Article II by virtue of the Tenth Amendment and principles of federalism. Those arguments were rejected in *Missouri v. Holland* discussed in Chapter 3A *supra*. Although the treaty power may not be

sion. Id. This type of condition arguably invades the President's foreign affairs power, but Clinton's forced acceptance of the condition illustrates the vulnerability of presidential foreign affairs power to political vicissitudes.

6.   580 F.2d 1055 (D.C.Cir.1978).

limited by the Tenth Amendment, it is clearly limited by the rest of the Bill of Rights. Moreover, it would seem that treaties would have to be genuinely a matter of international concern, and not a sham, to provide a basis for congressional regulation of matters of no concern to a foreign nation or American foreign policy.

A related question involving the limits of constitutional authority to conclude treaties (and congressional-executive agreements as well) grows out of the increasing tendency to delegate authority to international institutions. Hence, under the UN Charter the United States delegates authority to the Security Council and to the International Court of Justice to make legally binding decisions in their respective spheres of operation, and the United States separately agrees to carry out those decisions. In the WTO, Dispute Settlement Panels have been delegated authority to render decisions regarding the compatibility of federal and state law with international norms and to prescribe remedies for their violations. In all these cases the decisions by international bodies are clearly non-self-executing, either because of the terms of the U.N. Charter or because of U.S. intent in accepting the obligations. Thus, the non-self-executing doctrine becomes the vehicle for the protection of Congress' and the states' ultimate authority over exercises of the delegated power, at least as a matter of formal law. In addition, the veto power of the United States in the Security Council precludes a decision to its detriment.[7] On the other hand, as a practical matter, once a negative decision by the ICJ, and especially by a WTO panel, is handed down, the formal protection offered by the non-self-executing nature of the decision may not mean much given the strong political forces—foreign and domestic—that can gather behind compliance with such a decision. In practice decisions by international institutions and their officials are not subject to the practical accountability checks that Congress and domestic courts exercise over the decisions of administrative agencies exercising comparable delegated legislative power.

By changing the scope of the treaty commitments the Senate's conditions effectively determine the scope of U.S. obligations under international law. The domestic law effect of Senate conditions is discussed below in Subchapter C.

Congressional–Executive Agreements. The principal alternative to the Article II procedure is for the President to conclude an international agreement on the basis of previously existing or concurrently enacted legislation. For example, if an existing law authorizes the President to ration gasoline in certain circumstances, the President may conclude an international agreement binding the United States to ration gasoline in those circumstances. Or, if there is no such law, the President may seek an act of Congress either specifically authorizing the international agreement he has negotiated or enacting

7. The ICJ may be less political, and thus more oblivious to U.S. political influence, but its decisions are relatively few in number and marginal in overall importance.

other general legislation that gives him domestic legal authority to carry out its terms, before he formally ratifies the agreement. Such agreements are known as congressional-executive agreements.

There is no direct-authority in the text of the Constitution for these agreements. However, in the parts of the Constitution that limit the authority of states to conclude treaties, reference is also made to "agreement or compact," thereby implying that the Framers contemplated international agreements concluded by means other than the Article II procedure.

Early practice quickly established the legitimacy of congressional-executive agreements. For example, in 1790 Congress authorized the President to borrow money, including contracts with foreign lenders, and the Second Congress authorized the conclusion of postal agreements with foreign countries. The practice continued sporadically throughout the nineteenth and early twentieth centuries including important agreements for the acquisition of territory and agreements governing tariffs and trade.[8] Significant international agreements in the early twentieth century were also approved as congressional-executive agreements. After the Senate failed to ratify the Treaty of Versailles, ending World War I, Congress declared the end of the war by a joint resolution; and Congress also passed a joint resolution approving the entry of the United

8. See, e.g., Field v. Clark, 143 U.S. 649 (1892); B. Altman & Co. v. United States, 224 U.S. 583 (1912).

States into the International Labor Organization (originally part of the rejected Versailles Treaty).

After the second World War, some internationalist academics even argued that the congressional-executive agreements were not only constitutionally legitimate, but also entirely equivalent to Article II treaties as a matter of constitutional law, and the two forms were therefore completely interchangeable.[9] Their concern was to avoid a repetition of the experience with the Treaty of Versailles in which a conservative minority in the Senate blocked American participation in the League of Nations. American internationalists feared a reversion to our traditional isolationism after World War II, and wanted to maximize the ability of the United States to participate in the post-war international institution-building without the potential roadblock created by the Article II requirement of a 2/3 vote which in turn gives a conservative minority the ability to dictate policy.

At that time several important agreements, such as those authorizing U.S. participation in the World Bank and the IMF, were concluded as congressional-executive agreements rather than Article II treaties. Since then Congress has on several occasions acknowledged in legislation that the two procedures are equally permissible, notably in Section 33 of the Arms Control and Disarmament Act, and in the

9. Myres S. McDougal and Asher Lans, Treaties and Congressional–Executive or Presidential Agreements: Interchangeable Instruments of National Policy, 54 Yale L.J. 181 (1945).

Case–Zablocki Act.[10] The use of executive agreements has grown dramatically in the twentieth century. From 1939 to 1982, the United States concluded 608 Article II treaties and 9,548 executive agreements. In 1982 alone the United States concluded 372 executive agreements and only seventeen Article II treaties.

In the 1990s, however, the Senate challenged the President's authority to use the congressional-executive agreement procedure in two separate areas. First, the Bush Administration considered sending a bilateral chemical weapons agreement to Congress for approval, rather than to the Senate under Article II, but Senator Biden objected. In its approval of the multilateral Chemical Weapons Convention, the Senate attached a condition, mirroring Section 33 of the ACDA Act, to the effect that future arms control treaties must be concluded either as congressional-executive agreements or as Article II treaties. In 1997, however, the Senate became more bold. In connection with the CFE Flank Agreement the Senate forced the Clinton Administration to abandon its decision to seek approval of the agreement by Congress, and when it submitted the agreement to the Senate under Article II, the Senate attached a

10. Section 33, redesignated § 303, 22 U.S.C. § 2573 provides that certain arms control agreements may be concluded only pursuant to Article II or Congressional legislation, thereby implying their equivalence. See Phillip R. Trimble and Jack S. Weiss, The Role of the President, the Senate and Congress with respect to Arms Control Treaties concluded by the United States, 67 Chicago–Kent L. Rev. 645 (1991). The Case–Zablocki Act, 1 USC § 112b (1988), requires submission of both types of agreement to Congress.

condition asserting that all major arms control treaties had to be approved under Article II. Clinton protested, but a precedent was set that undercuts the President's discretion to determine the appropriate source of domestic authority, at least for arms control agreements.

Another debate over Article II was precipitated by the accession of the United States in 1994 to the new World Trade Organization (WTO). The WTO encompassed a comprehensive set of rules regulating international trade, new rules on services, investment and intellectual property, and a strong adjudication system. The WTO was attacked on the grounds that it would undermine U.S. sovereignty, and opponents argued that it must be approved by the Senate under Article II, even though historically trade agreements had normally been concluded as congressional-executive agreements. Professor Tribe argued that Congress had not been delegated any legislative power, or any other power, specifically to approve international agreements.[11] He therefore concluded that Congress had no such power, with the result that congressional-executive agreements are of dubious legitimacy. This omission however, may be explained by distinguishing the executive and legislative acts involved. International agreement making rests on executive powers. The role of the Senate or Congress is limited to providing advice and legal support for discharging

11. Laurence H. Tribe, Taking Text and Structure Seriously: Reflections in Free-form Method in Constitutional Interpretation, 108 Harv. L. Rev. 1221 (1995).

the resulting obligations, either through Article VI (in the case of a Senate approved treaty), or through legislation (in the case of a congressional-executive agreement). That legislation may be comfortably based, inter alia, on the Necessary and Proper Clause. Only the President has the power to make or conclude international agreements. That executive power is exercised when the instrument of ratification is exchanged or defeated. Neither the Senate nor Congress may make or conclude an international agreement. Of course a President would be foolish to conclude an agreement, e.g. to ration gasoline, if he did not have domestic legal authority to do so. Concluding an agreement without the requisite domestic legal authority to assure its execution would risk placing the United States in violation of an international legal obligation, with the prospect of retaliation. Consequently the President may need an act of Congress to support his international agreement making, or he may need the support provided by Article VI in the case of Article II treaties.

Another argument in the recent trade agreement debates was that the WTO threatened to undermine the federal structure of government because it had significant consequences for the regulatory powers of the states.[12] The Senate is the principal part of government where the states are represented as states, and where their interests as states can be protected. Therefore, the argument went, agree-

12. Letter of Laurence H. Tribe to Sen. Robert Byrd, reprinted in 140 Cong. Rec. S10584–5 (daily ed. August 4, 1994).

ments like the WTO had to be submitted under Article II. Those arguments did not withstand scrutiny. State regulatory power could be just as deeply affected by acts of Congress under the legislative powers delegated by Article I, including the Foreign Commerce Clause. Moreover, numerous trade agreements going back to before World War II had been concluded as congressional-executive agreements.

Notwithstanding the arguments to the contrary, and the Senate's assertion of its prerogative, the President must in the first instance determine the procedure to be used to bring an agreement into force. The criteria for distinguishing the alternatives available to him are unclear at best. The President's choice is theoretically guided by the State Department's Circular 175 Procedure.[13] This State Department regulation requires that due consideration be given to such factors as the formality, importance and duration of the agreement, the preference of Congress, the need for implementing legislation by Congress, the effect on state law, and past U.S. and international practice. Under Circular 175 officials of the executive branch may consult with the Senate Foreign Relations Committee as to the choice of constitutional procedure. However, the Circular 175 factors are general, indeterminate and may sometimes suggest inconsistent choices. They seem too vague and uncertain to guide actual decisions.

13. Dep't of St. Circular No. 175 (Dec. 13, 1955) reprinted in 50 Am. J. Int'l L. 784 (1956).

Notwithstanding the academic argument that Article II treaties and congressional-executive agreements are interchangeable, and notwithstanding the obscurity of Circular 175, no President has indiscriminately mixed the alternatives. In almost all cases the executive follows tradition. In the past international agreements dealing with boundaries, war and peace, arms control, military alliances, human rights, extradition, diplomatic and consular privileges, immigration, intellectual property, taxation, the environment and commerce have almost always been submitted to the Senate as Article II treaties. Most, but not all, agreements to join international organizations have been concluded pursuant to Article II.[14] On the other hand, international agreements dealing with trade, finance, energy, fisheries and bilateral aviation relations have normally been concluded as congressional-executive agreements. It is also undoubtedly true that, historically, most important treaties have normally been concluded under Article II, even though the frequently heard argument that major treaties *must* be so concluded is not supported by the historical record.

It may seem surprising that more agreements are not treated as congressional-executive agreements. The political impetus for favoring the congressional-executive agreement is the obvious difficulty in satisfying the requirement for a 2/3 vote in the Senate.

14. For a list and categorization, see Kevin C. Kennedy, Conditional Approval of Treaty by the U.S. Senate, 19 Loyola L.A. Int'l & Comp. L.J. 89, 135–72 (1996).

The Article II process also gives disproportionate power to small states which tend to be more rural and less internationally oriented. A conservative minority can thus extract concessions, hold up agreements (assisted by the Senate's tolerance of the filibuster), and even defeat treaties. In the early twentieth century the Senate acquired the reputation of being the "graveyard of treaties."

For these reasons congressional-executive agreements are less problematic from the point of view of democratic principles than Article II treaties. Both the Senate and House participate in the process, so neither the House, representing the people directly and proportionately to population, nor the Senate, representing the states equally without regard to population, is excluded from the process. Overriding prior federal legislation is similarly unproblematic since both Houses of Congress participate, just as they would in repealing or amending domestic law. Another factor suggesting more use of the congressional-executive agreement alternative is that, under the impact of globalism, the distinction between the domestic and foreign spheres often fades, so that agreements increasingly deal with matters that historically were of domestic concern and thus regulated by Congress. Nevertheless, the textual legitimacy of Article II treaties and the strong Historical Practice supporting their widespread use in important matters seem likely to assure that their traditional preeminence will continue. An increased congressional role can be assured by providing that treaties are "non-self-executing" (see infra Sub-chapter C).

In addition to the predictable resistance from Senators to the use of the congressional-executive agreement alternative, sometimes members of the House of Representatives as well as Senators have objected to the practice of presidential reliance on *existing* legislation to carry out agreements. For example, pre-existing legislation gave the President the right to ration gasoline in the event of an emergency. When the President concluded an international agreement that would require gasoline rationing in certain circumstances, the President cited the existing legislation as authority for carrying out the new agreement. Some members of Congress objected that the prior legislation did not contemplate international action and accordingly should not be used to support a treaty. In another case Congress granted the President authority to impose export controls for foreign policy and other reasons, but in an agreement with the Soviet Union the executive branch agreed *not* to impose such controls on specified exports of wheat. Again some members of Congress believed that this practice amounted to overreaching by the President. However, both agreements went into force and were implemented without further challenge or controversy.

Presidential Executive Agreements. Another alternative basis for authority that the President may draw upon to conclude an international agreement is his constitutional foreign relations power inherent in the Vesting Clause. That power, which revolves around the conduct of diplomatic relations and international negotiations, includes authority to conclude a discreet category of agreement called presidential–executive agreements, which are concluded without the participation of the Senate or Congress. Critics have pointed out that they are not expressly mentioned in the text of the Constitution, and have argued that they were not explicitly contemplated by the Framers. Nevertheless, such agreements were clearly part of Crown prerogative and the eighteenth century concept of executive power. Not having been removed from the executive, like participation in the treaty power, they fall comfortably within the Vesting Clause. Early practice, moreover, established the legitimacy of this alternative authority to conclude international agreements on behalf of the United States. For example, in 1799 the President settled a claim against Holland arising out of the destruction of an American national's ship.

Most presidential-executive agreements deal with minor, technical or routine matters of diplomacy. Occasionally, however, they have been used to deal with matters of great national concern. Those situations continue to generate considerable controversy. The opposition comes from the Senate, Congress as a whole and opponents of unpopular Presidents and of presidential prerogative. Their complaints concern both the political and the legal consequences. For example, President Roosevelt agreed with Great Britain to exchange "over-age" destroyers for military bases, thereby materially helping our future ally in its war with Germany at a time when the United States was officially neutral, and thereby significantly moving the United States toward involvement in that war. Furthermore, Roosevelt, and then Truman, in conjunction with the U.S.' wartime allies, delineated post World–War II settlements, all without the advice and consent of the Senate, at Yalta and Potsdam. Similarly the Eisenhower Administration engaged the United States in a defense agreement with Franco's Spain in 1953 that led to the establishment of U.S. bases in Spain without using the Article II ratification process. The President has also concluded cease-fire agreements (the one with North Korea is still in force) and agreements for military bases or other facilities around the world. Nuclear weapons were deployed under presidential-executive agreements in potentially unstable environments. In response the Senate Foreign Relations Committee examined the use of executive agreements in a series of investigations and hearings in the late 1960s. As a result the Senate passed the National Commitments Resolution in 1968. Under this resolution the Senate declared that a commitment to the defense of another nation or to the use of force to defend another nation could only be made pursuant to an Article II treaty or an act of Congress. The purpose of the Resolution was to check what the Senate saw as the usurpation of congressional prerogative by an increasingly imperial President. The resolution expressed the "sense of the Senate" and did not purport to be legally binding. It has been generally ignored.

Another congressional response to the controversial use of presidential-executive agreements was the Case–Zablocki Act, passed in 1972,[15] which required the executive branch to transmit to Congress a copy of all executive agreements, even secret agreements (under appropriate protections), so that Congress at least would be informed about the extent of the executive practice and could take further steps if it decided that additional regulation were warranted. Subsequently Congress debated a bill which would have required the reporting of all proposed executive agreements to Congress at least 60 days before they entered into force and would have subjected those agreements to a legislative veto. The executive branch strenuously resisted this proposed legislation on the grounds that it unconstitutionally burdened the President's foreign relations power and that legislative vetoes were defective on the grounds eventually endorsed by the Supreme Court in the *Chadha*[16] case. Congress did not pass the proposed legislation.

Presidents have avoided the need for legislative approval, and even reporting under the Case Act, by entering into "agreements" that were "political" commitments not intended to be "legally binding." Some of these "political" commitments represented quite significant measures of U.S. foreign policy,

15.   Supra note 10.

16.   Immigration and Naturalization Service v. Chadha, 462 U.S. 919 (1983).

such as the Helsinki Accords, trade policy declarations issued in anticipation of the Tokyo and Uruguay rounds of trade negotiations, and declarations made by the United States and the Soviet Union in connection with various military affairs and strategic nuclear weapons negotiations. The motivation for this approach was to get the agreement in place quickly and without potentially entangling legislative conditions (or even rejection). Since many international agreements do not have any formal adjudication or enforcement procedures, the difference between a legally binding and a politically binding agreement is blurred, at least superficially. Presidents have also made unilateral commitments, even of a military nature, as when President Reagan promised to defend Saudi Arabia, that are taken quite seriously as a matter of foreign policy but which exclude congressional involvement. The 1968 National Commitments Resolution of the Senate does not seem to have had any impact on executive decision-making.

The use of presidential–executive agreements has engendered controversy by virtue of their legal, as well as their political, consequences. It may seem anomalous to think of the President as a domestic law-maker, but some of these agreements have had legal effect, for example overriding inconsistent state law and policy, and even superseding a federal statute. Most presidential–executive agreements deal with technical or minor matters, like consulting with other governments in specific circumstances and the many "housekeeping" aspects of diplomatic operations. Occasionally, however, the President has concluded a presidential–executive agreement that affects private causes of action.

In the *Belmont*[17] and *Pink*[18] cases the Supreme Court upheld the validity of a presidential–executive agreement against the claim that Article II required the participation of the Senate. Moreover, the Court held that the executive agreement in question superseded the otherwise applicable state law. The cases involved highly important and controversial foreign policy, i.e. the diplomatic recognition by President Roosevelt in 1933 of the Bolshevik government of the Soviet Union, and the effect of the presidential–executive agreement conferring that recognition on state law. After the Bolshevik revolution the Soviet government nationalized Soviet assets located in New York without paying compensation. However, the New York courts would not recognize a foreign law that violated state public policy, and they regularly had found the Soviet confiscatory laws to violate that public policy. Accordingly, under New York law and state public policy the former owners of those assets would have continued to be entitled to them. The presidential–executive agreement with the Soviet Union, however, specified that those New York assets were to be transferred to the U.S. government (to pay different claims, notably those of U.S. nationals whose property in Russia had been seized by the Soviets). The Supreme Court upheld the validity of the presiden-

17.   United States v. Belmont, 301 U.S. 324 (1937).

18.   United States v. Pink, 315 U.S. 203 (1942).

tial–executive agreement, giving priority to the U.S. Government whose claim rested on the executive agreement over the former owners and their New York successors whose claims rested on New York law and policy. In doing so the Court decided that there was no constitutional requirement that all international agreements be approved by the Senate under Article II (*Belmont*) and that the presidential–executive agreement was a constitutional act of power with as much legal validity as if authorized by the legislature (*Pink*). In the latter case the Court stated: " 'All constitutional acts of power, whether in the executive or in the judicial department, have as much legal validity and obligation as if they proceeded from the legislature, ...' The Federalist, No. 64. A treaty is a 'Law of the Land' under the supremacy clause, Art. VI, Cl. 2, of the Constitution. Such international compacts and agreements as the Litvinov Assignment have a similar dignity."[19]

The legal consequence of the holding in the *Pink* case was to override New York state law and policy, but the dictum quoted above suggests that a presidential-executive agreement would also override an earlier, inconsistent act of Congress. This implication incensed conservative opponents of the President and presidential power. The rationale for such a result would be that these executive agreements are similar to treaties in that they are international obligations concluded by the President under a recognized constitutional power, Article II in the case

19. Id., at 230.

of treaties and the implied foreign relations power in the case of presidential-executive agreements. Treaties derive their status as domestic law by virtue of the "law of the land" language in Article VI which also covers other federal "laws" and arguably was intended to establish the supremacy of all federal acts (in its sphere of competence) over the states. Such a purpose would support extending legal supremacy to constitutionally permissible executive agreements. Textually it is not too much of a stretch to regard them as "treaties" or "laws." Moreover, the Supreme Court has recognized that the President has domestic law-making authority in other contexts involving foreign policy and the rights of foreigners in U.S. domestic courts. Where foreign policy and foreign interests are primarily at stake it is accordingly not unprecedented to accord domestic law-making authority to the President.

In the 1981 *Dames & Moore*[20] case, which involved the President's settlement of claims growing out of the Iranian revolution and related hostage crisis, the scope of presidential law-making was extended even to the point of superseding an act of Congress as well as applicable state law. In 1976 Congress passed the Foreign Sovereign Immunity Act (FSIA),[21] conferring jurisdiction on the federal courts over causes of action in commercial claims against foreign government-owned entities. At the time of the Iranian revolution many American companies had such claims against Iranian entities, and

20. Dames & Moore v. Regan, 453 U.S. 654 (1981).

21. 28 U.S.C. §§ 1602–1611.

some had even received a judgment. Nevertheless, in order to secure the release of hostages held in Tehran, the United States agreed under a presidential–executive agreement to terminate those claims in U.S. courts and to submit them instead to an ad hoc, tri-national arbitration in the Hague, thereby effectively overriding the FSIA and eliminating state-law-based causes of action. The Supreme Court approved the agreement and enforced the executive order issued to carry it out.

Two contrasting lower court cases in the trade field suggest limits on the use of presidential–executive agreements in non-crisis situations. The *Consumers Union*[22] and *Capps*[23] cases involved presidential-executive agreements that affected domestic and foreign commerce in ways that were arguably inconsistent with existing acts of Congress. In both cases the executive branch concluded agreements under which foreign producers agreed not to export specific products to the Untied States. Congress had already provided procedures under which the President could have restricted those imports, but the President did not use those procedures (probably because they were too cumbersome or too public to allow quick action). Congress had not purported to state that the procedures were exclusive. In both cases the President's authority under the Constitution to conclude such presidential–executive agree-

22. Consumers Union of the United States v. Kissinger, 506 F.2d 136 (D.C.Cir.1974).

23. United States v. Guy W. Capps, Inc., 204 F.2d 655 (4th Cir.1953).

ments was challenged. The *Capps* case condemned the agreement on the grounds that only Congress could regulate commerce. The *Consumers Union* case affirmed presidential authority on the grounds that the agreement did not purport to be judicially or legally enforceable under domestic law. The cases can be reconciled on that ground. In *Capps* the executive branch sought to enforce the agreement's prohibitions through an action in U.S. courts. In *Consumers Union* no domestic legal enforcement was contemplated. Hence it can be said that the President may conclude executive agreements, outside of congressionally authorized procedures, so long as those agreements do not purport to be enforceable under U.S. domestic law, and in extreme situations like that in *Belmont* and *Dames & Moore* presidential–executive agreements can even have full federal law status.

B.   Treaty Interpretation and Termination

Interpretation of a Treaty. Once a treaty has been ratified, the President oversees its implementation, monitors compliance with its norms, and asserts rights that the United States may have under it. This activity may be grounded on his duty to execute the laws or, more persuasively, on the Vesting Clause as it encompasses the President's foreign relations power. In this regard the President has the power to interpret the treaty, either unilaterally or in agreement with treaty partners. The power to interpret has been an executive function since Washington, and is not ordinarily controversial. Moreover, if the meaning of a treaty is contested in the courts, the executive branch interpretation is normally accepted as binding. The standard doctrine has been stated by the Supreme Court as follows:

"although not conclusive, the meaning attributed to treaty provisions by the Government agencies charged with their negotiation and enforcement is entitled to great weight."[24]

A court is still entitled under the Constitution to interpret a treaty differently from the executive branch's interpretation. Such a judicial interpretation, however, would not be binding as a matter of international law (no unilateral interpretation can bind other parties) or even necessarily on the executive branch in international dealings. The result could be that U.S. domestic courts would end up interpreting a term differently than that term would be interpreted internationally, e.g. by court or arbitrator or by a treaty partner, so that the United States could be considered to be in violation of international law by that court, arbitrator or treaty partner.

The possibility of such a conflict is at least theoretically increased by the differences between the international canons of treaty interpretation and the domestic rules for contract and statutory interpretation which domestic judges seem instinctively

24. Sumitomo Shoji America, Inc. v. Avagliano, 457 U.S. 176, 184–5 (1982).

to follow, at least partially, when deciding treaty cases. Domestic courts frequently refer to treaties as international contracts which can lead them by analogy to the rules for interpreting ambiguous domestic contracts. In the interpretation of contracts the international and domestic rules are not so different. The parole evidence rule normally limits the use of material outside the document, such as prior drafts and statements made during a negotiation. International practice only permits use of negotiating history as a supplemental means of interpreting ambiguous terms. The strong preference is to stay within the document itself, analyzing the "ordinary meaning" of the text in its context and in light of the object and purpose of the treaty. It has been said that the purpose of interpretation is to ascertain the objective meaning of the text, as opposed to the intent of the parties. Consequently international practice is reluctant to consider the negotiating history of a treaty. Moreover, unilateral statements by one party to the treaty would ordinarily not be credited, at least in the absence of evidence that the other party or parties acquiesced or agreed to a unilaterally stated position.

U.S. courts, however, have not always followed the contract approach, but instead have sometimes approached the interpretative task as they would approach the interpretation of statutes. In this mode they seem more willing to refer to negotiating history and especially to statements by the President or the Senate or Congress (the staple of legislative history). For example, the courts look to executive branch explanations offered to the Senate or Congress, testimony at hearings on the treaty, and a uniform course of executive interpretation (e.g. in diplomatic exchanges with treaty partners). In addition, the courts look to legislative sources, such as Senate or congressional committee reports and statements of individual members in the course of deliberations relating to the treaty. These practices seem well embedded as a matter of domestic constitutional law, but under international law such sources of treaty interpretations are not authoritative.

These differences seem highly abstract, to say the least, and cases where the different approaches make a difference in result are hard to find. In any event domestic courts regularly defer to executive branch interpretation of treaties, and the President normally does not commit the interpretation of treaties to third-party dispute resolution, such as arbitration or ad hoc adjudication by the International Court of Justice, without Senate or Congressional acquiescence or approval. After the Senate or congress give any necessary approvals to the President's ratification of an international agreement, it is well established doctrine that the legislators have no further role with respect to its interpretation. A congressional or Senate declaration or opinion has no more authority than the interpretation of a statute by a subsequent Congress.[25] Consequently treaty interpretation is an executive prerogative.

25. Fourteen Diamond Rings v. United States, 183 U.S. 176 (1901).

Reinterpretation and Amendment. The power to interpret a treaty is conceptually distinct from the power to amend it. Interpretation clarifies an ambiguous term; amendment changes it. Interpretation is an executive function; amendment may require Senate or congressional involvement. Of course in practice interpretation and amendment may blend. The problem is further complicated because under international law, state practice under a treaty, or even a new rule of customary international law, may establish or modify the meaning of a treaty term. The President plays the predominant role in carrying out state practice for the United States. Yet the Constitution does not permit him to modify significant treaty terms even when such a modification would be permitted by international law. Where the line is drawn remains unclear. It would seem at a minimum to depend on the importance of the matter to Congress or the Senate.

This problem was graphically raised by President Reagan's attempt to "reinterpret" the ABM Treaty. In that situation Congress used its legislative and appropriations powers to force the President to reconsider. The reinterpretation controversy involved the 1972 U.S.–U.S.S.R. Treaty on the Limitation of Anti–Ballistic Missile Systems (hereinafter called the "ABM Treaty"). When the President sent the ABM Treaty to the Senate for its advice and consent to ratification, executive branch officials told the Senate that the treaty prohibited the development and testing of space-based ABM systems based on "other physical principles" than those existing in 1972, such as lasers. Thirteen years later the Reagan Administration "reinterpreted" the treaty to permit the development and testing of those space-based ABM systems. However, several senators, former officials who negotiated the treaty and academic commentators vigorously disputed the Administration's case. Congress used its legislative and appropriation powers to force the executive branch to limit development and testing of ABM systems to activities permitted under the original interpretation.

In addition to the controversy over the substantive question of how the ABM Treaty should be interpreted, the ABM reinterpretation attempt sparked a dispute over the constitutional limits on presidential interpretation power. The Senate considered, but declined to adopt, S. Res. 167, 100th Cong. 1st Sess. (1987), which was a general resolution stating that the meaning of a treaty cannot be unilaterally changed by the President from "what the Senate understands the treaty to mean when it gives its advice and consent to ratification." After another round of debate on the constitutional issue, the Senate attached a similar condition in its consent to ratification of the 1987 U.S.-U.S.S.R. Treaty on the Elimination of Intermediate-range and Shorter-range Missiles (hereinafter called the "INF Treaty"), applicable only to that treaty. The President questioned the constitutionality of that condition, but only after he had ratified the INF Treaty. Similar conditions were attached to subsequent arms control treaties.

After all the controversy little is settled. It seems clear that the executive branch has some authority to create or modify some treaty terms on its own. Established practice confirms the authority to correct errors, to make a treaty "provisionally applicable," to add technical annexes to maritime pollution and safety treaties, and to change uncontroversial terms of treaties dealing with migrating birds and fish. In addition, a treaty may contemplate, and hence implicitly authorize, subsequent agreements to carry out its provisions. If the subsequent agreement merely fills in a detail within an earlier approved understanding, the subsequent agreement would seem to be authorized on the basis of the original authorization. For example, some arms control treaties have established commissions with authority to adopt more elaborate verification procedures and to settle disputes by adjusting such procedures. A similar practice of granting commissions authority to adjust technical norms has been followed in treaties with Canada protecting migrating birds and the allowable catch of salmon. Similarly the executive can approve changes in technical treaty rules by voting or otherwise acting in an international organization, like the IMO or ICAO. On the other hand, if the subsequent agreement covers a new matter or especially if it revises in a nontrivial manner an earlier provision, then additional authorization would seem to be called for.

Most commentators would probably agree that the President may not "reinterpret" important treaty provisions in major respects, even with the agreement of a treaty partner, without seeking Senate or congressional consent. Such a change would properly be classified as a "major amendment" to the treaty and, as such, would require that consent. It would also seem that other reinterpretations—those covering minor matters or uncontroversial changes—could be made by the President with Senate or congressional acquiescence. If Congress disagrees with a presidential interpretation, it may reflect its non-acquiescence through its legislative or appropriations power. In recent years the executive branch has been highly sensitive to congressional views, especially on matters of arms control, so here again an exclusive executive prerogative is strongly tempered in practice. Finally, conditions formally adopted, like that to the INF Treaty, should bind the President if he chooses to ratify the treaty.

A decade after the "reinterpretation" controversy, the United States and Russia became embroiled in a dispute over how to treat so-called "theatre" missile defense systems (as opposed to "strategic" missile defense systems) under the ABM Treaty. Congress was pushing the President to deploy such a system, while Russia resisted. The legality of deploying a theatre missile defense system was disputed. The executive branch of course had to interpret the treaty initially and to discuss that interpretation with Russia. Chastened by the earlier controversy the Administration informed Congress of the interpretation discussions. Eventually a new treaty, clarifying the applicability of the existing

ABM Treaty to theatre missile defense systems, was negotiated, but Russia declined to sign at first. U.S. President Clinton and Russian President Yeltsin finally signed a joint statement in Helsinki on March 21, 1997, affirming the principles for an agreement on demarcation between ABM systems and theater missile defense systems. In this way the President maintained the executive prerogative of interpreting treaty terms.

Termination of a Treaty. The text of the Constitution deals with the power to make treaties, but is silent about their termination. Historical practice has been mixed. Madison terminated a 1782 treaty with Holland on his own authority, but Congress itself terminated treaties with France at the end of the eighteenth century. Polk was supported by an 1846 Congressional Joint Resolution in terminating a treaty with Great Britain, while Buchanan received Senate authorization for terminating a treaty with Denmark in 1858. The issue was joined in the contemporary era when President Carter terminated an Article II defense treaty with Taiwan in accordance with its terms, despite a "sense of the Congress" expression that he should consult with Congress before any such change in policy. In *Goldwater v. Carter*[26] the Supreme Court dismissed a complaint filed by some conservative members of Congress to enjoin the presidential action, although only one Justice opined in favor of the executive branch on the merits. The plurality opinion invoked the political question doctrine. Since that time the

26.   444 U.S. 996 (1979).

President has claimed the right to terminate Article II treaties in accordance with their terms in the case of the U.S.–Nicaragua Friendship, Commerce and Navigation Treaty and with respect to U.S. acceptance of compulsory jurisdiction of the International Court of Justice. Congress has acquiesced to all these recent presidential claims of independent authority to terminate treaties.

In 2001 President Bush informed Russia that the United States would terminate the ABM Treaty in accordance with its terms (requiring six months notice). The Bush Administration's plans for a National Missile Defense were inconsistent with the Treaty, which the Administration sometimes characterized as an obsolete relic of the Cold War. In response, Russia proposed to amend the Treaty to accommodate U.S. plans for the NMD. Either course of action raised an issue regarding participation of the Senate or Congress in the decision. An amendment of the Treaty would have to be sent to the Senate for its approval under Article II, but the President's plan to withdraw from the Treaty altogether did not envision Senate participation. Administration critics argued that because the power to make a treaty is a shared power, terminating it should similarly be a shared responsibility. They also argued by analogy that a treaty is law of the land by virtue of Article VI, like an act of Congress; the President cannot unilaterally revoke a statute, so he should not be able to unilaterally withdraw from a treaty.

Nevertheless, the opposing arguments seem more persuasive, and the D.C. Circuit Court of Appeals in the *Goldwater* case so held for the executive on the merits in that case.[27] The fact that the text of Article II grants the power to make treaties to the President with the consent of the Senate, but does not address the question of termination, can be read to create a negative implication: the Framers did not intend Senate participation in treaty termination or they would have said so. The fact that several Framers specifically remarked on the importance of making it difficult to get into treaty obligations similarly suggests they were less concerned about getting out of them. The analogy to the repeal of statutes is not as compelling as the analogy to the appointment of ambassadors. The Supreme Court has held that the President may fire an official, even though his appointment was approved by the Senate,[28] and the same is the case with ambassadors. Unilateral power to fire officials may be important to enable the President to see that the laws are faithfully executed, just as unilateral power to fire ambassadors is important to enable the President to control the conduct of foreign relations.

Although it is true that a treaty may have the force of domestic law, its role as an international obligation is more prominent, especially in view of the fact that not all treaties are self-executing and

27. Goldwater v. Carter, 617 F.2d 697 (D.C.Cir.1979) (en banc), vacated, 444 U.S. 996 (1979) (political question).

28. Myers v. United States, 272 U.S. 52 (1926).

hence enforceable by private parties in the courts. Rather than thinking of treaties as an odd form of domestic statute, it is more compelling to view them as an instrument of foreign policy, and to view treaty termination as one facet of the spectrum of activities conducted in the life of a treaty, ranging from negotiation through interpretation and supervision, all of which are within the domain of the executive branch. For example, the President has successfully asserted the right to declare a treaty partner to be in "material breach" of its terms, so that under international law the United States may withdraw from the treaty. Finally, the President has successfully asserted the right to violate the terms of a treaty or other norms of international law in the course of conducting the nation's foreign relations, at least in the absence of congressional action prohibiting such a violation. Those rights are based on the President's foreign relations power. Because the acts leading to termination of a treaty normally would involve an assessment of foreign government behavior—compliance or not—and reaction, the executive's functional advantages are fully engaged in this situation: the relevant events may be secret, or the information and analysis leading to the decision to terminate the agreement may be based on executive knowledge and expertise. Foreign reaction is clearly within executive expertise. Increasingly termination may have an effect within the United States, but the executive branch can estimate that effect as easily as Congress could. Often the decision to terminate requires a balance of negative and positive consequences, foreign as well as domestic, and the executive can more effectively perform a genuine balancing analysis since Congress would ordinarily credit domestic consequences almost exclusively. And, as in other areas of foreign relations law, the President's actions are accountable—through congressional review and public reaction—in a way that actions of Congress would rarely be scrutinized.

C. The Multiple Domestic Effects of a Treaty

Article VI of the Constitution provides that a treaty is "the supreme Law of the Land; and the Judges in every State shall be bound thereby, any Thing in the Constitution or Laws of any State to the Contrary notwithstanding." This provision dealt with a notable weakness in the Confederacy, when some state courts refused to honor national treaties and gave precedence instead to state law. Article VI accomplishes two objectives: First, it establishes the supremacy of treaties over all inconsistent state law or policy, even a state constitution. Second, it gives treaties additional status as "law of the land." Accordingly Article VI confers a kind of legislative power on the Senate and President acting as "Treatymakers." In that regard the Supreme Court has held that a treaty has the same status as an act of Congress.[29] Hence a treaty may supersede inconsistent federal legislation that is prior in time,

29. Whitney v. Robertson, 124 U.S. 190 (1888).

just as later statutes supersede earlier inconsistent statutes and (as domestic law) earlier inconsistent treaty obligations. Moreover, a treaty, like some federal statutes, may give rise to rights enforceable by private parties thorough litigation in the courts.

Not all treaties, however, create rights that are judicially enforceable by private parties. For example, treaties requiring reductions in nuclear arms cannot be judicially enforced. This kind of treaty is called "non-self-executing," and will be explained below. On the other hand, a treaty affecting the treatment of private persons or their activities, relations or interests is more likely to be judicially enforceable by private litigants. These treaties are called "self-executing treaties." This term means that the treaty obligations in question may be enforced by a court at the behest of a litigant, without the need for any independent action by a legislature or executive officials. For example, the U.S. Supreme Court struck down a Seattle city ordinance which excluded Japanese nationals from a specified business activity because that exclusion violated a U.S.-Japan treaty.[30] The treaty thus was functionally the same as a civil rights statute. The treaty provision banning discrimination was the basis of the cause of action which the plaintiff could invoke without the need for legislative or executive action beyond the treaty itself. Self-executing treaties include those guaranteeing prescribed rights of aliens to inherit property, to carry on business, to trademark protection, and to enter and leave the coun-

30. Asakura v. City of Seattle, 265 U.S. 332 (1924).

try. Other examples of self-executing treaties include the U.N. Convention on the International Sale of Goods, which is like a federal Uniform Commercial Code (UCC) for international contracts for the sale of goods, and the Warsaw Convention, which provides a cause of action for injuries suffered during international air travel (and limitations on recovery for those injuries).

It has been argued that the Framers expected that all treaties would be self-executing,[31] or at least that the courts would apply treaties to the fullest extent possible. However, in an early case Chief Justice Marshall created an exception which forms the basis of the modern concept of "non-self-executing" treaties:

> Our constitution declares a treaty to be the law of the land. It is, consequently, to be regarded in courts of justice as equivalent to an act of the legislature, whenever it operates of itself, without the aid of any legislative provision. But when the terms of the stipulation import a contract—when either of the parties engages to perform a particular act, the treaty addresses itself to the political, not the judicial department; and the legislature must execute the contract, before it can become a rule for the court.[32]

31.   Jordan J. Paust, International Law as Law of the United States (1996); Stefan A. Riesenfeld and Frederick M. Abbott, The Scope of the U.S. Senate Control Over the Conclusion and Operation of Treaties, 67 Chi.-Kent L. Rev. 571 (1991).

32.   Foster v. Neilson, 27 U.S. (2 Pet.) 253, 314 (1829).

The criteria for deciding whether a treaty is self-executing have never been very clearly established. The *Foster* case involved the effect of a treaty provision that certain Spanish land titles "shall be ratified and confirmed." Marshall interpreted this language to require future legislative action. Accordingly, he said the treaty was not self-executing, so that the plaintiff's claim for a confirmed land title was denied. In a later case, *United States v. Percheman*,[33] the Chief Justice examined the Spanish text of the same treaty provision, but this time he said that the language should be read to mean that the Spanish land titles "are hereby confirmed." Accordingly, legislative action was not required; the treaty was self-executing; and plaintiff's land title could be confirmed. From this one might conclude that the determination of whether a treaty is self-executing depends on the language of the treaty and, by extension, the intent of the parties to the treaty. Although that has been the normal inference from these cases, a closer look suggests that another factor—the attitude of Congress toward the subject matter of the treaty—is also important.

The *Foster* and *Percheman* cases are significantly different in this regard. In *Foster*, plaintiff sought confirmation of a land title in a disputed part of West Florida, where Congress had expressly nullified Spanish grants, so that the Court would have had to invalidate an act of Congress to find for the plaintiff. In *Percheman*, there was no similar legis-

33. 32 U.S. (7 Pet.) 51 (1833).

lation; plaintiff sought confirmation of a title in East Florida that a congressional commission had declined to confirm simply because of the plaintiff's failure to submit a proper survey. Marshall emphasized that it was a property right protected by natural law, and Congress not having acted against the plaintiff's interests, it was just to find for the plaintiff. Thus, it was consistent with the attitude of Congress to regard the treaty as self-executing in East Florida, but not in the disputed part of West Florida involved in *Foster*.

Contemporary courts have applied a variety of tests. The most important element in determining whether a treaty is self-executing seems to depend on whether the parties, or at least the U.S. Government as a party, *intend* it to be self-executing. The determination of intent as to the self-executing nature of a treaty involves examination of the language of the treaty. If the parties choose language such as "agree to enact appropriate legislation" or "agree to take appropriate steps" to accomplish the treaty's objectives, the normal inference would be that the parties intend the treaty to be non-self-executing, i.e., they contemplate that additional, implementing action will be taken beyond ratifying the treaty. On the other hand, if the language creates an unqualified right or obligation, such as "nationals of each party are entitled to equal treatment with respect to carrying on a manufacturing business," the inference would normally be that the parties intended the treaty to be self-executing, i.e., operational without further legislative action.

In addition to intent, other factors may be considered in determining if a treaty is self-executing. The reasoning of the *Asakura* case described above suggests that the court found the treaty to be self-executing because it was an important and common treaty obligation whose achievement would be advanced by holding for the plaintiff. Moreover, no legislation was necessarily required, so it was an obligation that the courts could enforce comfortably within their tradition of enforcing individual civil rights. Other courts have listed factors, such as the availability of alternative enforcement mechanisms, the purpose of the treaty, the existence of domestic procedures and institutions appropriate for direct implementation, and the consequences of holding one way or the other.[34]

The Reporter's Notes to the Restatement (Third) of Foreign Relations Law suggest certain presumptions for determining whether a treaty is self-executing;

> ... Since generally the United States is obligated to comply with a treaty as soon as it comes into force for the United States, compliance is facilitated and expedited if the treaty is self-executing. Moreover, when Congressional action is required but is delayed, the United States may be in default on its international obligation. Therefore, if the Executive Branch has not requested implementing legislation and Congress has not enacted

---

34. See, e.g., People of Saipan v. U.S. Dept. of Interior, 502 F.2d 90 (9th Cir.1974); U.S. v. Postal, 589 F.2d 862 (5th Cir. 1979); Frolova v. U.S.S.R., 761 F.2d 370 (7th Cir.1985).

such legislation, there is a strong presumption that the treaty has been considered self-executing by the political branches, and should be considered self-executing by the courts. (This is especially so if some time has elapsed since the treaty has come into force.) In that event, a finding that a treaty is not self-executing is a finding that the United States has been and continues to be in default, and should be avoided.

In general, agreements that can be readily given effect by executive or judicial bodies, federal or State, without further legislation, are deemed self-executing, unless a contrary intention is manifest. Obligations not to act, or to act only subject to limitations, are generally self-executing.[35] [emphasis added]

The Restatement thus creates a presumption that treaties which can be judicially enforced will be judicially enforced. It is unclear whether the courts have actually followed this prescription.

As to intent the Restatement adds:

§ 111, Comment h. *Self-executing and non-self-executing international agreements.* In the absence of special agreement, it is ordinarily for the United States to decide how it will carry out its international obligations. Accordingly, the intention of the United States determines whether an agreement is to be self-executing in the United States or should await implementation by legisla-

35. Restatement (Third) of Foreign Relations Law § 111 Reporter's Note 5 (1987).

tion or appropriate executive or administrative action. If the international agreement is silent as to its self-executing character and the intention of the United States is unclear, account must be taken of any statement by the President in concluding the agreement or in submitting it to the Senate for consent or to the Congress as a whole for approval, and of any expression by the Senate or by Congress in dealing with the agreement.... Whether an agreement is to be given effect without further legislation is an issue that a court must decide when a party seeks to invoke the agreement as law....

This part of the Restatement is controversial in two respects. First, some commentators argue that the self-executing nature of a treaty depends on the intent of *all* the parties, not just the United States, so statements by the President, the Senate or Congress should not be given probative value in determining the issue. One problem with this point is that not all the parties to a treaty may have a relevant intent because they may not apply a doctrine of "self-executing" or "non-self-executing" treaties in the first place. Second, some argue that the determination of a treaty's self-executing nature should be made by the courts, applying judicial criteria, not by the political branches of government like the President or the Senate. Although the Restatement clearly indicates that the courts indeed must make the ultimate decision, it seems ambiguous as to how much weight the courts should give to statements of the President or Senate. As a practical matter the courts have normally gone along with the positions adopted by the political branches, but whether the courts must do so raises an important issue, discussed below, of the scope of the Senate's legislative authority under the treaty power.

It is generally accepted doctrine that a treaty may not be self-executing if it raises taxes, requires an appropriation of funds or creates criminal responsibility. The first case reflects acknowledgment of the constitutionally mandated role of the House of Representatives in initiating revenue bills. The last two cases—appropriating funds and creating criminal responsibility—do not seem to be literally required to be self-executing by the Constitution, but their extreme importance may suggest a need to involve the House of Representatives. Finally, in areas where the House has been actively involved it would seem inappropriate to change the law without again involving the House. One can even read the early Marshall opinions discussed above—*Foster & Neilson* and *Percheman*—as reflecting a respect for the Congress as a basis for the creation of the doctrine of non-self-executing treaties.

The doctrine that a self-executing treaty and a federal statute are of equal value, so that whichever is subsequent in time prevails, is an old, well-established doctrine. Nevertheless, this doctrine has rarely been applied in practice. There is apparently only one case where the Treatymakers have overridden a prior act of Congress. In the converse situation the courts bend over backwards to construe statutes in such a way as not to override a prior treaty. The courts require a very clear expression of congressional intent, in some cases almost an explicit declaration, to violate the treaty norm. Professor Janis recounts the story of the recent *PLO* case:

In the *Palestine Liberation Organization* (PLO) case [695 F.Supp. 1456 (S.D.N.Y.1988)], a federal district court heard a suit brought by the U.S. Justice Department, seeking to close the PLO's U.N. observer mission in New York. This seemed to be the intent of the Anti-terrorism Act of 1987, albeit the closure would probably violate the international obligations of the United States under its treaty as a host country for the United Nations. The federal court, noting that "statutes and treaties are both the supreme law of the land" and that "the Constitution sets forth no order of precedence to differentiate between them," concluded that the text and legislative history of the Anti-terrorism Act failed "to disclose any clear legislative intent that Congress was directing the Attorney General, the State Department or this Court to act in contravention of the Headquarters Agreement." There seemed to be "unanimous belief" in the Justice Department that the *PLO* decision should have been appealed, but the State Department felt that it would have been "a grave mistake" to close the PLO office. The interagency dispute was settled by President Reagan who, citing "foreign policy considerations," chose not to appeal the district court's judgment.[36]

There are good arguments for never overriding a treaty obligation, even by subsequent act of Congress. After all, a treaty's international obligations imposed on the United States remain intact despite its supersession as domestic law by a later statute. Accordingly, the United States can be put in a position of having violated international law and therefore being subject to retaliation. Some countries regard treaties as always superior to domestic legislation. This approach would foster greater stability in international relations which is increasingly important in the modern world. Nevertheless, the authority of Congress to override treaty norms as domestic law is well settled and explicable as a necessary corollary to its role in democracy.

Non-Self–Executing Treaties. One solution to the problem of giving the Senate too much legislative power through the treaty process would be to make all treaties non-self-executing. That means that the treaty obligation would only be discharged within the U.S. domestic legal system by some means independent of the treaty itself, thereby preserving the role of Congress and state legislatures in the domestic law-making process. The major alternative means of discharging obligations under non-self-executing treaties include (1) an act of Congress passed specifically to carry out the treaty, (2) existing legislation that authorizes or mandates action required to be taken by the treaty, (3) existing

36. Mark W. Janis, An Introduction to International Law 91 (2d ed. 1993).

executive or administrative authority to carry out such action, and (4) existing state legislation authorizing or requiring the treatymandated action. To say that a treaty is non-self-executing simply means that its obligations must be enforced by some means other than judicial action based on the treaty at the behest of an affected private party. Non-self-executing does not mean that the Government is not going to enforce the treaty obligation through the domestic legal system. It just means that private parties may not enforce the treaty itself in domestic courts.[37] A non-self-executing treaty should still be regarded as "law of the land" even if it is not enforceable in the courts. Hence executive officials and legislators have a duty to carry out the treaty in good faith, and the treaty's norms serve as standards by which their conduct can be measured. Their accountability is political, not judicial, but the treaty should still be thought of as legally binding. Furthermore, a non-self-executing treaty is still an international obligation (with whatever remedies may be available in the international system); and governments normally do not conclude treaties that they do not intend to honor.

37. Even if a treaty is non-self-executing, and hence cannot be invoked by a party in litigation, the treaty could still theoretically override inconsistent state law. Hence, in this view, a state official, sworn to uphold the Constitution and laws of the United States, would not enforce an inconsistent state law, even though she would not be compelled by a court not to enforce it. Alternatively a treaty could be used as the basis of a defense in a criminal proceeding, even if the defendant could not use it as the basis of a cause of action. These possibilities have been explored in the academic literature, but not endorsed by the courts.

Some recent examples of non-self-executing treaties illustrate the variety of means by which the U.S. Government has chosen to implement treaty obligations. Congress passed a statute in 1988 specifically making genocide a crime in order to carry out the Genocide Convention. The 1992 Montreal Protocol requires each party to eliminate production of ozone-depleting chemicals within its territory by certain dates. The United States has carried out this obligation by using an existing act of Congress (the Clean Air Act). Treaties on the law of the sea are implemented through Coast Guard regulation, e.g., the prohibition against stopping vessels on the high seas except with the consent of the flag state. In these situations coast guard and naval vessels should be required by administrative regulation to follow procedures dictated by treaty. The President used his constitutional authority as Commander-in-Chief to assure U.S. compliance with obligations under nuclear test ban treaties. With respect to the International Covenant on Civil and Political Rights, the U.S. Government did not ask Congress to pass any special implementing legislation on the grounds that existing civil rights legislation, federal and state, was adequate for the United States to carry out the international obligations assumed under the Covenant. For example, the Covenant provides that "no one shall be subjected to torture." Presumably the Constitution's Fifth and Fourteenth Amendments, coupled with ordinary criminal and tort law, already provide sufficient legal protection against torture so that the

U.S. could safely join the Covenant without seeking new legislation or applying the Covenant as a self-executing treaty. Where existing legal authority is not adequate to assure U.S. compliance with a treaty, the President will usually not formally ratify the treaty (which brings it into force as an international legal obligation of the United States) until the requisite implementing legislation has been passed.

The major disadvantage of making treaties non-self-executing is the delay in having to wait for the legislature to pass implementing legislation. Delay not only defers domestic implementation of a desirable norm (if the norm were not desirable, presumably the Treatymakers would not have concluded the treaty in the first place). Delay also defers the changes in foreign government behavior sought through the treaty negotiation, and may risk backsliding from the commitments undertaken. Furthermore, there is always the risk that an act of Congress will not exactly track or fully implement the treaty norm. With an unpopular treaty, opponents in the Senate have another opportunity to try to undercut the commitments undertaken, and members of the House, who have been left out of the process, may assert their influence in a negative way. Moreover, when the President asks for congressional action there is inevitably the chance that political bargains will have to be made to get Congress to act. These may seem high prices to pay in exchange for the extra political support provided by full congressional approval.

The choice as to whether a treaty is self-executing or non-self-executing is important politically as well as a matter of constitutional law. Self-executing treaties exclude the House of Representatives, the more democratic of the two branches of Congress, from the law-making process. There seem to be few fixed guidelines for deciding whether a treaty should be self-executing or not. The Restatement says that treaties requiring the payment (and hence appropriation) of money, raising taxes or creating criminal responsibility cannot be self-executing, out of deference to the constitutional role of the House, at least with respect to the former two categories.[38] Presumably on other matters where Congress was traditionally or actively involved, such as environmental, health or labor regulation, a self-executing treaty would also be inappropriate. There is, however, no judicial guidance.

Domestic Effect of Senate Conditions to Ratification of Treaties. Although not explicitly authorized by the text of the Constitution, the Senate historically has asserted the power to attach conditions to its consent to ratification of a treaty under Article II. As indicated above, those conditions may require the President to attach a reservation to United States adherence to the treaty or to amend the treaty by agreement with the other treaty party or parties. Senate-imposed conditions may also require the President to make a specified declaration to the other treaty party or parties in connection with

38. Restatement (Third) of Foreign Relations Law § 111 comment i (1987).

ratification. Finally, Senate-imposed conditions may state an understanding or interpretation of the treaty that the Senate seeks to impose on the President or on the U.S. courts. For example, in approving human rights treaties the Senate has recently attached "reservations" and "understandings" dealing with the interpretation of particular terms of a treaty, a "declaration" stating that part of the treaty will not be self-executing, and attempting through a "proviso" to negate the holding of *Missouri v. Holland*. In its resolution of ratification approving the International Covenant on Civil and Political Rights, the Senate prescribed:

I.   The Senate's advice and consent is subject to the following reservations: . . .

(3) That the United States considers itself bound by Article 7 to the extent that "cruel, inhuman or degrading treatment or punishment" means the cruel and unusual treatment or punishment prohibited by the Fifth, Eighth and/or Fourteenth Amendments to the Constitution of the United States. . . .

III.   The Senate's advice and consent is subject to the following declarations:

(1) That the United States declares that the provisions of Articles 1 through 27 of the Covenant are not self-executing. . . .

IV.   The Senate's advice and consent is subject to the following proviso, which shall not be included in the instrument of ratification to be deposited by the President:

Nothing in this covenant requires or authorizes legislation, or other action, by the United States of America prohibited by the Constitution of the United States as interpreted by the United States.[39]

These provisions purport to accomplish several different objectives. First, the reservation regarding cruel, inhuman or degrading treatment or punishment seeks to limit the scope of the U.S. obligation under the treaty. Because this condition relates to the scope of the international obligation, the President would be bound to communicate that reservation to the other parties to the treaty (if the President chooses to ratify the treaty), and the Senate condition will accordingly define the scope of the U.S. obligation under international law.

There is nevertheless an international law problem that in turn may become a domestic law issue: Under international law, reservations which are incompatible with the object and purpose of the treaty are not permitted. In such a case, the United States is either not considered to be a party to the treaty, in which case there is no legal problem because the United States would have no obligations at all. Or, under another view of the effect of reservations that are incompatible with the treaty, the United States could be considered to be a party to the treaty without regard to the proffered,

39.   U.S. Senate Resolution of Advice and Consent to Ratification of the International Covenant on Civil and Political Rights, 138 Cong. Rec. 8070 (1992), reprinted in Barry E. Carter and Phillip R. Trimble, International Law Selected Documents, 2001–2002 Edition 403–05 (2001).

but invalid, reservation.[40] In that case the President would have blundered by depositing a ratification that bound the United States to treaty obligations beyond those authorized by the Senate. The domestic issue then would become: what is the domestic effect of the treaty with the invalid Senate conditions?

Article VI literally provides that the "treaty" is also law of the land. If "treaty" refers to the bundle of international law obligations assumed by the United States, then a domestic court would apply all the international law obligations as domestic law. Under this approach a reservation that is invalid under international law would be ignored by a domestic court in a domestic lawsuit because that reservation is not part of the "treaty" within the meaning of Article VI. On the other hand, the President only has constitutional authority to ratify the "treaty" as approved by the Senate. If he ratifies a treaty with a Senate-required reservation that is invalid under international law, the President has bound the United States to international obligations greater than he was permitted by the Sen-

---

40. Ten states objected to the reservations to U.S. acceptance of the ICCPR, and the United Nations Human Rights Committee stated that the United States was not entitled to rely on them. If the reservations are indeed severable, then the President has ratified a treaty establishing obligations beyond those authorized by the Senate. Professor Henkin criticized the entire package of reservations, declarations, understandings and provisos, which have become standard practice in U.S. ratification of human rights treaties. See Louis Henkin, U.S. Ratification of Human Rights Conventions: The Ghost of Senator Bricker, 89 Am. J. Int'l L. 341 (1995).

ate to do. In short the President blundered. In that situation, whatever the international consequences, the domestic courts should not compound the constitutional blunder of the President by enforcing the treaty without the reservation.

Another theoretical issue raised by this reservation is that the Senate seeks to impose a particular interpretation of a general treaty term. In this way the Senate arguably intrudes into the Article III territory of the judiciary, one of whose core functions is to interpret treaties. Whether the Senate's reservation constitutes defining the scope of the treaty obligation, which is permissible, or interpreting its terms, which may be dubious, is an open question.

The non-self-executing declaration raises another set of issues concerning the domestic legal effect of Senate action, viz. the extent of the Senate's (and the Treatymaker's) legislative power under Articles II and VI, and how that power can be reconciled with the judicial power of the courts enshrined in Article III. No doubt the Treatymakers have an irrefutable claim to some measure of legislative power. That is what Article VI literally states, and self-executing treaties have been recognized for over 200 years. The difficult problems arise when the Treatymakers attempt to legislate beyond the text of the treaty, for example by specifying the treaty's domestic legal, even constitutional, effect. One way by which the Treatymakers can legislate beyond the text of the treaty is to attach a condition that the treaty will not be self-executing. Such an under-

standing can be viewed as a concession to the
political importance of the House of Representatives
and to democratic values. The Senate willingly es-
chews its legislative role by in effect turning "law"
of the land into non-law. Chief Justice Marshall
seems to have done the same thing selectively in the
Foster and *Percheman* cases[41] when he created the
concept of non-self-executing treaties that the
courts would not apply without action by Congress
as a whole. In recent years, however, some commentators have questioned the Senate's authority to
legislate beyond the text of the treaty. They argue
that in the case of a non-self-executing declaration,
the Senate is doing what is normally done by the
courts. The courts regularly interpret general treaty
terms, and decide whether treaties are self-executing or not.

This line of reasoning is not persuasive. If the
Senate can make law within the scope of the treaty's subject matter, why should it be debarred from
a more modest role.[42] It still makes law of the land,
but law binding only on the political branches and
not on the courts. Congress does likewise when it

41. Supra notes 32 and 33.

42. In Power Authority of New York v. Federal Power Commission, 247 F.2d 538 (D.C.Cir.1957), the court declined to give
effect to a Senate "reservation" to a treaty with Canada dividing
the water of the Niagara River, on the ground that the reservation was only of domestic concern. The reservation reserved to
Congress in future legislation the right to determine how to use
the U.S. share, although an existing act of Congress gave authority to do so to the Federal Power Commission. This situation is
unusual in that the Senate was trying to defer to Congress
(which had been actively considering the issue) but by overriding
existing legislation. Non-self-executing declarations could be similarly seen as solely of domestic concern, and therefore not part

passes statutes that create legal obligations enforceable by an administrative agency but not through private causes of action. In any event it seems inconceivable that the courts, which are accustomed to deferring to the political branches on similar matters ranging from the interpretation to the very existence of treaties, would not similarly defer to the Treatymakers as to this question as well.

Apart from the question of whether the Treatymakers have law-making authority to decide whether a treaty is non-self-executing, some commentators have raised more fundamental issues. Some, for example, have argued that the Framers intended that all treaties be self-executing so Chief Justice Marshall was simply wrong to create the non-self-executing category.[43] Alternatively it can be argued that the *Foster* case, and the non-self-executing category, should be limited to treaties that literally could not be executed by the courts, such as treaties calling for an appropriation of funds. On the other hand, as noted above, *Foster* and contemporary cases suggest that the courts should look at the attitude of Congress in determining whether a treaty is non-self-executing. If Congress has legislated actively or contemporaneously, the courts should find the treaty non-self-executing.[44]

of the treaty, but such a limitation of Article II domestic effect seems disrespectful of the political branches.

43.   Jordan J. Paust, International Law as Law of the United States 51–57 (1996).

44.   Professor Yoo goes further and argues that self-executing agreements should be limited to those covering matters beyond

Through its Reservations and Understandings, especially not allowing the independent judiciary to fashion its own interpretations of the treaty, the Senate may also have sought to convey another command to the courts. In interpreting the Covenant, courts could be expected in the ordinary course of interpretation to look to the interpretations adopted by foreign courts, including Human Rights Courts, and UN bodies. By adopting Reservations and Understandings the Treatymakers probably wanted to preclude both prospects, reflecting a conservative minority in the Senate who have regularly attempted to insulate the domestic legal system from foreign review or influence.

Reflecting the same constituency, the final Proviso may reflect an attempt to negate *Missouri v. Holland.* In some ways this attempt extends Senate legislative power even further than the non-self-executing declaration, to changing constitutional law. Surely the Senate cannot reduce the power of Congress under the Constitution! Nevertheless, Congress has sometimes in fact reversed Supreme Court constitutional decisions so perhaps the Treatymakers can do likewise. At one point the Supreme Court also said that the Tenth Amendment was only politically, not judicially, enforceable. This type of Understanding can be seen as an attempt at the political enforcement endorsed by the Court. The Understanding can also be read as an invitation to

Congress' Article I powers. John C. Yoo, Globalism and the Constitution: Treaties, Non–Self–Execution and the Original Understanding, 99 Colum. L. Rev. 1955 (1999).

the Court to reconsider *Holland*, perhaps a remote but not inconceivable result, given the current Court's revival of states rights and principles of federalism.

Other Impacts of Treaties on Domestic Law. Even if a treaty is not applied directly or does not lead to the enactment of implementing legislation, it may still have an impact on domestic law. First, there is a maxim of statutory construction to the effect that Congress is presumed not to violate international law. Consequently a court will interpret an ambiguous statute to be consistent with, rather than to violate, a treaty obligation (or even a norm of customary international law). For example, the Supreme Court construed federal labor legislation not to apply to workers on Honduran flag vessels serving U.S. ports, in part because international law reserved exclusive authority in such matters to the flag state.[45] In addition, a statute making it a crime to unload liquor from a vessel except at designated ports was construed not to apply to conduct 20 miles off the U.S. coast because the international law of the sea limited U.S. jurisdiction to a 12–mile coastal zone. In considering the application of the immigration laws to Haitian refugees, the Court reviewed the treaty requirements which those laws were designed to implement.[46] Most recently the Court indicated that it would apply international law, or at least principles of comity, in some cases to

45.   McCulloch v. Sociedad Nacional de Marineros de Honduras, 372 U.S. 10 (1963).

46.   Sale v. Haitian Centers Council, 509 U.S. 155 (1993).

limit the extraterritorial application of the antitrust laws.[47]

A related maxim of statutory construction, also recently reaffirmed by the Supreme Court, is that an act of Congress will ordinarily be construed to apply only within the territory of the United States. Thus the sex discrimination laws of the Civil Rights Act were held not to apply to discrimination in Saudi Arabia, even when carried out by a U.S. corporation against U.S. nationals. Similar presumptions have been employed in construing other legislation, like that covering age discrimination and ordinary criminal law. This territorial presumption probably reflects traditional international law limitations on territorial sovereignty. Although in recent decades international law has changed to permit some extraterritorial legislation, the presumption that a statute must be construed to be consistent with international law remains at least rhetorically intact.

The presumption that Congress does not intend to violate international law, and the presumption that Congress normally intends to legislate only territorially, are only judicial presumptions. It is clear that Congress may legislate both extraterritorially and in violation of international law. The courts have not placed any significant *constitutional* limits (such as through the Fifth Amendment Due Process Clause) on Congress' authority. Neverthe-

47. See, e.g., Hartford Fire Insurance v. California, 509 U.S. 764 (1993).

less, Congress, like the executive branch, in fact, normally respects international law.

Finally, international law, even in the form of non-self-executing treaties, can also have an indirect impact on the substantive content of U.S. and state constitutional law, statutory law and common law. In the area of human rights, for example, treaty norms may be used to fill out the content of general, related concepts in U.S. constitutional or statutory law, such as "due process," or "equal protection." This potential is perversely illustrated by the Senate's "understanding" quoted above to the effect that the Covenant's prohibition of "cruel, unusual or degrading treatment or punishment" did not go beyond the Eighth Amendment's bar of "cruel and unusual punishment." Without that understanding, the Covenant's textually more sweeping coverage, reflecting accepted international standards, could influence judicial interpretation of the Eighth Amendment. Moreover, interpretations of the Covenant and similar provisions in other human rights treaties by other courts, such as the European Court of Human Rights, together with commentary of the Covenant's Human Rights Committee, provide sources of reference for filling out the meaning of the general constitutional language. The Covenant also has a number of provisions that are more specific than the U.S. Constitution, such as an express right of family privacy and a broad prohibition of sex discrimination, that could be drawn upon in interpreting the Equal Protection Clause. There are a few lower court cases employing standards from human rights treaties in constitutional adjudication, and perhaps that approach will be more widely followed now that the United States has ratified the Covenant (even if it is considered technically non-self-executing) and as the United States joins other international human rights treaties.

D. Formal International Law Making Through the Creation of Customary International Law

The President's constitutional foreign affairs authority supports another type of international lawmaking by the United States, viz. U.S. participation in the development of "customary international law." Although all the branches of government may participate in the development of customary law by the United States, the President again is the dominant branch.

Customary international law is defined as the practice states follow out of a sense of legal obligation. There are two components of this definition: (1) "state practice" in following a particular rule, and (2) a psychological element—that practice must be followed out of a sense of legal obligation. State practice refers simply to what states do or refrain from doing, e.g. not searching the bags of diplomats in transit through the state, or asserting the right to apply and enforce its law in the ocean up to 6, 12, or 200 miles off the coast. State practice encompasses all acts of government, including legislation, judicial decisions, administrative regulations and making official statements. Consequently evidence of state practice can be found in the actions of any branch of government—administrative, legislative, executive, or judicial. Thus a customs regulation speaking to the treatment of diplomats in transit would be evidence of state practice on that issue. Similarly an act of Congress purporting to extend the criminal law to a 12–mile band of territorial sea would be evidence of U.S. state practice. Judicial decisions like the *Filartiga*[48] and *Marcos*[49] cases would count as U.S. state practice recognizing that government-sponsored torture was a violation of customary international law. Pursuant to his foreign relations power the President may make declarations of the U.S. position on a matter of customary law. The Department of State is normally the executive branch agency through which such declarations are made. The executive authority to make declarations would of course be subject to any applicable act of Congress but in many areas of customary law Congress has not spoken. Recent examples of important declarations concerning customary international law include a series of pronouncements regarding coastal state jurisdiction under the law of the sea and declarations reiterating the U.S. position on expropriations of property.

48. Filartiga v. Pena–Irala, 630 F.2d 876 (2d Cir.1980), on remand 577 F.Supp. 860 (E.D.N.Y.1984).

49. Trajano v. Marcos, 878 F.2d 1439 (9th Cir.1989).

Because these sources of state practice are so vast and diverse, ascertaining the state practice of more than 150 nations obviously presents a daunting challenge. One of the more accessible sources of state practice can be found in diplomatic correspondence, i.e., the innumerable statements, protests and counter protests issued by the executive branches of governments, and in related opinions of legal advisers to governments, press releases and official statements in the course of dealing with other governments. These official statements and responses of governments are known as "diplomatic correspondence", and form abundant evidence of state practice. They are frequently published by the governments involved, and hence are more accessible to library researchers than wading through the legislative and administrative records of all the states of the world. The use of diplomatic correspondence as a major source of customary law enhances the executive branch's power in this area.

The Restatement also points out that practice need not be universal to be binding and that inaction as well as action may constitute state practice:

Inaction may constitute state practice, as when a state acquiesces in acts of another state that affect its legal rights. The practice necessary to create customary law might be of comparatively short duration, but ... it must be "general and consistent." A practice can be general even if it is not universally followed; there is no precise formula to indicate how widespread a practice must be, but it should reflect wide acceptance among the states particularly involved in the relevant activity.... A principle of customary law is not binding on a state that declares its dissent from the principle during its development.[50]

Since the President conducts the diplomatic relations of the country, in the course of which new developments are most likely to be discovered or monitored, he is obviously in the dominant position to accept new developments in the law. In this way, the President may make new customary law binding on the United States through inaction, as well as expressing dissent on behalf of the United States to a newly developing rule.

The Reporters Notes and Comment to § 102 of the Restatement add:

The practice of states that builds customary law takes many forms and includes what states do in or through international organizations. The United Nations General Assembly in particular has adopted resolutions, declarations, and other statements of principles that in some circumstances contribute to the process of making customary law, insofar as statements and votes of governments are kinds of state practice, and may be expressions of *opinio juris*. The contributions of such resolutions and of the statements and votes supporting them to the lawmaking process will differ widely, depending on factors such as the subject of the resolution, whether it purports to reflect legal principles, how large a majority it

50. Restatement (Third) of Foreign Relations Law § 102 cmt. b (1987).

commands and how numerous and important are the dissenting states, whether it is widely supported (including in particular states principally affected), and whether it is later confirmed by other practice. "Declarations of principles" may have greater significance than ordinary resolutions. A memorandum of the Office of Legal Affairs of the United Nations Secretariat suggests that:

> in view of the greater solemnity and significance of a "declaration," it may be considered to impart, on behalf of the organ adopting it, a strong expectation that Members of the international community will abide by it. Consequently, insofar as the expectation is gradually justified by State practice, a declaration may by custom become recognized as laying down rules binding upon States. . . .

> International conferences, especially those engaged in codifying customary law, provide occasions for expressions by states as to the law on particular questions. General consensus as to the law at such a conference confirms customary law or contributes to its creation ... e.g., as to the law of the sea, ...[51]

Because the executive branch represents the United States and votes in international organizations, the President may make customary international law in this way as well.

51. Id., Reporters' Note 2 on customary law at 32.

The psychological element required to establish the existence of a rule of customary international law may be more difficult to show. If Congress asserts the right to apply fishing regulations up to 200 miles off the U.S. coast (but not beyond), or the Customs Service does not assert authority over diplomats in transit, how would you know if those actions were motivated by a sense of legal obligation? Governments normally do not specify a motivation when they act. Diplomatic correspondence may be clearer because, in asserting a position or protesting an action, a government often will bolster its claim by arguing that its position is in accordance with international law. In that case it is easier to identify both the state's practice and its belief that the practice is required by international law. Again, diplomatic correspondence is an important source of authority which is controlled by the President.

Customary international law is not written or formally established like treaties, but it rests on the same notion of a state's consenting to be legally bound. Through practice states demonstrate their consent to be bound. A rule or practice that is accepted as law is law. Acceptance may be explicit or implicit. For example, by common understanding a state has authority to make and enforce law within its territorial borders, and may not enforce its domestic law in the territory of another state without that state's consent. The FBI may not legitimately make an arrest in Canada. There are no treaties prescribing these rules. They are simply assumed and generally followed as part of the international system. Similarly the practices of government-sanctioned human torture, summary executions, and holding people indefinitely without charges or trial, are considered to be violations of customary international law, binding on all states even though all states may not be parties to treaties or may not have made statements condemning those practices. The executive monopoly on speaking for the United States assures its dominant position in these situations.

Therefore the President plays a predominant role in customary international law-making on behalf of the United States. This presidential power has been established since the eighteenth century. The Framers understood the "law of nations" (which then was almost entirely customary practice, as opposed to treaties) to be part of the "law" of the United States. President Washington claimed authority to execute the law of nations by executive order, e.g. by declaring neutrality in the 1793 war between France and Great Britain. He also issued regulations defining specific offenses against the law of nations which provided the governing law until Congress passed applicable legislation. In modern times Presidents have initiated changes in customary international law through executive orders proclaiming jurisdiction over fisheries, the continental shelf, air space and the 200 mile zone adjacent to the coast known as the Exclusive Economic Zone. In almost all the cases where the President declares customary law Congress has concurrent authority to regulate, and frequently does so by ratifying the executive initiative. For example, Congress legislated the executive positions on the law of the sea.

Customary international law has the status of federal common law and thus supersedes inconsistent state law and policy, like a treaty; it must be applied by state courts; and it provides a basis for federal question jurisdiction in the federal courts. The U.S. courts have applied customary international law in two contemporary situations—providing relief for victims of human rights abuses under customary human rights law, and providing relief for corporations whose property was expropriated without compensation by foreign governments—in addition to old cases applying the law of prize. On the other hand, the courts have normally declined to strike down U.S. Government action that violates customary international law, such as when the United States Government held undocumented aliens indefinitely in detention if they did not qualify as refugees and their government would not take them back, and in the case of the recent kidnapping in Mexico of a Mexican national to stand trial in the United States.[52]

The *Paquete Habana*[53] is the principal case cited for the proposition that American courts apply the law of nations as a rule of decision. In that case the Supreme Court ruled that the 1898 capture of a fishing vessel during the U.S. blockade of Cuba in

52. United States v. Alvarez–Machain, 504 U.S. 655 (1992).

53. The Paquete Habana, 175 U.S. 677 (1900).

the Spanish–American War violated international customary law. The Court said:

> International law is part of our law, and must be ascertained and administered by the courts of justice of appropriate jurisdiction, as often as questions of right depending upon it are duly presented for their determination. For this purpose, *where there is no treaty, and no controlling executive or legislative act or judicial decision*, resort must be had to the customs and usages of civilized nations; and, as evidence of these, to the works of jurists and commentators, who by years of labor, research and experience, have made themselves peculiarly well acquainted with the subjects of which they treat. Such works are resorted to by judicial tribunals, not for the speculations of their authors concerning what the law ought to be, but for trustworthy evidence of what the law really is.

It should be noted that the Court left open the ability of Congress or the President to override the otherwise applicable customary international law (in the italicized language). Moreover, the President had ordered the Navy to conduct operations in accordance with international law, so the Court can also be seen as implementing the presidential proclamation.

In *Garcia–Mir v. Meese*,[54] the Eleventh Circuit Court of Appeals upheld the ability of both Congress and the President to detain Cuban refugees

54. Garcia–Mir v. Meese, 788 F.2d 1446 (11th Cir.1986).

indefinitely, in explicit violation of customary international law. These decisions stand for the proposition that the President, under the authority of his constitutional foreign affairs power, may violate customary international law, just as Congress can violate international law (recall that a later-in-time statute will override an inconsistent treaty obligation as a matter of domestic law). The court implicitly assumed that the President had constitutional authority to detain the aliens in question. The basis for this act is the foreign relations power. The President has historically exercised governmental authority at the border to regulate cross border pipelines, airports and bridges, as well as to control the entry of foreign ships and aliens. The President's authority has been based on his independent constitutional foreign affairs power, although of course Congress could regulate these matters itself if it chose to do so.

A contrary result would be profoundly undemocratic, especially with respect to customary international law. When Congress or the President acts within its recognized constitutional provenance, they do so with the safeguards of public publicity and accountability. Customary international law, on the other hand, may be formed in an obscure manner largely or even entirely outside the U.S. political system. Although some academics have argued that the President should be restrained by customary international law,[55] that position has not been

55. See, e.g., Jordan J. Paust, The President Is Bound by Customary International Law, 81 Am.J.Int'l L. 377 (1987).

endorsed by the courts. Indeed it would be anomalous to concede that the President has constitutional foreign affairs authority to declare U.S. positions on customary law, but to deny him authority to change that position.

The courts have been generally reluctant to apply customary international law because it lacks legitimacy as "real law." There are several reasons to question the legitimacy of customary law. First, as outlined above, it is often vague and rests on innumerable diffuse sources that may be difficult to find. It is not formal or even written like a treaty. Most significantly, in the U.S. context, its political foundation is not well grounded. The Constitution does not expressly endorse it as "law of the land." Neither the Senate nor Congress has approved it. To the extent that the President declares official U.S. positions on customary international law, its recognition seems to enhance presidential law making authority under his foreign affairs power, which is always potentially controversial. Finally, the evidence of customary law is often found in UN General Assembly resolutions and other declarations that are by their terms not legally binding, in treaties that have been negotiated by diplomats but not yet ratified (or widely ratified) by governments, and in the writings of scholars. None of these materials are usually considered sources of formal law.

In the well known *Filartiga* cases, the court's subject-matter jurisdiction and the plaintiff's cause of action depended on a finding that government-sponsored torture violated customary international law. In finding the law the court relied on unanimously-adopted UN General Assembly resolutions; generally accepted human rights treaties, even though not ratified by the U.S.; the constitutions of 55 countries that prohibited torture; statements by the U.S. Department of State; European judicial decisions; and the opinions of academic international law scholars. The United States Government, through the executive branch, filed an amicus brief in the *Filartiga* case urging the court to make its finding, so at least as a practical matter the court was carrying out the President's policy. Since then other courts have occasionally drawn upon similar sources in "finding" customary international law. Yet they have not yet "found" a norm contrary to the position of the political branches. When the courts "find" or apply customary international law, they have normally only done so when one or more of the political branches had clearly endorsed the result.

The future role of customary international human rights law in U.S. courts is highly uncertain. The Supreme Court has not addressed the issues, and there are significant theoretical obstacles to applying customary human rights law in the manner of the *Filartiga* decisions. First is the anomaly of ignoring the actual practice of governments, which regularly violate human rights norms, and instead taking "law on the books" as evidence of state practice. Second, much of the "law on the books" is not technically legally binding on the target state, such as General Assembly Resolutions and treaties that have not been ratified or have been adopted only with many reservations. Third, international law itself is law between states, and does not in general provide for individual official responsibility or for private causes of action. Fourth, the determination of actual state practice, the significance of declarations by Human Rights Treaty Committees and the consequence of imposing random liabilities in the context of widespread abuses are matters in which the functional advantages of the political branches far exceed those of the judiciary. Accordingly, it seems reasonable to view the judicial application of customary international law as strongly dependent on guidance from the political branches. The fact that the Treatymakers have uniformly provided that ratified human rights treaties, which include a large body of customary law, are non-self-executing should lead courts to look carefully for solid political branch support before proceeding in this area.

Bibliographic Note

The major works on the general Treaty Power on which I have relied are Louis Henkin, Foreign Affairs and the United States Constitution, Chapters 7 and 8 (2nd ed. 1996); Michael J. Glennon, Constitutional Diplomacy, Chapters 4–7 (1990); Jack N. Rakove, Solving a Constitutional Puzzle: The Treatymaking Clause as a Case Study, 1 New Series, Perspectives in American History 233 (1984); and the studies of the subject by the Congressional

Research Service. The current version is Congressional Research Service, Treaties and Other International Agreements: The Role of the United States Senate, 103d Cong. 1st Sess. (1993).

See also the following works with respect to congressional-executive agreements: Bruce Ackerman and David Golove, Is NAFTA Constitutional?, 108 Harv. L. Rev. 799 (1995) (expansive view of such agreements); and John C. Yoo, Laws as Treaties?: The Constitutionality of Congressional–Executive Agreements, 99 Mich. L. Rev. 757 (2001). On presidential executive agreements, see Michael D. Ramsey, Executive Agreements and the (Non) Treaty Power, 77 N.C.L. Rev. 133 (1998) (arguing for limited scope extending only to minor agreements without domestic legal effect).

On reservations, see Curtis A. Bradley and Jack L. Goldsmith, Treaties, Human Rights and Conditional Consent, 149 U. Pa. L. Rev. 399 (2000).

On interpretations and reinterpretations, I have relied on David Koplow's articles; When Is an Amendment Not an Amendment?: Modification of Arms Control Agreements Without the Senate, 59 U. Chi. L. Rev. 981 (1992); and Constitutional Bait and Switch: Executive Reinterpretation of Arms Control Treaties, 137 U. Pa. L. Rev. 1353 (1989); and my response, The Constitutional Common Law of Treaty Interpretation: A Reply to the Formalists, 137 U. Pa. L. Rev. 1461 (1989). See also John C. Yoo, Politics As Law: The Anti–Ballistic Missile Treaty, The Separation of Powers, and Treaty Interpretation, 89 Cal. L. Rev. 851 (2001).

A comprehensive account of the history of the non-self-executing doctrine is John C. Yoo, Globalism and the Constitution: Treaties, Non–Self–Execution and the Original Understanding, 99 Colum. L. Rev. 1955 (1999). Rejoinders by Martin S. Flaherty and by Carlos Manuel Vazquez are in the same issue, at 2095, and 2154, respectively. See generally Carlos Manuel Vazquez, The Four Doctrines of Self–Executing Treaties, 89 Am. J. Int'l L. 695 (1995); and John H. Jackson, Status of Treaties in Domestic Legal Systems: A Policy Analysis, 86 Am. J. Int'l L. 310 (1992).

There is considerable skepticism about the genuine force of CIL (Jack L. Goldsmith and Eric A. Posner, Understanding the Resemblance Between Modern and Traditional Customary International Law, 40 Va. J. Int'l L. 639 (2000)), its basic legitimacy and its claim to status as law (Trimble, A Revisionist View of Customary International Law, 33 UCLA L. Rev. 665 (1986)), and its status as federal common law and its utility as a means of actually advancing human rights (Curtis A. Bradley and Jack L. Goldsmith, Customary International Law as Federal Common Law: A Critique of the Modern Position, 110 Harv. L. Rev. 815 (1997), and The Current Illegitimacy of International Human Rights Litigation, 66 Fordham L. Rev. 319 (1997)). The conventional wisdom is codified in the Restatement of the Foreign Relations Law of the United States (Third) §§ 111–15 (1987); and Louis Henkin, International Law as Law in the United States, 82 Mich. L. Rev. 1555 (1984).

CHAPTER FIVE

MILITARY FORCE AND INTELLIGENCE OPERATIONS

There has been as much controversy over war powers as over any other single issue involving presidential and congressional authority. The debate started in Philadelphia in 1789, if not earlier, and continues today. After World War II the President continued to claim extensive war powers, while Congress fitfully resisted. Most dramatically in legal terms, President Truman committed major U.S. forces to the Korean War without prior congressional authorization. Conservatives vigorously protested Truman's assertion of unilateral power, but Congress funded the war. Two decades later the war in Vietnam provided a defining experience for my generation that brought the question of presidential power again to the fore. This time the political stripes were reversed. Liberals pleaded the old conservative cause in favor of restoring congressional prerogative over military affairs that had been lost to the "imperial President." This constitutional struggle culminated in 1974 when Congress finally terminated funding for the war in Southeast Asia and passed the War Powers Resolution[1] (WPR) over President Nixon's veto.

1. 50 U.S.C. §§ 1541–48 (1973).

Although called a "resolution," the WPR has the force of statutory law and was designed to recapture some of the "lost" congressional prerogative by inserting Congress into the decision-making process, and especially by firmly limiting the President's ability to use military force without express, advance congressional support. The debates of the 1960s and 1970s were intensely passionate and partisan. The bitter unpopularity of President Nixon added to the intensity of the debate. A few months after the WPR was passed, Nixon was forced to resign the presidency as the Watergate scandal engulfed his Administration.

Although the debate was partisan, politicians and academics often employed constitutional law argument to advance their causes. In so doing they invoked the usual sources of law and methods of constitutional interpretation: the text of the Constitution, Original Intent, Historical Practice, and Functionalism. In the end little was definitely settled, and the debate continues. In the last decade of the twentieth century presidential war-making in the Balkans did not generate much constitutional controversy, and the President received the immediate support of Congress to respond militarily to the September 11 attacks (see Chapter Six). Nevertheless, members of Congress emphasized that their authorization did not extend to war against Iraq or other targets unconnected to the September 11 attacks. Moreover, they reiterated their commitment to the restrictions of the War Powers Resolution. Given the probability that President Bush (and his successors) will maintain a prerogative to initiate at least limited war without congressional authorization, the controversy will continue.

In this Chapter, I follow the standard pattern for presenting a constitutional law analysis: I outline the textual division of authority, summarize the main elements of Original Intent (including a dimension missing in the discourse on the Vietnam War, viz. that provided by the historical context in which the Constitution was drafted), and describe Historical Practice. I divide Historical Practice into minor wars and major wars, which the political branches seem to have recognized as a distinction of constitutional significance. In approaching the major wars I point out the legal effect of a formal Declaration of War and note the cases where Congress has chosen other means to authorize a war. For those major wars of most recent significance— Korea, Vietnam and Iraq—I outline the political and historical background, the President's claims for authority, the attitude of Congress, and the precedential lesson. Then I analyze the War Powers Resolution, why Presidents claim it is unconstitutional, how it has been implemented, and the case for its repeal or reform. Finally, I note the distinctive arguments and problems raised by U.S. participation in U.N. Peacekeeping Operations. The war in Afghanistan following the September 11 attacks on the United States is covered in Chapter Six.

Because there have been few relevant judicial decisions on these issues, it is especially important to see how the political branches have interpreted the war power. By looking at practice since 1950, and especially considering the extensive constitutional dialog between Presidents and Congresses since the Vietnam War, certain principles of law can be extracted.

A. Background

Framing the Legal Issues. The protagonists in this debate typically frame the argument as a contest between Congress' War Power and the President's role as Commander-in-Chief. That formulation is both misleading and incomplete. It is misleading because Congress' power is "to declare war," which may or may not encompass an exclusive power to initiate war. The formulation is incomplete because both Congress and the President have additional powers that bear on the use of military force. Congress has the power, first of all, to authorize and fund the Armed Forces, with the concomitant ability to attach conditions thereto. Congress has the power to oversee the military's operations, to make rules for the regulation of the armed forces, and to guide their activities by legislation. And of course Congress can declare war, with all the legal consequences that flow from that act. On the other side, in addition to being Commander in Chief, the President has the "executive power" of the Vesting Clause which incorporates any military functions not allocated to Congress in the Declare War Clause.

Even asking the question in the usual way—which branch has authority to authorize the initiation of war—assumes a model of conflict that does not actually conform to the dynamics of most contemporary situations. The standard model assumes that a controversy develops, military forces are assembled, and a decision is taken to start the war. In fact many decisions bearing on the use of force are made along the way, and may make war inevitable or at least a matter of self-defense where all concede the President may act. Viewed as a series of steps in a larger process of making war, Congress is regularly involved at several points in the process, under the powers referred to above. Of course there may be a moment, even if seen only clearly in hindsight, when the President orders the armed forces to a point of inevitable conflict or authorizes the troops to fire the fateful shots. Consequently a narrow legal issue, which admittedly may be obscured in any particular situation, can be framed in terms of which branch has power to *initiate* the use of force. That power is at least not literally allocated in the constitutional text, leading us into the other sources of constitutional interpretation.

The Text. In colonial times the war power was a Crown prerogative. The Framers clearly deviated from that model. Yet they also were determined to correct the problems of congressional indecision and fractiousness experienced under the Confederacy. Consequently the constitutional text divided the relevant authorities among the political branches, and in the process created some ambiguity. Congress has power to raise and to regulate the armed forces, including the power to call up the militia, to declare war, to issue letters of marque and reprisal (a form of private war), and to make rules concerning capture, in addition to Congress' exclusive Appropriations power and its legislative power under the Necessary and Proper Clause.[2]

The President, on the other hand, is designated as "Commander-in-Chief of the Army and Navy of the United States,"[3] has the duty (and implied power) to "take care that the Laws be faithfully executed," and has a broad foreign relations power (including powers relating to treaties) inherent in the Vesting Clause.[4] The war power formerly vested in the Crown was thus divided, with ample checks and balances embedded in the resulting scheme.

The text is obviously ambiguous in important ways. Most importantly Congress' power to "declare" war can be read literally to refer to making a formal declaration of war, with all the attendant legal consequences, or it can be read broadly to mean "authorize" war. A declaration of war is a formal act, well known and understood in eighteenth century law and practice, with widespread legal consequences. To "declare" war, at least in a technical or legal sense, is different from "authorizing" or "making" war (the importance of this difference will be reinforced when we consider Original Intent below).

2. U.S. Const. art. I, § 8.

3. Id., art. II., § 2, cl. 1.

4. Id., art. II., § 3.

Second, the term "war" is undefined. In the eighteenth century, as now, the use of military force covered a broad spectrum, ranging from punishing pirates and coercing weak foreign rulers on the one hand to formal, large scale war against major world powers. How much of that spectrum is encompassed in the constitutional term "war" is unclear. The term "war" also had a widely understood technical meaning under the eighteenth century law of nations. It could be declared or undeclared, "perfect" or "imperfect," with different legal consequences. Nevertheless, it is obviously not necessary to give the term "war" in the Constitution the same meaning as "war" in international law. Moreover, international law has changed so much—war is now illegal under the UN Charter—that it is entirely uncertain how the eighteenth century conception of war should be translated into a modern context, even if the text so required.

Third, the Marques and Reprisal Clause[5] covers practices that are now obsolete. However, by analogy the Clause could be interpreted to give Congress the power to authorize the use of force in situations, perhaps minor hostilities, that are not covered by the Declare War Clause. Some early Supreme Court cases applied acts of Congress to award prize from captures,[6] creating a possible in-

5. Id., art. I, § 8, cl. 11.

6. The Brig Amy Warwick; the Schooner Crenshaw; the Barque Hiawatha; the Schooner Brilliante (the Prize Cases), 67 U.S. (2 Black) 635 (1862).

ference that Congress needed to authorize the waging of limited war, and that the executive would be bound to respect conditions attached to the congressional authorization. Such a conclusion, like the assumed contemporary relevance of the Marque and Reprisal Clause, is hardly self-evident. The constitutional language can also be read simply to confirm the removal of the letters and marque power from the states and to assure that Congress had the power to bring into effect the legal consequences that followed issuance of letters, specifically the law of prize, and to alter the otherwise applicable law of nations. The clause may have been intended to do no more than to give Congress control over the then common practice of authorizing privateers to disrupt enemy shipping by seizing its vessels. Cases like *Little v. Barreme*,[7] which are sometimes cited as authority for the correct distribution of presidential or congressional power, actually involved the adjudication of disputes among private parties concerning the law of prize. Accordingly they do not necessarily stand for anything beyond illustrating the availability of judicial enforcement of that specific constitutional provision to enforce the private rights created by the acts of Congress.

Finally, the term "Commander in Chief" is equally obscure, as is the scope of the Vesting Clause. The Commander in Chief power is normally invoked synergistically with other presidential powers, and as such has figured significantly in the justification for major presidential initiatives, in-

7. 6 U.S. (2 Cranch) 170 (1804).

cluding deployment of troops in troubled regions, the initiation of limited war, and the conclusion of armistice agreements. As an isolated, independent power, it can be read merely to assure civilian control over the military and the President's ability literally to make tactical decisions during a conflict. Thus decisions about when to engage opposing forces in a hostile situation, whether to use the marines or the army in a specific context, and what weapons to use would seem to fall within the parameters of Commander-in-Chief authority. On the other hand, Congress can presumably legislate generally as to the deployment of the armed forces, such as prohibiting any deployment in a specified area like the Persian Gulf or the continent of Africa, and Congress could generally prohibit use of specified weapons, like nuclear or chemical weapons, or establish conditions for their use. Its powers to raise armies, provide rules for their regulation, and appropriate funds, together with the Necessary and Proper Clause, would support such legislation. The key is general application. As legislation becomes more specific or more concerned with an already existing crisis, it approaches the point at which it would seem to encroach upon executive authority.

In the final analysis the text is significantly ambiguous on the important questions surrounding the exercise of the Federal Government's war power.

Original Intent. The evidence of Original Intent is inscrutable. Thousands of pages of passionate argument have addressed the question of Original Intent. Dozens of scholars have sifted the records and presented conclusions, some in partisan tones, others more objective. Some of the writing consists of not much more than selective quotations isolated from context to support one position or another. Other contributions are more thorough and seemingly dispassionate, but the record requires so much interpretation that persuasive, "objective" conclusions seem impossible. More fundamentally, the scant evidence is fragmentary and subject to all the defects of Original Intent analysis summarized in Chapter One. There was little discussion of the relevant issues at the Philadelphia constitutional convention, and none at the ratifying conventions. The Framers included men with sharply contrasting views on executive power. It is hazardous to impute the intent of a Jefferson or a Hamilton to the collective body of Framers. Virtually nothing can be said about the Ratifiers (whose views would seem to be at least as or more important than those of the Framers). The record consists mostly of silence, from which contradictory inferences can readily be drawn.

I will summarize the most prominent aspects of the ancient lore, which provides important source material for legal argument. Discerning the Framers' intent can start with trying to reconstruct their assumptions about government and the "normal" or generally understood allocation of functions thereunder, in light of the intellectual context in which they operated. Hence, the ideas of the dominant political philosophers of the day, the operation of the British constitution, the practices of colonial governments and state governments immediately after the Revolution, and the experience under the Articles of Confederation all combine to create an intellectual framework that conditioned the Framers' thought about constitutional issues and the language they chose to reflect that thinking.

Some matters seem generally clear. The British Crown had the authority both to wage and to declare war. Waging war was conceptually and legally distinct from declaring war. The Crown's powers were checked, by the middle of the eighteenth century, by Parliament's prerogative to raise armies and navies, to fund all military operations, and to impeach officials.

The early state constitutions established during the Revolution sharply limited the exercise of executive power (which no doubt was associated in their minds with the Crown). In almost all cases the executive branch was elected by, and responsible to, the legislature. The governor usually had short term limits or was subject to frequent elections. The executive could often act only with the advice of a legislatively controlled council. The limitations on executive power, however, generally took the form of procedures to assure that the executive would exercise power in conformity with legislative wishes, not dilutions of the substantive content of executive power itself. Most state constitutions made the governor "commander in chief" (or similar title) of the state militia, but were silent about the war power. Several prominent states—Virginia, Massachusetts, Delaware and New Hampshire—expressly gave the war power to the governor, and New York's governor exercised that power.

The Articles of Confederation placed legislative, executive, and judicial powers in the Continental Congress. The Articles used different terminology in different places. Congress had the sole power of "determining on" war and peace, but required the consent of nine states to "engage in" war, and the states were forbidden to grant letters of marque and reprisal unless Congress had issued a "declaration of war." The Articles thus recognized a distinction between "determining on" war, "engaging in" war, and "declaring war." Whether the distinctions were considered to be significant, or merely involved different phrases meaning the same thing, is unclear. In any event, since Congress exercised both executive and legislative powers, no inference can be drawn about the location of the power to initiate war, even assuming that it is distinct from the power to declare war.

Congress was not very good at exercising executive power while waging the Revolutionary War. It first delegated authority to smaller committees, and then to General Washington. Congress also had trouble raising money for the troops, and later struggled with treaty negotiations and getting states to comply with the results. All these defects were addressed at the Philadelphia convention.

The 1787 Philadelphia Convention and the Ratifying Conventions. Against this background the textual provisions dealing with war can be interpreted two different ways, either to confirm or to deny an executive war power. If Congress' power to declare war refers only to the formal legal declaration, then the power to initiate war may be seen as having been vested in the President, as it had been under many of the state constitutions, either by virtue of the Vesting Clause or the Commander in Chief Clause. Under this view the Framers did not spell out this part of executive power because it was implicitly understood to encompass the power to initiate war. The inference from silence would therefore be that the initiation of war, a traditional executive power, remained an executive power.

On the other hand, clearly some part of traditional executive power—the power to "declare" war—was taken from the President and given to Congress. There is no necessary reason to believe that the Framers used "declare" in a legalistic sense, The Articles of Confederation used three different terminologies in the context of war, and the Constitution itself uses different terms to refer to the same, or similar, concepts (like treaties, agreement, and compact). The Constitution was not drafted with the precision of a trust indenture. Given the general revulsion against the British monarchy in the period immediately before and during the Revolution, one might expect that a text giving the power of initiating war to the executive would have been greeted with expressions of outrage and opposition. Since there were no such expressions, the inference from the silent record could therefore be that everyone understood that Congress had the power to initiate, as well as declare, war.

A third possibility is that the Framers simply did not think that the issue as we conceive it would ever come up or be important. If there were no standing army a President wishing to initiate military force would first have to get Congress to raise one. The ensuing debate would give Congress ample opportunity to debate the wisdom of the proposed engagement in a focused way. Accordingly the Framers may have assumed that the political branches would be forced to work together when using military force, synergistically combining their textual powers, and that in case of differences Congress could always prevail by denying funding.

One can find statements in the accounts of the Philadelphia convention to support all conclusions. The progress of the text through various drafting stages, and a critical change in the draft, provides the only clearly traceable evidence of Original Intent. During early deliberations, in the course of discussions about whether the executive should be a unitary or a collective body, several delegates stated that the executive power should not include war and peace. Later the convention considered a draft presented by the Committee on Detail clause by clause. That draft gave Congress the power to "make" war, and the Senate the power to "make" treaties and send Ambassadors. Both of the last two powers were subsequently relocated to the executive branch, subject to a requirement of Senate consent for their exercise. As to the power to make war, Pinkney proposed that it be given to the Senate, and Butler proposed that it be given to the President. Neither was accepted, so Congress still had the power to "make" war when a famous amendment was proposed by Madison and Gerry. They proposed to change "make" to "declare." Such a change seems to suggest a narrowing of Congress' power. Such an inference would be reinforced if the term "declare" was understood to have a technical, legal meaning. Madison, however, explained that the change would enable the President to "repel sudden attacks."

The intended effect of this amendment is inscrutable. At least one delegate thought the President already had that power. Even if the President did not have that power, the simplest way to give it to him would have been to clarify Article II, which deals with presidential authority, not to change Article I which deals with the power of Congress. But legislative drafting is not always technically impeccable. Connecticut changed its vote from opposing to approving the amendment after Mr. King explained that "make" was the same as "conduct," which was properly an executive function. This can be interpreted to suggest that the Framers made the change to reinforce the apparent purpose of locating the Commander-in-Chief power in the executive. Another approach would be to measure the change against the legal and historical background above. Substituting "declare" for "make" suggests that Congress got the formal power to create legal changes in legal relationships, consistent with its role as a law-making body, while the rest of the power to "make" war went to where it traditionally rested, the executive.[8] But why was that not made explicit? Moreover, Butler's proposal to do something like that was not accepted, and his proposal excited outraged comments from two or three of his colleagues. Perhaps the Framers were not of a legalistic mind when they changed "make" to "declare," or perhaps they just wanted to shroud the issue in ambiguity, or perhaps they did not regard this issue as a practical problem because at the time most people assumed that there would be no standing army.

The discussion of the commander in chief power, which is often invoked by the President in contemporary situations, does not offer much support for executive claims. The discussion was primarily concerned with whether the clause permitted the President to actually command troops in the field, and his authority over state militias.

Historical Practice. Executive branch lawyers have often invoked Historical Practice relating to the use of force by the United States as a way of bolstering claims to a presidential war power. As Justice Frankfurter wrote in the *Youngstown* case, ". . . a systematic, unbroken, executive practice,

8. To the Virginia ratifying convention Madison explained: "The sword is in the hands of the British King; the purse in the hands of Parliament. It is so in America, as far as any analogy can exist." 3 Elliot's Debates at 393 (John Elliot ed. 1836). This remark too contains an element of inscrutability.

long pursued to the knowledge of the Congress and never before questioned, engaged in by Presidents who have also sworn to uphold the Constitution, making as it were such exercise of power part of the structure of our government, may be treated as a gloss on 'executive Power' vested in the President by § 1 of Art. II...."[9] Between 1798 and today there have been over 200 examples of the use of armed force by the President without a Declaration of War or other advance, specific authorization by Congress.[10] On the basis of this history Presidents have claimed a general, open-ended war power, even including the authority to wage a full-blown general war.

B. Minor Wars

Such an undifferentiated claim is not tenable. A cursory examination of the history shows that almost all the examples involved minor conflict, or no conflict at all, with militarily weak adversaries that in some cases consisted merely of pirates, bandits, poorly armed insurgents and other non-state actors. From the historical record we can infer several categories of situations in which the President has used the armed forces without specific, advance congressional authorization, including (1) defense of

9. Youngstown Sheet & Tube Co. v. Sawyer (The Steel Seizure Case), 343 U.S. 579, 610–11 (1952).

10. Congressional Research Service Report for Congress, Instances of Use of United States Armed Forces Abroad, 1789–1989, (Ellen C. Collier ed., Dec. 4, 1989).

U.S. territory, including disputed territory; (2) protection of American armed forces, diplomats, diplomatic premises, nationals and their property; (3) punishment of pirates and other criminals; and (4) protection of "U.S. interests" and advancement of specific foreign policy goals.

The power to defend U.S. territory is often based on the remark of Madison at the Philadelphia convention in which he explained that the change in the text from "make" to "declare" with respect to Congress' war power was intended to confirm that the President had the power to "repel sudden attacks." Such presidential authority may also be confirmed on the basis of Article I, sec. 10. That section authorizes the states to engage in war if "actually invaded, or in such imminent Danger as will not admit of delay." It would seem anomalous to accord the President less emergency power than the states would have. In addition, the First Congress passed legislation assuming that the President had the power to defend the border, and Washington used it to do so and to engage in punitive offensive operations as well. The functional advantages of the executive branch, especially the ability to act quickly and with unified resolve, suggest allocating such a power to the President. As to the armed forces, no one would deny their right to defend themselves against hostile attack, although this power presumably does not extend beyond responding proportionately to the immediate circumstances.

Early practice may suggest a distinction between defensive action, which the President may undertake, and offensive action for which congressional approval is required. For example, in 1801 Jefferson dispatched the Navy to the Mediterranean to protect American shipping. In the ensuing hostilities one Tripolitan vessel was captured, but released because, the President explained to Congress, it would have been unlawful to "go beyond the line of defense" without congressional approval, the President being unauthorized by the Constitution to do so on his own authority.[11] Washington and Adams arguably followed a similar path,[12] but—inconsistently—Washington and the first Congress seemed to assume that the Commander in Chief would use forces for retaliation, and Jefferson himself actually authorized offensive action without congressional support. Subsequent practice has undercut the clarity of this distinction. For one thing the transition from defensive to offensive action may be seamless, making it difficult to identify the point when military action becomes illegal (e.g. the U.S. response to the September 11 attacks, discussed more fully in Chapter Six, illustrates this difficulty). Moreover, the President's power as Commander in Chief to move troops around, and thereby put them in harms way, potentially expands his power as a practical matter. Also, many of these situations implicate other presidential powers, or involve un-

11. David P. Currie, The Constitution in Congress: The Jeffersonians 1801–1829, 123–24 (2001).

12. David P. Currie, The Constitution in Congress: The Federalist Period 1789–1801, 83–88 (1997).

controversial action of which Congress would approve.

The largest category of historical precedents involves the protection or rescue of American nationals, including diplomats, or punishment of their mistreatment. In addition, the President has frequently acted to protect U.S. diplomatic premises and the property of Americans generally. All these interventions also implicate the President's constitutional power to conduct foreign relations, and it thus is natural to ground the authority in the same place—the Vesting Clause. As indicated in Chapter Two, this authority includes the authority to send diplomats to foreign countries, to extend diplomatic protection to Americans abroad, and to assert their claims under international law. Given these powers it seems reasonable to imply the additional power for the President to use all the resources available (which have been provided by Congress) to effectively discharge those functions.

The courts have so recognized. In the *Neagle* case the Supreme Court upheld the President's inherent or implied power to provide armed defense of a federal judge. The Court asked rhetorically: "... who can doubt the authority of the [P]resident, or of one of the executive departments under him, to make an order for the protection of the mail, and of the persons and lives of its carriers, by ... providing a sufficient guard , whether it be by soldiers of the army or by marshals of the United States [as was done in the case before the Court]...."[13] The

13. Cunningham v. Neagle, 135 U.S. 1, 65 (1890).

Court regarded it as self-evident that judges were as important as mail carriers, and at the time of the decision carrying the mail was more important and more dangerous than it is today. The court also invoked a precedent from foreign affairs to support its conclusion It recounted the story of the Koszta affair in which an American naval commander rescued an American (who was not even technically a citizen, but who was apparently about to become one) by demanding the victim's release and training the U.S. vessel's guns upon an Austrian vessel until the victim was released. The Court noted that the naval commander's intervention was popular and Congress even gave him a gold medal.[14] The Court plainly endorsed this example of presidential authority. On the basis of the *Neagle* case the President has authority to use the threat of military force to protect American diplomats and nationals in distress.

Extending this principle a lower court upheld executive authority to attack and destroy the town of Greytown in Nicaragua, in order to redress threats to an American diplomat and property in which Americans apparently had an interest. The court opined:

> As the executive head of the nation, the president is made the only legitimate organ of the general government, to open and carry on correspondence or negotiations with foreign nations, in matters concerning the interests of the country or of its citizens. It is to him, also, the citizens abroad

14.   Id., at 64.

must look for protection of person and of property
. . . . [15]

The President's authority to use the armed forces to protect American diplomats, nationals and property is therefore well-established and does not seem to be at least generally controversial. Nevertheless, this power has sometimes been used as a pretext to cover other objectives having more to do with general foreign policy goals, as in the interventions in Grenada and Panama. For such situations another justification would seem to be required.

A third category of situation where the President is authorized to use military force without specific, advance congressional approval includes actions taken to punish pirates, bandits, poachers, highjackers, drug dealers and other criminals. This power may be squarely based on the President's duty (and implied power) to enforce the laws, including international law. Here too law enforcement may be a pretext for intervention that is more plausibly explained by reference to foreign policy objectives. In such a case (like the military engagements with Libya in the Gulf of Sidra and with Panama) another justification would be more persuasive.

The fourth (and second largest) category drawn from the list of over 200 examples of presidential war making is the deployment of armed forces into potentially dangerous or hostile situations where the objective was the general protection of "U.S. interests" or the advancement of general foreign

15. Durand v. Hollins, 8 F. Cas. 111, 112 (Case No. 4,186) (S.D.N.Y.1860).

policy goals. Some of these precedents involved very important matters, for example the deployment of troops in Iceland and Greenland on the eve of U.S. entry into World War II, dispatching the navy to the Taiwan Straits to deter a Communist invasion of the island, and the naval quarantine of Cuba during the missile crisis. Authority to move the army and navy around seems literally within the Commander-in-Chief power, but such decisions obviously can lead to war. Since the executive has the power of self-defense, the power to deploy forces blends into a power to commit the nation to war as a result of that deployment without advance congressional approval.

To each of the above categories there are counter examples where Congress denied a presidential request for advance authorization of the use of force, particularly in the early nineteenth century. Congress declined to authorize reprisals by Presidents Jackson and Buchanan against France, Mexico and elsewhere in Latin America, as well as declining to authorize occupation of West Florida in 1805. The Historical Practice with respect to each of the three categories described above is therefore not unbroken.

Moreover, Congress is unquestionably the final arbiter. Congress has limited and even terminated executive-initiated military actions, as was the case in Southeast Asia at the end of the Vietnam War. One should also not underestimate the importance of informal congressional influence. Presidents are all political figures, responsive to congressional and public opinion. If public opinion opposing a military engagement has coalesced, and Congress reflects that opinion, even in a non-binding resolution, Presidents may normally be expected to defer to that viewpoint. Nevertheless, as contemporary practice vis-a-vis Somalia, Sudan, Haiti and the Balkans demonstrates, as a matter of constitutional principle the President retains the basic authority to initiate the use of military force in the four categories described.

Finally, there are a few cases (under 20) where the President unilaterally initiated the use of force and his action led to an actual military engagement. The precedents in this category suggest a presidential authority to use military force for general foreign policy purposes. Examples include the military engagements with Libya and the interventions in Grenada, Panama, Haiti, and Serbia (Kosovo). The legal basis for this category of action may seem more troublesome because foreign policy concerns are virtually unlimited in scope and magnitude. On the other hand, a President cannot sustain major war without substantial congressional support, so perhaps the spectre of an open-ended presidential war power is not as troublesome in practice as it may seem in the abstract. In any event the precedents established by Historical Practice clearly justify a presidential power to initiate military action without advance, specific congressional approval when the potential or actual engagements are limited in time, scope and potential American casualties.[16]

C. Major Wars

Between 1812 and 1945 the United States engaged in five major foreign wars: 1812 (Great Britain), 1848 (Mexico), 1898 (Spain), 1914 (World War I), and 1941 (World War II). In each of these major wars Congress passed a declaration of war, authorized armed forces for the particular purpose, and appropriated the necessary funds. Each war for the most part was broadly supported by the general public. None of these wars raised any major constitutional problem because the plain structure of the text was followed: Congress declared war and the President and his generals commanded the troops.

A declaration of war has widespread consequences under both international law and under domestic law. As to the former a formal declaration of war triggers rights and obligations under the law of war, the international law protecting neutral shipping, the suspension of treaty obligations between the belligerents, etc. As to domestic law several statutory emergency powers are activated[17] and enemy property may be confiscated regardless of the Fifth Amendment's requirement of compensa-

16. The same conclusion was reached by Peter J. Spiro, Old Wars/New Wars, 37 William and Mary L. Rev. 723, 734–37 (1996); Jane E. Stromseth, Rethinking War Powers: Congress, the President, and the United Nations, 81 Geo. L. J. 597 (1993).

17. See Harold Hongju Koh, 46 St.L.Univ. L. J. (forthcoming) (2002).

tion for public takings of property. The fact that domestic legal consequences flow from a declaration of war makes it especially appropriate to place that power in the hands of Congress.

Since World War II the United States has fought in three major wars. In each case the President claimed constitutional authority to commit the nation to war without the advance authorization of Congress. The executive branch relied on the express and implied constitutional authority of the President as chief executive , as "sole organ" of the nation in the conduct of foreign affairs, and as Commander in Chief, in addition to relying on treaty commitments and the Historical Practice described above. However, in two of the three wars these claims were never tested because Congress authorized U.S. participation in the conflict in sweeping terms prior to the engagement by the United States in major hostilities. Only in the Korean War did the President initiate war without the advance authorization of Congress.

Next I will briefly discuss the two major wars in which Congress authorized U.S. participation—Vietnam and Iraq—and then I will explain the issues surrounding the Korean war, especially the effect of U.N. Security Council Resolutions, which in turn is important background for the concluding part of this Chapter dealing with U.N. peacekeeping operations.

Vietnam. The Vietnam war precipitated unprecedented debate over presidential power. Congressional and academic critics fostered the image of an imperial President who had usurped the constitutional prerogatives of Congress. In response to such supposed presidential aggrandizement Congress eventually passed the War Powers Resolution[18] to rectify the imbalance and restore a congressional role in military decisions. Yet Congress had actually been involved in supporting the President's policies in Southeast Asia for two decades, through authorization of military advisors and funding assistance to the government of South Vietnam, in addition to Senate approval of the SEATO Treaty.[19] Most ironically in 1964 Congress itself directly and expressly authorized the war by passing the sweeping Tonkin Gulf Resolution.[20] The story of the Vietnam war still shows that Congress can terminate an ill-advised war, which it did in 1974 by cutting off appropriations. Although the President said he was pursuing the same policy, and the war was lost anyway, Congress' actions at the end showed that it indeed retained and theoretically could use its powers to shape decisions about the United States' use of force.

American involvement in Vietnam started in 1950 with economic assistance, authorized and funded by Congress, to France (which was the colonial power governing Indochina). As France was ensnared by the civil war waged by Ho Chi Minh and the Viet

18. Supra note 1.

19. Southeast Asia Treaty Organization, 6 U.S.T. 81 (1955).

20. Gulf of Tonkin Resolution, House Pub. L. No. 88–408, 78 Stat. 384 (1964).

Minh, the United States increased its financial support to France and considered military intervention. The Chair of the Joint Chiefs of Staff proposed using nuclear weapons in support of France, but only a few military advisers actually went to Vietnam before the defeat of the French at Dienbeinphu in 1954.

In 1956 President Eisenhower commenced covert action in Vietnam, consisting of psychological and military action against North Vietnam, under the authority of the National Security Act of 1947.[21] The Diem government in South Vietnam proved corrupt, brutal, and incompetent and was threatened by an insurgency led by the Viet Cong. In the late 1950s North Vietnam sent its own armed forces into the South.

During the Kennedy Administration the United States dispatched more than 15,000 military personnel to bolster the South Vietnamese government. The President determined that U.S. policy was to support South Vietnam to prevent a Communist takeover, which it was believed would produce a domino effect throughout Southeast Asia. U.S. covert operations included raids against rail, highway and coastal installations in the North. Following such raids on two islands in the Gulf of Tonkin, the North Vietnamese attacked U.S. destroyers in the area over a period of 2 or 3 days. The attacks were minor. One may never have occurred. But President Johnson used the occasion to mobilize public and congressional support for his policy in

21. 50 U.S.C. 403 (1947).

Southeast Asia. He briefed Congress and addressed the nation, outlining a plan of limited reprisal. "We still seek no wider war" he said. Congress responded by passing the Gulf of Tonkin Resolution (which had been drafted months before by executive branch officials):

> [T]he Congress approves and supports the determination of the President, as Commander in Chief, to take all necessary measures to repel any armed attack against the forces of the United States and to prevent further aggression.... [T]he United States is therefore prepared, as the President determines, to take all necessary steps, including the use of armed force to assist any member ... of ... [SEATO] requesting assistance. ...[22]

On the basis of the Resolution, President Johnson conducted a steadily escalating air and ground war, ultimately involving more than 500,000 American combat troops.

Opponents of the war argued that it was unconstitutional. They claimed that the President had usurped Congress' powers and was waging war without authority. The executive branch defended the legality of the President's actions, not just by invoking the Tonkin Gulf Resolution (which seems to provide ample textual support), but also by arguing that the President had Article II powers (Chief Executive, Commander in Chief and foreign affairs) that confer "very broad powers, including the pow-

22. Supra note 20.

er to deploy American forces abroad and commit them to military operations when the President deems such action necessary to maintain the security and defense of the United States."[23] The lawyers also invoked Historical Practice in which the President has used military force abroad in more than 125 cases without specific, prior congressional authorization. Finally, they argued that the SEATO treaty justified the President's acts because it was law of the land which the President had power to execute.[24]

The executive branch's legal opinion is interesting for its structure and its emphasis on constitutional, as opposed to statutory, claims. The statute would seem to have been sufficient. The emphasis on constitutional and treaty arguments may have reflected lawyerly caution, or it may have been thought to be more persuasive (the audience was the public), or it may have anticipated a congressional change of mind (which subsequently happened).

The arguments against the legality of the war seem less than persuasive. First it has been argued that the President did not furnish all the relevant information regarding future plans and the uncertainties concerning the actual incidents in the Gulf of Tonkin. Congress was thus misled. Such an argument, even if true, would be irrelevant because

23. Department of State, The Legality of United States Participation in the Defense of Vietnam, 75 Yale L. J 1085, 1100 (1966).

24. Id., at 1101–02.

fraud or even bribery of the legislature does not vitiate the legal effectiveness of its formal acts. The second argument was that, notwithstanding the clear, broad language of the Tonkin Gulf Resolution, Congress did not intend to authorize such an extensive war. This argument has been refuted by John Ely's exhaustive study of the congressional deliberations.[25] Applying the normal conventions of determining legislative intent, such as crediting floor statements by the manager of a bill discussing ambiguous provisions, and colloquies, it is quite clear that members of Congress well understood that they were conferring open-ended authority on the President, with potentially far-reaching consequences. In short, applying the normal rules of statutory construction, Congress authorized general war in Southeast Asia.

The U.S. participation in the Vietnam war started at a very low level of intensity, with a few advisers and covert assistance. Then it escalated to a small number of combat forces, then more, and finally it became the most costly U.S. commitment since World War II. At each stage the President probably could have advanced a plausible claim to authority to proceed to the next stage without seeking congressional authorization—Commander in Chief power and the power to protect U.S. forces, nationals and property. President Johnson sought a broad authorization at a time when it was not clear that there would be a major war, so Congress did

25. John Hart Ely, War and Responsibility: Constitutional Lessons of Vietnam and Its Aftermath 15–30 (1993).

not examine the matter as closely as it did, e.g., before World Wars I and II. The Vietnam war did not conform to the old model of war as a conflict that starts at a single, clearly identifiable moment and is waged by the regular armies of two or more internationally recognized states. The Vietnam war thus illustrates the difficulties of applying traditional legal analysis to a modern war situation, although any legal difficulties were avoided because of Congress' (in retrospect) unwise Tonkin Gulf Resolution. The next major war presented no such difficulties. The Gulf war fit the traditional model perfectly.

The War against Iraq. On August 2, 1990, Iraq launched a classic invasion of the neighboring state of Kuwait. Within a few days it conquered the entire country. The United Nations Security Council condemned the invasion, demanded that Iraq withdraw, and passed a series of mandatory sanctions designed to coerce Iraqi compliance with its demand for withdrawal. Over a period of four months the United States lead the formation of a coalition of states to counter the Iraqi aggression. The United States deployed over 500,000 troops, including naval and air forces, into Saudi Arabia and the adjacent region. On November 29, 1990, the U.N. Security Council issued an ultimatum which Iraq did not heed.[26] The coalition forces counterattacked starting on January 17, 1991 with air strikes. Ground operations began on February 24

26. U.N.S.C. Res. 678, Nov. 29, 1990.

and within four days the Iraqi forces were expelled from Kuwait.

President Bush deployed U.S. forces to the Gulf on the basis of his constitutional powers, including the Commander in Chief power, and existing appropriations. He led the diplomatic effort to secure U.N. action and to assemble the coalition under his foreign affairs powers. Congress adjourned after the invasion of Kuwait and after the deployment of U.S. forces had begun. The President had made his policy clear: His statement to the effect that the Iraqi invasion "will not stand" was reiterated many times. However, the major deployment was not made until after the November election. Congress had then adjourned "sine die," and the President was prepared to go to war on the basis of executive power alone. Congressional leaders were reluctant to reconvene Congress to take up the issue, but eventually the pressure of public opinion, the press and opponents of U.S. involvement forced the leadership to reconvene on January 3, 1991. On January 12, 1991, after a thorough and sophisticated debate, Congress authorized U. S. participation in the war that was soon to follow. The President continued to maintain his claim of independent power to commit U.S. forces unilaterally, but in the end he agreed with the congressional leadership to state that he would welcome congressional support. As a result the constitutional issues were averted.

Korea. The war in Korea was the only major war waged by the United States without the prior authorization of Congress. Communist forces from

North Korea suddenly invaded South Korea on June 25 (Korean local time, June 24 in the U.S.), 1950. In the United States it was a time when the concerns about the spread of "international communism" and fears of Communist subversion at home were high. The North Korean invasion seemed to be another step—following Communist take-overs in Eastern Europe and threats in Greece—threatening the "free world." It was also the first major test of the new collective security system established by the United Nations. The invasion was a classic act of aggression, following the model of Nazi Germany, of the sort the United Nations was designed to deal with. The opportunity was especially ripe because the then Soviet Union was boycotting sessions of the Security Council because the China seat on the Council was held by the government on Taiwan. Accordingly the Security Council could act without the threat of a Soviet veto.

On June 25 the Security Council condemned the invasion and called on North Korea to withdraw. Two days later the Security Council called on member states to assist South Korea militarily to defend against the North Korean aggression. The Truman Administration publicly justified its decision to commit U.S. forces to war without prior Congressional approval on the basis of the U.N. Charter. Yet the orders to commit troops were given on June 26, and a State Department legal memorandum argued that the United States committed troops (on the basis of the President's foreign relations authority) to support the United Nations, not the other way around.[27] In subsequent discussion the war was characterized as a "police action," to avoid admitting it was a "war" within the meaning of the Constitution and to bring it within the legislative history of the U.N. Charter in which the Secretary of State said the executive could dispatch troops without congressional approval "if we are talking about a little bit of force necessary to be used as a police demonstration."[28] In retrospect it is clear that the President was prepared to commit U.S. forces to a major war on the basis of his constitutional powers. The public justifications, however, relied on the U.N. Charter as authority. That basis of authority in turn was used by Presidents Bush in the Iraq war and Clinton in the Haiti intervention. A similar argument was made during the Vietnam war. The basic argument is that the United States is a party to a treaty (the U.N. Charter or SEATO) which is law of the land under Article VI, which the President in turn is bound to faithfully execute under Article II. Another variation of this argument would hold that the Vesting Clause confers power on the President to administer or carry out the intended operation of the treaty.

This claim is very controversial. Opponents point out that the treaties do not require the United

27. See 23 Dept. of St. Bul. 173 (1950).

28. John Foster Dulles in The Charter of the United Nations: Hearings Before the Senate Committee on Foreign Relation, 79th Cong., 1st Sess. 197 (1945) *quoted in* Louis Fisher, The Korean War: On What Legal Basis did Truman Act?, 89 Am. J. Int'l L. 21, 28 (1995).

States to commit troops; they only authorize it to do so. Moreover, the collective defense treaties like SEATO and NATO state that the parties will act "in accordance with their constitutional processes," and the Senate was similarly assured in the course of considering the U.N. Charter. Most fundamentally reliance on the Senate excludes the House, sometimes called the "most democratic" branch, from a decision that the Declare War clause arguably vested in the whole Congress. On the other hand, collective defense treaties clearly contemplate military actions. The references to "constitutional processes" do not specify what those processes are, and do not preclude the possibility that the requisite constitutional process is executive alone. And Congress of course participates in the process by authorizing and funding troops without conditions.

A more sophisticated argument for presidential power focuses on the original scheme of the United Nations, and Congress' enactment of the U.N. Participation Act of 1945.[29] The basic idea of the U.N. Charter was to make war illegal unless it is in self-defense. Moreover, it was contemplated that the Security Council would take the necessary measures to deal with aggression, including using military force to repel the aggressor. To that end Article 43

29. See Thomas M. Franck and Faiza Patel, UN Police Action in Lieu of War: "The Old Order Changeth," 85 Am. J. Int'l L. 63 (1991). The counter arguments are presented in Jane E. Stromseth, Rethinking War Powers: Congress, the President and the United Nations, 81 Geo. L. J. 597 (1993); and Michael J. Glennon, The Constitution and Chapter VII of the United Nations Charter, 85 Am. J. Int'l L. 74 (1991).

provided that members would enter into special agreements with the U.N. to make armed forces available to the Security Council. During the Senate and congressional debates on the Charter and the Act, there was much discussion of the role of Congress in the operation of the new system. Conservatives were concerned that the Congress would be excluded from future decisions about the use of armed force. The solution was that any U.S. Article 43 agreements would be submitted to Congress for its approval. It was understood that, after such approval, Congress would have no further role in authorizing the use of the committed forces in a specific crisis. It was probably also assumed that Congress would only approve a relatively small U.S. contribution, and that U.N. actions with the Article 43 forces would be limited (hence the term "police actions").

Article 43 agreements were never concluded because of the Cold War. From this story, opposite inferences may be drawn. One conclusion would be that since the contemplated system did not come into place, the original rules—whatever they may be—stay in place. Another conclusion would be that, as a result of ratification of the Charter, Congress surrendered its role in authorizing use of force in specific crises and instead retained only a general supervisory power, either through approval of Article 43 agreements or through the normal legislative process, either of which processes would be concluded in advance of any decision to go to war in a specific context and thus would not focus on a specific war. There is some support for this view in the legislative history of the U.N. Participation Act. The Senate Foreign Relations Committee reported its understanding of the future situation:

> Although the ratification of the Charter result-ed in the vesting in the executive branch of the power and obligation to fulfill the commitments assumed by the United States thereunder, the Congress must be taken into close partnership and must be fully advised of all phases of our participation in this enterprise. The Congress will be asked annually to appropriate funds to support the United Nations budget and for the expenses of our representation. It will be called upon to approve arrangements for the supply of armed forces to the Security Council and thereafter to make appropriations for the maintenance of such forces.[30]

During consideration of the Act the key Senate leaders, Connally and Vandenberg, agreed that in "certain emergencies" the President and the Security Council might be able to act without first obtaining authority from Congress.[31] This record can be read to reflect acceptance of a distinction between small wars and large wars. For the former the President could act under Security Council authorization, with the forces being authorized by an

30. S. Rep. No. 717, 79th Cong., 1st Sess. 5 (1945).

31. 91 Cong. Rec. 10,965 (1945) (statement of Sen. Connally) *quoted in* Jane Stromseth, Rethinking War Powers: Congress, the President, and the United Nations, 81 Geo. L. J. 597, 616 n.97 (1993).

approved Article 43 agreement or by whatever other arrangements Congress approved for the supply of armed forces to the Security Council. In this view the regular authorization process is the functional equivalent of Article 43 agreements. The remarks of Connally and Vandenburg can also be taken to accept the idea that when the President carries out Security Council decisions, he is engaging in collective self-defense which today may be comparable to defending the country against invasion. At the same time, this line of reasoning may be academic because it appears that the President already has the constitutional authority to commit forces in limited wars. In any event, as to the war in Korea, Congress quickly appropriated funds and reauthorized the draft, thereby ratifying the President's actions.

Although the Korean war is cited as a precedent by the executive branch for a general presidential war-making power, it is the only major war that Congress did not authorize in advance. Its "precedential" value seems limited given the unique political context in which it occurred. Like the War Powers Resolution two decades later, it seems in retrospect to have been an assertion of constitutional power by one branch based on the unusual political context of the moment. The Korean war precedent was created at a time of extreme national fear of Communism and a time of extreme optimism about the potential of the United Nations to prevent future wars. Both factors contributed to the President's decision, but neither factor remains viable today.

D. The War Powers Resolution

In 1973 Congress passed the War Powers Resolution ("WPR")[32] into law over President Nixon's veto. The WPR was enacted in immediate reaction to the Vietnam war and in the general context of the perception that after World War II an imperial President had usurped congressional prerogatives. Nixon's veto was overridden at a climactic moment of the Watergate investigation, leading to Nixon's resignation in the face of probable impeachment. The purpose of the WPR was to restore the constitutional balance and assure a congressional role in decisions to use military force.

However, the WPR failed to achieve that objective. President Nixon and all his successors took the position that one or more parts of the Resolution was unconstitutional. In this subchapter I will outline the major provisions of the WPR, identify those which raise constitutional problems, analyze the respective arguments, and describe the experience of the WPR in operation. This legislation is called a "resolution," but that label is misleading. The "resolution" is in fact an act of Congress with the full force of statutory law.

The WPR starts with a "purposes" section which catalogs situations in which the President may use military force on his own authority.[33] The catalog is

32. Supra note 1.
33. Id., § 1541.

obviously incomplete since it does not refer to the President's authority to rescue Americans abroad, which is generally uncontroversial, and in any event the "purposes" section has no legal effect under the operative provisions of the Resolution.

The operative provisions of the Resolution set forth consultation[34] and reporting obligations[35] and, most significantly, they establish an automatic termination of the President's authority to continue military operations after 60 days if Congress does not affirmatively act to approve it.[36] The 60 day period can in some cases be extended to 90 days, but in this book I will refer to this provision as the "60 day cut-off." The Resolution states that congressional approval of presidentially initiated uses of military force must specifically refer to the WPR and cannot be inferred from other congressional action such as general military authorization and appropriations legislation.[37] The WPR also provides for termination of the President's authority to continue military operations upon adoption of a concurrent resolution of both Houses of Congress, i.e., an act of a simple majority of Congress that is not subject to presidential veto.[38] Finally, the WPR disclaims any intention of expanding or contracting power that the President may have under the Constitution.[39]

34. Id., § 1542.
35. Id., § 1543.
36. Id., § 1544(b).
37. Id., § 1547(a).
38. Id., § 1544(c).

The Resolution was, like most legislation, the product of compromise between the House and the Senate. The Senate's version of the bill would have directly and absolutely limited the use of military force to specified situations. For example, the Senate version limited the President's war powers to "necessary and appropriate retaliatory actions in the event of [an armed attack upon the U.S., its territories or possessions]," "to forestall the direct and imminent threat of [an attack against the armed forces of the United States located outside of the United States]," and "to protect evacuating citizens and nationals of the United States ... from [certain situations] involving a direct and imminent threat to [their] lives."[40] The House approach was much less restrictive of executive discretion, and the final bill dealt only with process and not with the substantive standards governing the legitimate use of force by the President. The enumeration of situations where the President may use force on his own authority is contained only in a non-binding "purposes" section which, as noted above, is manifestly incomplete.

The event that triggers the most significant provisions of the law is a decision by the President to introduce the armed forces into "hostilities" or into situations where "hostilities" are imminent.[41] In

39. Id., § 1547(d).

40. S. 440, 93d Cong., 1st Sess. § 3 (1973) *quoted in* Stephen Dycus, et al., National Security Law 125–26 (1990).

41. Supra note 1, § 1542.

those situations the law imposes consultation and reporting requirements and, most significantly, a 60–day limit on the President's authority to use military force.

Consultation. First, the President is required "in every possible instance ... [to] consult with Congress" before introducing the armed forces into hostilities or imminent hostilities.[42] The consultation requirement is obviously weak and has not led to significant congressional involvement in the decision-making process. First, it only applies "in every *possible* instance" (emphasis supplied). The President of course must initially decide whether it is "possible" to consult in any given situation. The term "possible" could mean physically possible or it could refer to a looser "feasibility" standard. It could also be interpreted to reflect respect for a presidential prerogative to keep some operations entirely secret. President Carter did not consult at all in advance of his secret attempt to rescue the hostages in Tehran. Second, and more problematically, the term "consultation" itself is not entirely clear. The House Report stated that "consultation ... means that a decision is pending on a problem and that Members of Congress are being asked by the President for their advice and opinions ... to be meaningful, the President himself must participate and all information relevant to the situation must be made available."[43] However, Presidents have in-

42. Id.

43. House Committee on Foreign Affairs, War Powers Resolution of 1973, 93rd Cong. 1st Sess., 1973, H. Rep. 93–287, pp. 6–7, reprinted in 1973 U.S.C.L.A.N. 2346, 2351.

terpreted the term more narrowly, more akin to simply giving notice. Reagan informed the congressional leadership of his decision to bomb Tripoli only after the bombers had been launched.[44] In general, the "consultation" that has occurred under the WPR has concerned decisions already made. It has failed to introduce the legislative branch into the decision-making process, as the WPR was said to be intended. Finally, by requiring consultation with the entire "Congress" (rather than with the leadership or with specified committees), Congress can be seen as not being too serious about the provision. It is obviously impractical to consult with the 535 members of the entire Congress, and Congress itself has not taken any formal steps to implement a procedure to carry out this provision. In the end the consultation provision has not had an effect on the constitutional balance.

Reporting. Second, the President is required to send periodic reports to Congress when the armed forces are introduced into "hostilities" or "imminent hostilities."[45] However, the WPR also imposes the same reporting requirements in other defined situations where the troops are simply deployed abroad while equipped for combat.[46] These additional reporting requirements are the source of fatal confusion.

The reporting requirements do not raise constitutional problems. Congress clearly has the power to

44. Stephen Dycus, et al., National Security Law 276 (1990).

45. Supra note 1, § 1543(a)(1).

46. Id., § 1543(a)(2)–(3).

demand information from the executive, and thousands of reports are called for and provided without objection by the executive during every legislative session. Indeed, Presidents have routinely submitted reports in response to the WPR, although the reports are drafted in such a way as not to concede that the Resolution is constitutional.

Sixty day Cut-off. The major point of contention over the WPR has focused on the 60 day cut-off of presidential authority. The operation of that procedure has several key ambiguities and shortcomings and is the focus of the constitutional problem. As noted above reports are required not only under section 4(a)(1) when forces are introduced into hostilities or imminent hostilities, but also reports are required in specified situations under subsections (a)(2) and (a)(3) when troops equipped for combat are deployed. The big problem stems from the fact that a perilous situation will often be covered by all three subsections (a)(1), (a)(2), and (a)(3), but the serious consequence of cutting off authority after 60 days only occurs when a report is filed under (a)(1). The critical operative section provides that 60 days after a report is submitted or is required to be submitted under (a)(1), but not after a report is submitted under (a)(2) or (a)(3), the President must terminate the use of military force unless Congress has in the meantime approved it. There is accordingly a strong incentive for Presidents to tailor their reports to (a)(2) or (a)(3), and to avoid falling under the terms of (a)(1). In all but one case Presidents have simply not specified which subsection their reports are submitted in response to. Consequently there is critical ambiguity as to when the 60 day clock starts to run.

Moreover, the term "hostilities" is not defined. Consequently it is often unclear whether any given situation actually triggers the 60 day cut-off. It is true that the statute provides for the cut-off either when a report under (a)(1) is filed or when it is "required to be filed." However, as in defining the meaning of "consultation," the President makes the initial decision as to whether a report is "required" to be filed. He has regularly decided that the statutory standard was not met, so that under the President's interpretation of the facts a report need not be filed. Several of these presidential determinations seemed quite dubious given the facts of the situations involved. For example, Reagan determined that sending the Navy to police the safety of oil tankers in the middle of the Iran–Iraq war did not involve introducing the armed forces into "hostilities" or "imminent hostilities," and Bush made a similar judgment when sending half a million troops to the Kuwait border on the eve of the Gulf war. However, Congress has never acted to counter the President's substantive interpretation of (a)(1), nor has it asserted a claim to interpret the provision independently. The courts have similarly declined to fill the gap. They have held that the determination of whether "hostilities" exist or are imminent, and therefore the question of whether a report under (a)(1) is "required to be filed," which in turn would start the 60 day clock, is a political question to be resolved by the political branches.[47]

More fundamentally, even if it were clear that hostilities existed or were imminent, and that the 60 day clock was accordingly triggered, Presidents have still claimed that the provision of the WPR purporting to automatically terminate authority to use the armed forces upon the expiration of the 60 day period is unconstitutional. This provision is the heart of the controversy over the WPR. The executive branch's argument runs along the following lines: Congress has raised an army and navy and provided for its funding under its Article I powers. The President then takes over as Commander in Chief. In that role he decides how to use the armed forces that Congress has provided. Moreover, in addition to being Commander in Chief, the President has several additional powers that synergistically support the use of force in support of the nation's foreign policy. They include (1) the implied foreign affairs power, (2) the express duty to take care that laws be faithfully executed, including the laws providing for the armed forces, treaty obligations and international law generally, and (3) the executive power reflected in Vesting Clause.

On the other hand, Congress has the power to declare war, which proponents of congressional prerogative argue places some limit beyond which the

47. See, e.g., Crockett v. Reagan, 558 F.Supp. 893 (D.D.C. 1982), aff'd, 720 F.2d 1355 (D.C.Cir.1983); and Lowry v. Reagan, 676 F.Supp. 333 (D.D.C.1987). There are at least twelve cases where plaintiffs have unsuccessfully attempted to enforce the War Powers Resolution.

President may not go, and Congress has authority to pass legislation to implement (and by implication to regulate) any power of the government, including powers held by the President like the foreign relations power, the Executive Power, and the Commander in Chief power. In the WPR Congress has simply legislated to regulate the collective war powers of the federal government.

The executive would respond by arguing that Congress may implement the war powers of the government, but it may not encroach upon a constitutional power of the President. In this view, the WPR is an invasion of the Commander in Chief and other executive powers. But what is the boundary between executing or properly regulating a power and encroaching upon it? Or how does one reconcile or balance the powers that plainly are divided between Congress and the President? The text of the relevant provisions, and what one can discern from Original Intent, simply do not provide answers.

Going beyond the duel of labels, the protagonists in this debate also invoke arguments drawing on logic, structure, functional necessity, and democratic theory to justify one or another position. Executive branch lawyers point out that it is at least anomalous, if not logically impossible, that presidential authority based on the Constitution could simply terminate after 60 days because of an act of Congress. An act of Congress cannot formally alter the Constitution. And 60 days is entirely arbitrary. True, Congress can delegate legislative authority and provide for its termination in a "sunset" provision (as by authorizing an administrative agency for a limited period of time), but the WPR is distinguishable because it implicates independent constitutional powers. In addition, sunset provisions usually are focused on specific agencies and are applied to domestic affairs, not foreign policy.

Perhaps most significantly, the automatic 60 day cut-off effectively means that a major policy decision can be made by indecision. This consequence seems similar to that which was condemned in *Chadha*,[48] where the Court said Congress cannot change the legal status of persons outside the legislature, including the President's legal powers, except by ordinary legislation that would be subject to the President's veto. Moreover, the practical operation of the WPR can lead to negative and indefinite consequences simply because Congress is unable to vote on the matter. Finally, by giving the President a free hand for 60 days, the WPR may also have the perverse effect of implicitly authorizing presidential use of force for any reason at all during the 60 day period. In recent years Congress seems to have acquiesced in the President's claims that the 60 day provision is unconstitutional. President Clinton continued to wage an air war against Serbia, and continued to keep ground forces in Kosovo, after the 60–day cut-off. This part of the WPR therefore seems to be defunct.

There are two other constitutional issues raised by the WPR. First, Congress provided that it could

48. Immigration & Naturalization Service v. Chadha, 462 U.S. 919 (1983).

terminate the use of force by its own action, viz. through a concurrent resolution of both Houses which requires only a majority vote for passage and is not presented to the President for signature or veto like a normal bill. Thus the act of Congress would produce a legal consequence—cessation of the President's authority to wage war—without going through the constitutionally prescribed process of presenting the legislation to the President and, if he vetoes it, overriding the veto by a 2/3 vote of both Houses. This kind of process was condemned by the *Chadha* case,[49] and is widely assumed to be invalid.

Second, Congress provided that subsequent acts of Congress, such as in the authorization or appropriations process, could not constitute authority for the President to use force unless the subsequent legislation specifically referred to the WPR and expressly stated that such legislation constituted the authorization required by the WPR. In other situations presidential authority has been inferred from appropriations or other legislation (like renewing the draft). This part of the WPR would therefore reverse established constitutional practice. One Congress of course cannot bind a subsequent Congress—statutes later in time always trump earlier inconsistent acts. Accordingly it seems doubtful that the 1974 Congress can limit the ability of subsequent Congresses to authorize military force in whatever ways they may then see fit to chose.

49. Id.

Repeal or Reform. The most significant parts of
the War Powers Resolution have not been operative. Consultation has been perfunctory and largely
after the decision to use force had been irrevocably
made. The 60 day cut-off has been finessed by the
executive practice of declining to specify a particular subsection of section 4 under which the required
reports have been filed. The ambiguity of the "hostilities" standard which would trigger the 60 day
cut-off has rendered uncertain the question of
whether the clock is running. Congress has not
taken any action, substantive or procedural, to force
a resolution of the question of whether the clock
has started to run, and the courts have not been
willing to play that role either.

In light of this situation some members of Congress and several commentators have called for
repeal of the Resolution. They reason that it is
undesirable to have a law on the books that is so
conspicuously ignored. They also point out that
there is no evidence that the Resolution has had
any impact whatsoever on executive branch decision-making. On the other hand, others have argued that repeal of the Resolution would send the
wrong political signal from Congress to the President regarding war decisions. Repeal could be seen
as another step in the process of congressional
abandonment of its constitutional prerogatives, or
at least abandonment of the principle that committing armed forces should result from a collective
judgment of the political branches. When repeal
legislation came up for a vote in the House of

Representatives during the Clinton Presidency, some Republicans argued against repeal because they did not want to appear to be giving the Democratic President any additional power. In 1995 the House declined by a vote of 201–217 to repeal the War Powers Resolution.

E. U.N. Peacekeeping

After the collapse of the Soviet Union, President Bush, Sr. called for a "new world order" in which the United Nations would become revitalized as an instrument of U.S. foreign policy and as a means for resolving international disputes. Democratic presidential candidates and President Clinton also regularly endorsed the principle of multilateral approaches to international problems. One manifestation of these positions is the increased use of U.N. peacekeeping operations to deal with international conflict, civil war, and anarchy. Since the end of the Cold War the United Nations has deployed 41 peacekeeping missions (as opposed to 13 in the preceding four decades). Their tasks have ranged from monitoring cease-fires in civil wars (as in Angola and the Western Sahara), supervising electoral processes (as in El Salvador), and protecting humanitarian assistance (as in Somalia), to major nation-building commitments as in Cambodia, Bosnia and East Timor. Peacekeeping and peacemaking (or enforcement) missions have been authorized by the U.N. Security Council pursuant to Chapters 6

or 7 of the U.N. Charter.[50] For the most part the
United States has played a very limited role in
these missions, often simply providing logistics and
technical support.

In a few situations, however, the United States
has deployed its armed forces and engaged in combat pursuant to authorization by the Security Council. Examples include the Korean war, the Gulf war,
and U.S. interventions in Somalia and Haiti. The
major legal issue is what effect does authorization
by the Security Council have on the President's
authority to commit U.S. armed forces to combat
without a specific authorization from Congress. As
set forth above in Subchapter B, the President has
authority to use military forces in minor war situations, as most U.N. peacekeeping operations are.
Hence the President does not need any additional
treaty-based authority. Further, as noted above, the
executive could claim that Congress has ceded its
ability to authorize armed engagements in advance
(through the U.N. Participation Act) to the executive and the U.N. Security Council. Such an argument seems less persuasive today, in light of the
U.N.'s uneven performance, than 50 years ago.
Moreover, Congress has adopted a much more skep-
tical stance regarding the value of the U.N. At the
time of the Haiti intervention, the Senate over-

50. Ordinarily these missions were invited into the affected
country by the government of that country, and the Security
Council acted under Chapter 6. In Bosnia and Kuwait, however,
the Council acted under Chapter 7 which enables it to take a
legally binding decision without the consent of the affected
government.

whelmingly passed a non-binding sense-of-the-Senate resolution to the effect that approval of the U.N. Security Council was not equivalent to approval by Congress. The movement against the U.N. has been led by conservatives, especially in the Senate, but the skepticism about the value of the U.N. as a leading component of U.S. foreign policy seems more general. Therefore, politically and legally, the United Nations Charter does not provide a very persuasive basis for unilateral executive use of military force.

The experience of U.S. troops in Somalia precipitated legislative action against U.S. participation in U.N. peacekeeping operations. In the face of anarchy and mass starvation, President Bush, Sr. supported the U.N. Security Council decision to dispatch a peacekeeping force to help assure the delivery of food and medicines to people caught between factions in a civil war and anarchy. A U.N. Peacekeeping Force was deployed with the United States providing logistical support but no forces. Instead the U.S. deployed a separate contingent of forces (separate from the U.N. forces). In 1993 eighteen Americans were killed and the popular reaction in the United States led President Clinton to withdraw the U.S. forces from Somalia. The popular but inaccurate perception was that the U.S. troops had been jeopardized because of their association with the U.N. The domestic criticism was directed at both the President and the United Nations. At that time Congress proposed limiting U.S. participation in future U.N. peacekeeping missions.

Two of the proposed limitations posed constitutional problems. First, one possible limitation would have required the President to notify Congress of impending actions by the Security Council, and give Congress time to consider the matter before voting for a new mission. This restriction would have placed a significant burden on the President's executive power. The President has the authority to represent the United States at conferences and to conduct diplomacy. Deciding how to vote is a traditional executive prerogative. Similar claims have been made by executive branch lawyers regarding congressional directions given to U.S. representatives to international financial institutions. In practice, however, the executive branch has often objected in principle, but cooperated with congressional committees in practice. The necessity for congressional funding of peacekeeping as a practical matter requires a joint decision on such a vote. Accordingly President Clinton adopted procedures in which he promised increased consultations with Congress regarding proposed peacekeeping operations.

Another limitation would have barred the President from placing U.S. troops under any separate U.N. command. This would have invaded the President's Commander-in-Chief power, and the provision drew a veto threat from President Clinton. The Secretary of Defense called such a limitation "a significant intrusion upon the constitutional prerogative of the Commander-in-Chief,"[51] and Clinton

51. Carroll J. Doherty, U.N. Command of U.S. Troops Restricted by House Again, Cong. Q. Weekly Rep., Sept. 7, 1996, at 2537.

placed U.S. troops under the command of non-U.S. NATO commanders in the Balkan interventions.

F. Intelligence Operations

The conduct of "intelligence" operations includes at least three distinct categories of activity, each with different legal implications. Intelligence refers to: (1) collecting information; (2) influencing foreign governments and events; and (3) supporting foreign insurgents and other armed forces, including the provision of military equipment and assistance from U.S. military and intelligence personnel.

The executive branch agencies involved include the Central Intelligence Agency (CIA), the Department of Defense Intelligence Agency (DIA), the National Reconnaissance Office (which runs satellite operations), the intelligence corps of each branch of the armed forces, the Bureau of Intelligence and Research of the Department of State, and the National Security Agency (which conducts satellite and electronic surveillance). Intelligence collection may be overt or covert. In this subchapter, I will focus on covert operations, which raise the most difficult legal issues.

The President has an independent constitutional power to engage in covert intelligence activities, at least with respect to the first two categories, but he needs the support of Congress for virtually any meaningful exercise of that power. Congressional support has been readily forthcoming, and Congress has now both recognized the President's constitutional prerogative and authorized covert intelligence operations in very broad terms.

Using secret agents to gather information and to influence foreign opinion and governments has a well-established pedigree. The Continental Congress dispatched agents to Great Britain to gather information and to influence public opinion in favor of the Colonies' demands. As in the case of limited uses of military force, there is an extensive Historical Practice showing presidential initiatives of this sort. The CIA General Counsel cited precedents involving more than 400 agents acting on the basis of executive authority.[52] For example, Presidents Polk and Grant sent agents to oppose foreign designs on California and to promote American designs on Canada. Many of the 400 examples are as insignificant as the examples of presidentially initiated uses of armed force, but the principle nevertheless stands. In the *Curtiss-Wright* case the Court justified a presidential foreign affairs power in part on the grounds that the President "has his confidential sources of information ... [and] agents in the form of diplomatic, consular and *other* officials."[53] Of course almost any significant covert action requires congressional support, such as an appropriation of funds, so Congress inevitably plays a role. However, the extent of that role is difficult to

[52]. Hearings Before the House Select Committee on Intelligence, 94th Cong., 1st Sess., part 5, 1729, 1731–33 (1976) *quoted in* Stephen Dycus et al., National Security Law 295–96 (1990).

[53]. United States v. Curtiss–Wright Export Corp., 299 U.S. 304, 320 (1936) (emphasis added).

assess because the intelligence budget is secret, known only to a few members of Congress. Nevertheless, as in other areas, it is clear that Congress may force its policy on the executive by attaching conditions to appropriations, as it did to halt covert support of insurgents in Angola and Nicaragua.

The National Security Act of 1947[54] created the CIA and authorized it to perform a wide variety of functions relating to intelligence, including advising and making recommendations to the President, correlating, evaluating and disseminating intelligence information, and performing "additional services of common concern" and "such other functions and duties related to intelligence affecting national security as the National Security Council may from time to time determine." This last authorization—known as the "Fifth Function"—is obviously, and perhaps intentionally, extremely ambiguous. The legislative history is cryptic, and much was secret. To understand the meaning and scope of the Fifth Function, an important source of information to examine would seem to be the practice of predecessor agencies and groups. However, those activities were secret at the time the 1949 Act was passed, and knowledge of them thus cannot be imputed to Congress as a whole. Moreover, some of the most dramatic activities took place during World War II, so it would be difficult to figure out what was done under the Declaration of War and what came under the President's constitutional intelligence authority.

54. 50 U.S.C. § 403 (1947).

Most of the activities conducted by the CIA under the Fifth Function continue to be secret, so it is difficult to define the executive practice that normally would form a "gloss" on the ambiguous provision. Some incidents, however, are known, and their breadth suggests that the executive branch has interpreted the legislative mandate broadly and Congress has regularly acquiesced. For example, in the 1950s the CIA influenced elections in Europe, subsidized labor unions, student and cultural groups, and political parties, as well as supporting the overthrow of governments in Iran and Guatemala. In the 1960s the CIA continued such activities, assisted in attempts to assassinate leaders in Cuba, Chile, and Zaire, supported civil wars in Iraq and Laos, and an invasion of Cuba. Throughout that period Congress' oversight was lax, and the CIA did not volunteer much information anyway.

The political climate was dramatically reversed in 1974. As the Watergate scandal engulfed the Nixon Administration, many CIA activities became public knowledge, and two aggressive congressional committees sought to reexamine the role of the CIA. Both the House and the Senate established special committees to investigate intelligence abuses. Among the practices uncovered were several attempted assassinations of Castro and other foreign leaders, use of journalists and academics in covert roles, destabilization of a democratically elected leftist government, and experimentation with LSD and other drugs on American subjects. Throughout an extensive public debate extending over a period of several years Congress considered a comprehensive charter for the CIA. In the meantime Congress adopted an immediate funding restriction.

The Hughes-Ryan amendment[55] provided that no funds could be expended by the CIA for non-traditional intelligence operations "unless and until the President finds that each such operation is important to the national security of the United States and reports, in a timely fashion, a description of such operation" to various congressional committees. President Ford complained about the number of persons who would thereby get access to highly secret information, and in 1980 Congress amended the law to require reports only to the intelligence committee of each house.[56] The new law contained three kinds of innovation, viz. (1) the law provided a substantive legal standard which a proposed action would have to meet, (2) the law established new procedural requirements applicable to executive decisions, and (3) the law imposed a reporting requirement. These innovations turned out to be less than revolutionary. The substantive legal standard, requiring that proposed actions be "important to the national security," was both vague and almost tautologically easy to meet. The procedural requirement did not specify how the President needed to make his finding or whether he could delegate his duties to others. Finally, the reporting requirement left open the question of when a report

55. Foreign Assistance Act of 1974, 22 U.S.C. § 2422 (1974).

56. The Intelligence Oversight Act of 1980, 50 U.S.C. § 1801 (1980).

is "timely." On the other hand, the law forced the President to take responsibility for covert operations, just as it impliedly endorsed the legitimacy of such operations.

For several years Congress considered a "charter" for the CIA. It would have established extensive substantive standards for covert operations, prohibited a number of acts like assassinations of foreign leaders, and created elaborate procedures for decision-making. At one point the proposed legislation was 263 pages long. It fell of its own weight. In 1980 Congress passed the Intelligence Oversight Act which added a new Section 501 to the National Security Act of 1947:

(a) To the extent consistent with all applicable authorities and duties, including those conferred by the Constitution upon the executive and legislative branches of the Government, and to the extent consistent with due regard for the protection from unauthorized disclosure of classified information and information relating to intelligence sources and methods, the Director of Central Intelligence and the heads of all departments, agencies, and other entities of the United States involved in intelligence activities shall—

(1) keep the Select Committee on Intelligence of the Senate and the Permanent Select Committee on Intelligence of the House of Representatives ... fully and currently informed of all intelligence activities which are the responsibility of, are engaged in by, or are carried out for or on

behalf of ... the United States, including any significant intelligence activity, except that (A) the foregoing provision shall not require approval of the intelligence committees as a condition precedent to the initiation of any such anticipated intelligence activity, and (B) if the President determines it is essential to limit prior notice to meet extraordinary circumstances affecting vital interests of the United States, such notice shall be limited to the chairman and ranking minority members of the intelligence committees, the Speaker and minority leader of the House of Representatives, and the majority and minority leaders of the Senate; ...

(b) The President shall fully inform the intelligence committees in a timely fashion of intelligence operations in foreign countries, other than activities intended solely for obtaining necessary intelligence, for which prior notice was not given under subsection (a) and shall provide a statement of the reasons for not giving prior notice....

(e) Nothing in this Act shall be construed as authority to withhold information from the intelligence committees on the grounds that providing the information to the intelligence committees would constitute the unauthorized disclosure of classified information or information relating to intelligence sources and methods.[57]

57. The Intelligence Oversight Act of 1980, 50 U.S.C. § 1801 (1982).

This law too has significant loopholes. First, it acknowledges an undefined constitutional prerogative of the President. Second, it assures an exception to its operation when intelligence "sources and methods" could be compromised. Third, it assumes that the required notices need not be given in advance, and acknowledges that no prior approval is required before the executive can act. Fourth, the ambiguities of the Hughes-Ryan amendment, especially the meaning of "in a timely fashion," are not clarified. Notwithstanding the law's loopholes and ambiguities, it does introduce a procedural system of decision-making that takes some limited steps toward assuring political accountability for covert actions and congressional oversight. The result is still blurred, however, by the secret nature of the process.

Nevertheless, at least Congress now has information about covert actions, and can respond with additional regulation if it considers such action to be warranted. Congress can convene in secret session, and on at least two occasions Congress has used its appropriations power to halt existing programs (in Angola and Nicaragua). On the other hand, the relevant information is secret and known to only a few members of Congress. Advance approval, or even notice, is not required, so there is little theoretical restraint of executive discretion. Because the system operates secretly, it hardly adds to public trust that the system works better than before. In short it does not confer much political legitimacy on this type of government action. The system does, nevertheless, give the Director of Central Intelligence an incentive to control his own intelligence bureaucracy, lest it proceed without satisfying even the minimum legal requirements. It also gives the executive a second opinion about proposed operations and forces the executive to articulate and defend its rationale for specific operations to an external body. And finally, it gives Congress an input which it can use to influence executive decision-making (e.g. by forcefully suggesting more assistance to the opposition in Iraq).

In 1986 the executive's conduct of covert actions again became a public controversy. The Reagan Administration secretly approved arms transfers and sold weapons to Iran without complying with the requirements of the Arms Export Control Act, and it channeled some of the proceeds of those sales to the Contras in Nicaragua. At the time Congress had restricted the use of appropriated funds to support the Contras. The executive also solicited funds for the Contras from foreign governments and private groups in the United States. Congressional Democrats exposed these activities in a series of hearings, and some of the executive personnel involved were later prosecuted.

The Reagan Administration justified the actions on the grounds that the arms sales and transfers were authorized by the National Security Act of 1949, which they viewed as a covert alternative to the overt procedures of the Arms Control Export Act. They justified their assistance to the Contras on the basis of a mixture of statutory and constitutional arguments. They argued that, as a matter of statutory interpretation, the rather complicated and convoluted appropriations restrictions did not apply, or at least did not apply to the NSC which directed the operations. They also argued that the President's foreign relations power covered their actions generally, or at least the power to solicit funds from foreign governments.

In the aftermath of the hearings the executive branch undertook procedural reforms, and Congress amended the law in rather minor ways. The amendments dealt quite specifically with some particular missteps taken by the executive, including requiring that presidential findings be in writing, that they not be retroactive, and that they specify any third countries involved in the operations. The new law also added new language to the substantive standard to be met for covert operation be approved by the President, and to the notice provisions. Neither change seems to have had much actual effect. The congressional reforms thus tinkered at the margins. Even so President Bush vetoed one version of the reform legislation that would have, first, subjected any request for foreign government funds to the notice and reporting requirements of the Act, and, second, clarified the notice requirement to be a specific time (almost always 48 hours) in advance of an operation. Congress backed down on both points, and the President agreed that normally notice would be provided "within a few days."[58]

58.   Stephen Dycus et al., National Security Law 373 (1990).

Another issue generated by the Iran–Contra affair involved the role of the NSC in actual intelligence operations (as opposed to planning and coordinating intelligence operations). By Executive Order the President provided a comprehensive procedure for review, approval and implementation of covert operations, including a requirement that they must be carried out by the CIA unless the President specifically determined otherwise in a specific case. In 1996 Congress attempted to regulate further the decision-making process by requiring the establishment of two specific subcommittees of the NSC, with prescribed missions. The President objected on grounds that the provision invaded the Vesting Clause, and said he would treat the matter as "advisory." He added that he planned to establish the committees anyway. Preserving constitutional principle, the President seems to have conformed to congressional wishes.

At this time a rough bargain seems to have been struck, with Congress acknowledging an executive power based on the Vesting Clause and providing a loose oversight that seems more to legitimate than to regulate executive activities. The President in turn pays some attention politically and informally to the wishes of the involved members of Congress.

Bibliographic Note

For my historical account I am indebted to W. Taylor Reveley III, War Powers of the President and Congress (1981); John C. Yoo, The Continuation of Politics by Other Means: The Original Understanding of War Powers, 84 Cal. L. Rev. 167 (1996), and Clio at War: The Misuse of History in the War Powers Debate, 70 U. Colo. L. Rev. 1169 (1999); Jack N. Rakove, Original Meanings: Politics and Ideas in the Making of the Constitution (1996); and David P. Currie, The Constitution in Congress: The Federalist Period 1789–1801 (1997). Other influential works include John Hart Ely, War and Responsibility (1993); Louis Fisher, Presidential War Power (1995); and Michael J. Glennon, Constitutional Diplomacy (1990). For an account of recent developments regarding the Appropriations Power, see Louis Fisher, Presidential Independence and the Power of the Purse, 3 U.C. Davis J. Int'l L. & Pol. 107 (1997).

Jules Lobel has interpreted the Marques and Reprisal Clause to require congressional authorization of limited war. See Covert War and Congressional Authority, 134 U. Pa. L. Rev. 1035 (1986). For a refutation, see C. Kevin Marshall, Putting Privateers in Their Place: The Applicability of the Marque and Reprisal Clause to Undeclared Wars, 64 U. Chi. L. Rev. 953 (1997).

A comprehensive Symposium on contemporary war powers, with a full spectrum of experts, is found in 50 U. Miami L. Rev. 1–208 (1995). A comprehensive analysis of limited war powers is set forth in Mark T. Uyeda, Note, Presidential Prerogative under the Constitution to deploy U.S. Military Forces in Low–Intensity Conflict, 44 Duke L.J. 777

(1995). On the Clinton Administration's practice and the question of whether the President may place U.S. troops under U.N. or foreign command, see John C. Yoo, Kosovo, War Powers, and the Multilateral Future, 148 U. Pa. L. Rev. 1673 (2000). See also Michael J. Glennon and Allison R. Hayward, Collective Security and the Constitution: Can the Commander in Chief Power be Delegated to the United Nations, 82 Geo. L. J. 1573 (1994).

On intelligence activities, see Lori Damrosh, Covert Operations, in Foreign Affairs and the U.S. Constitution 87 (Henkin, Glennon and Rogers ed. 1990); and Kent A. Jordon, The Extent of Independent Presidential Authority to Conduct Foreign Intelligence Activities, 72 Geo. L. J. 1855 (1984).

Chapter Six

The September 11 Attacks

The September 11 attacks on the United States raise issues that encompass much of the substantive coverage of this book—the roles of the President and Congress, War Powers, Covert Intelligence Operations, and the Treaty Power, as well as some topics that the Bush Administration had declined to engage, such as international criminal law and the International Criminal Court. Accordingly it is appropriate to devote a separate chapter explaining some of the international law and foreign relations law problems that have been raised during the initial phase of the US response. This summary has been prepared in February 2002, and hence can only serve as an outline of the issues presented; the definitive precedents set will not be evident for some time to come.

After its election the Administration repeatedly emphasized that it would reject many of the multilateral approaches to world problems favored by its predecessors, in favor of a unilateral foreign policy based on rigorously defined *national* interests. Thus the new Administration criticized U.N. peacekeeping and nation-building in general, multilateral environmental cooperation (the Kyoto Protocol), treaty-based arms control (the Comprehensive Nuclear

Test Ban Treaty, the Land Mines Treaty, the ABM Treaty, and the development of a Protocol to the Biological Weapons Convention), and the establishment of an International Criminal Court. In the immediate aftermath of the September 11 attacks, however, it seemed possible—even likely—that the Administration would revise its commitment to unilateralism as it sought and welcomed support from the international community, including support from friendly governments, regional security organizations like NATO, and the United Nations. Nevertheless, it turned out that the Administration's fundamental shift away from multilateralism remains intact. First, even as it enjoyed broad international support for its initial responses to the attacks, the Administration did not deviate from a unilateral course in terms of its legal justifications for an immediate military response and for applying criminal justice to the perpetrators. Moreover, after the military successes in Afghanistan, the United States resisted involvement with United Nations sponsored nation-building and—at the time of this writing—threatened to continue its war on terrorism, presumably next against Iraq, on a largely unilateral basis. Finally, the Administration reiterated many of its previous positions favoring unilateral action over multilateral cooperation.

In crafting a legal framework in which to understand and analyze the September 11 attacks, one can view the attacks as a problem of foreign policy, military security and war. Or they can be viewed as a problem of law enforcement and criminal justice (involving either domestic or international criminal law). Neither approach is mutually exclusive, but neither quite captures the reality of the situation. The attacks were not "war" in the classic sense of a national army attacking another, or even in the sense of a civil war with insurgents attempting to displace an established government. Nor were the attacks common crimes in the sense of acts deviating from societal norms. They were attacks on the norms themselves, an assault on the United States as a society and on its government, its foreign policy, its economic success and dominance, and its reflection of modern culture. The attacks can thus be viewed from at least three different, but not mutually incompatible, perspectives: as a domestic crime, an international crime, or as an act of war. The Administration responded on all three fronts, but most prominently it treated the attacks as an act of war.

On the basis of mostly secret information the United States concluded that Osama bin Laden and the Al Qaeda network was responsible for the attacks, while the Taliban government of Afghanistan shared responsibility by virtue of its symbiotic relationship with Al Qaeda and its protection of the organization on its territory. The Bush Administration immediately invoked the rhetoric of war. But the enemy was not, at least initially or primarily, another state, but instead was a nebulous network of individuals and organizations operating in many countries.[1] Indeed, the Administration's initial rhet-

1. Al Qaeda has been estimated to include up to 10,000 terrorists operating in up to 60 countries.

oric pointed to a general campaign against all terrorist organizations with a global capability and the governments that harbored them, a daunting prospect at best. Congress responded accordingly, treating international terrorism as the declared enemy. Some members of Congress actually introduced a Declaration of War, but Congress instead adopted a Joint Resolution, following the format used for the Vietnam and Gulf wars, authorizing use of the U.S. armed forces against those responsible for the "attacks." The targets of the legislation included both the responsible terrorist organizations and the governments that harbored them. Accordingly, the conceptual framework implicitly adopted by the President and Congress was the model of inter-state war (even though the terrorist targets did not fit the classical model).

Under both international and domestic law, a unilateral U.S. response was clearly justified. Examining domestic law first, under the Constitution the President has the constitutional authority, in Madison's words, "to repeal sudden attacks." Of course in the eighteenth century an attack would have been a land or naval invasion by a foreign state, not internal violence orchestrated by a foreign sub-state terrorist organization. Nevertheless, the legitimacy of an immediate response of a military nature seems implicit in the original understanding of executive power. The difficult issue is drawing the line beyond which the response requires additional legal justification. To state the extreme, waging war for several years against states uninvolved with the initial attack would seem to go beyond that line. On the other hand, in the current context, it would seem reasonable that the executive could at least persist until the forces that initiated the attack were disabled from renewing it, and perhaps until those forces were substantially destroyed or captured. In addition, as pointed out in Chapter Five, Presidents since Truman have claimed authority to use military force beyond merely responding to an attack, extending at least to the use of force for a limited duration where the potential for casualties was small. This presidential authority is independent of explicit congressional authorization, and has sometimes in the past been buttressed by a resolution of the U.N. Security Council. As this manuscript goes to press, the U.S. military response has been limited to Afghanistan and the goals of dislodging the Taliban from power and disabling Al Qaeda. It would not be surprising for the President to claim broader constitutional power if he decides to expand operations, e.g. to Iraq.

In any case President Bush was not required to rely on an independent constitutional power. Congress responded to the attacks with a Joint Resolution that authorized "all necessary and appropriate force" against the persons and organizations that conducted the attack and those states that aided or harbored them. The President was authorized to identify those persons, organizations and states. Congress also provided that its action constituted the "specific" authorization required by the War Powers Resolution, thereby disabling the 60 day cut-off provision.[2] Finally, Congress provided that "[n]othing in this resolution supercedes any requirement of the War Powers Resolution." Although the language of the Joint Resolution was broad, and reminded some commentators of the Gulf of Tonkin Resolution, during the debate several members of Congress noted one significant limitation embodied in the law—it applied only to those who were involved in the September 11 attack, not to terrorists generally. They also took some comfort in the fact that the War Powers Resolution was still applicable. Such comments, like the Delphic reference in the Joint Resolution to the continuing requirements of the War Powers Resolution, presumably referred to its reporting and consultation requirements. It is clear that the President does not need additional congressional authorization after the 60 day cut-off period expires, either to escalate action in Afghanistan or to attack other states, so long as the action is aimed at those responsible for the September 11 attacks.

Apart from this limitation, the Joint Resolution is broad and grants the President unreviewable authority to determine who participated in the attack or harbored the perpetrators. From the limited facts initially known to the public, the scope of the law at least covers military action against Al Qaeda and Afghanistan. At the time the Joint Resolution was enacted the anthrax attack was not known. Whether the perpetrators of that attack, and those who harbored them, are covered by the Joint Resolution

2. See infra pp. 236–41.

depends on whether they were connected to the perpetrators of the attacks on the World Trade Center and Pentagon. That in turn depends on whether the President so certifies. If he cannot so certify, or if he wants to use military force against "terrorist states" that he cannot connect to the September 11 attack, new congressional authorization, or independent constitutional authority, will be needed.

In addition to an extensive bombing campaign, much of the immediate U.S. response took the form of covert intelligence operations—ranging from information gathering, encouraging opposition to the Taliban government, assistance in organizing resistance operations, and actual Special Forces raids. These were presumably covered by the "fifth function" of the National Security Act of 1947, as amended, and associated secret presidential findings. The question of whether covert raids by the U.S. armed forces are covered by the War Powers Resolution, or whether their authorization under National Security Act procedures is sufficient, was rendered moot by the Joint Resolution.

Some operations were specifically aimed at killing the head of the Taliban and leaders of Al Qaeda. The Executive Order banning "assassinations" either would not apply because it does not deal with war, or it would have been superseded by the September 11 Joint Resolution and/or Presidential Findings issued in connection with the covert intelligence response. Similarly other restrictions imposed by previous executive policies, such as the inhibition against dealing with foreign agents associated with human rights abuses, seem to have been cast aside. As the above analysis suggests, the Bush Administration had ample domestic legal authority to support its immediate responses to the September 11 attacks.

The United States also had ample authority to justify its response under international law. Article 51 of the U.N. Charter recognizes a nation's inherent right of self-defense, and also contemplates regional collective self-defense, like NATO. The United Nations Security Council, General Assembly, and Secretary General adopted resolutions and made statements of support for the United States as it prepared its anticipated military response. The Security Council condemned the attacks as a "threat to international peace and security," which is the threshold for action, including authorization of military force, by the Council. The Council, however, did not authorize or call on states to execute a military response. It did recognize (in the preamble to the Resolution) a nation's "inherent right of individual or collective self-defense" which is reflected in Article 51 of the Charter, and called on states to "bring to justice" the perpetrators, organizers and sponsors of the attacks and to prevent and suppress terrorist acts. The U.S. Ambassador informed the Council that it was exercising its inherent right of self-defense against Al Qaeda and the Taliban government, and he noted that, pending its continuing investigation into the facts, the

United States may act against "other organizations and other states."

The Security Council also adopted a Resolution that is legally binding on all states to take a series of steps to suppress recruitment of terrorists, prevent planning and financing of terrorist acts, deny safe haven to terrorists, bring them to justice, and cooperate in related criminal proceedings. The resolution complemented earlier U.S. unilateral action to freeze the assets of named organizations in the United States and parallel efforts in other countries.

At the regional level, NATO members invoked Article 5 of the NATO Treaty, declaring the attack as an "attack against them all," so that each of them is obligated "to take such action as it deems necessary, including the use of armed force, to restore and maintain the security of the North Atlantic area." By February 2002 several NATO allies had committed troops for action in Afghanistan.

The United States thus had extensive multilateral support in international institutions for its military and other actions against Al Qaeda and the Taliban. In addition, the Administration built a series of coalitions, of different states playing different roles, to deal with different facets of its attack on terrorism. In this process the President determined the adjustments in prior foreign policy positions and the compromises to be made pursuant to his constitutional foreign relations power. Most of the diplomacy was bilateral. For example, engaging with Russia to secure intelligence cooperation and access to Central Asia required downplaying human rights concerns. The unilateral economic sanctions policy against Pakistan (based on a longstanding U.S. policy supporting nuclear non-proliferation) was abandoned to secure critical cooperation. And the President negotiated for the use of military facilities in Uzbekistan, Kyrgyzstan, and Tajikistan.

Nevertheless, in the exercise of its war powers under international law, the Administration rested its legal authority on its unilateral right of self-defense, not on the collective authorization of the Security Council. The multilateral support from NATO and the United Nations, at least at the initial stage, was politically important but not legally necessary. In the aftermath of the military engagement, on the other hand, the United Nations may provide a critical legal basis for government in Afghanistan and long-term peacekeeping.

In the course of the war the United States captured or took control of hundreds of Taliban and Al Qaeda soldiers, primarily for the purpose of extracting intelligence information from them regarding the location of Osama bin Laden, the operation of Al Qaeda worldwide, future plots against the United States, and like matters. These individuals are held by U.S. forces in camps outside the United States, in Kandahar and subsequently at Guantanamo Bay in Cuba. Their legal status is uncertain, both under international law and under the U.S. Constitution. The issues to be resolved are whether the Third Geneva Convention of 1949 applies, whether the detainees are "prisoners of war" for purposes of that Convention, and whether they have any rights at all, being non-citizens held outside the territory of the United States after waging war against the United States, under the U.S. Constitution.

Their status and treatment served as a focus of criticism by human rights groups and opponents of U.S. policy. The Administration first stated that the captives would be treated humanely and generally in accordance with standards set forth in the relevant Geneva Convention. Critics argued that the captives were "prisoners of war" under the Convention, with resulting limits on the ability of the United States to interrogate them and other restrictions on the ways in which they may be treated and put on trial. The United States took the position that the Geneva Convention did not apply, presumably because it was framed in terms of traditional inter-state and civil war, and the war against terrorists did not fall within the treaty's intended scope (although, as noted above, the Administration in general has adopted the framework of war in its justifications for its responses to the September 11 attacks). In addition, although Afghanistan was a party to the Convention, the Taliban forces were not forces of the recognized government of Afghanistan (the Taliban had been recognized as a government only by Pakistan, Saudi Arabia, and the United Arab Emirates).

Despite the plausibility of the Administration's positions, after harsh criticism in which the treatment of the captives was linked with their possible trial by even more controversial presidentially established military tribunals discussed below, the

Administration agreed that the Taliban captives, but not those of the Al Qaeda, were covered by the Geneva Convention. The Administration nevertheless decreed that they were not "prisoners of war," presumably because they did not wear distinctive uniforms or follow the rules of war. The captives were instead described as "unlawful combatants." Opponents pointed out that the Geneva Convention required that "[s]hould any doubt arise" about their status, captives have a right to a *judicial* determination of that status. The blanket determination by the Administration that the captives were not prisoners of war seems justified on the facts (none of the Taliban wore uniforms and their commitment to the international laws of war seems dubious), and it is not clear that the Convention always requires a judicial determination. Representatives of the captives sought judicial relief in the federal courts, initially in Los Angeles, but the case was dismissed on grounds of lack of jurisdiction. The additional litigation that will undoubtedly ensue will present and perhaps resolve the full range of constitutional and international law issues, if any court reaches the merits of any of the lawsuits.

After the defeat of Taliban forces the military campaign focused on attacking the Al Qaeda network and trying to kill or capture its individual leaders. As noted at the beginning of this Chapter, the September 11 attacks may also be approached from the perspective of criminal law. The acts of course were crimes under U.S domestic law, and the perpetrators could be tried as ordinary criminals, as were the perpetrators of the earlier World Trade Center bombing and that of the U.S. embassies in Nairobi and Dar es Salaam. Such trials would not be easy. Most of the participants and evidence are abroad, and perhaps not in jurisdictions willing to cooperate with extradition and information sharing. Much of the evidence would probably be based on intelligence sources and methods that cannot be disclosed in open court or shared with the defendants. And finding an impartial jury would be challenging. Moreover, one could readily imagine a reincarnation of the OJ Simpson trial, in which protracted proceedings could degenerate into a trial of U.S. foreign policy or the merits of globalism. In any event, even though American lawyers may not doubt that the United States could conduct a fair trial for Osama bin Laden, it is likely that many foreign observers would not be as generous.

Consequently, some commentators suggested an international trial of some sort, perhaps an ad hoc tribunal established by the Security Council or a tribunal established by special international agreement. The crimes committed on September 11 were not only U.S. domestic crimes; they were also international crimes, viz. crimes against humanity and possibly war crimes. These are crimes of the sort that the International Criminal Court (ICC) could deal with once it is established, and of the sort dealt with by special War Crimes Tribunals established by the U.N. Security Council for the former Yugoslavia (ICTY) and for Rwanda (ICTR). The Bush Administration, however, had rejected participation in the International Criminal Court, and it did not seek a U.N. Security Council resolution to establish a special tribunal for the perpetrators of the September 11 attacks. Instead it decided to proceed unilaterally against those associated with the terrorist attack, creating a U.S. military tribunal to try offenders, apparently on the basis of the international criminal law of war.

Viewing the acts as international crimes requires a framework of analysis quite different from that applicable to domestic criminal law. International crimes are created, defined and limited by international law, and they are applied by tribunals that are not subject to the same constitutional limitations that apply in trials of domestic crimes. Because international crimes grow out of war (and indeed comprise part of the law of war), their classification more comfortably fits within the war paradigm than the domestic crime framework. The same constitutional authority—the Commander in Chief Clause, reinforced by congressional support and Historical Practice—supporting the President's use of military force also supports his creation of military tribunals applying international criminal law.

By Military Order the President provided for the establishment of military tribunals for the purpose of trying any non-citizen that the President determined was a member of Al Qaeda or was a person who engaged in, aided or abetted, or conspired to commit, acts of terrorism, or who was a person who knowingly harbored a terrorist. Such individuals could be tried for "violations of the laws of war and other applicable laws by military tribunals." The procedures to be followed by the tribunals would be established by the Secretary of Defense, would not necessarily embody the same protections provided by the Bill of Rights for domestic civilian trials, and the only appeal would lie to the Secretary or the President. Moreover, the Order provides that the defendant "shall not be privileged to seek any remedy or maintain any proceeding ... in any court ..." including federal, state, foreign and international tribunals.

The immediate reaction to the Military Order was sharply critical. Civil liberties groups criticized its sweep. Internationalists objected to its unilateral nature. International lawyers questioned its legality. And some European officials, including a Spanish judge who had ordered the arrest of Al Qaeda members, stated that they would not extradite suspects to the United States for a military trial.

Much of the criticism was premature. Many of the problems cited with the Order could evaporate when the Defense Department issues the regulations governing the tribunals. Nevertheless, the Order is striking for its breadth. It covers all noncitizens, even those permanently residing in or otherwise legally present in the country. It also covers anyone accused of terrorist activity, not just members of Al Qaeda. Furthermore, it seems to authorize the military tribunal to try defendants for federal crimes as well as for violations of the laws of war. And it seems to amount to an attempt by the President to suspend habeas corpus. The Order ignores protections that ordinary criminals would have under the Bill of Rights, including the presumption of innocence, grand jury indictment, public trial, the requirement of a unanimous verdict for the death penalty, right of judicial appeal, right to choose one's counsel, and other Fifth and Sixth Amendment guarantees. Some of those rights are also accorded prisoners of war under the Geneva Convention.

In the face of substantial criticism from members of Congress and others, the Administration promised to narrow the coverage of the Order and address the civil liberties problems in the regulations governing the tribunals. Government lawyers eschewed the denial of habeas corpus, and indicated that only persons captured on the battlefield would be tried by military tribunal. The only non-resident connected to the attacks who was present in the United States was indicated for trial in the regular federal courts, as was a U.S. citizen actually captured on the battlefield. The Government thus would limit the intended coverage of the proposed tribunals' jurisdiction to battlefield combatants, and not non-residents generally or those in the United States, and it would only try defendants for violations of the laws of war, and not for other crimes. Defendants were also promised a right of appeal beyond that specified in the Order.

The criticism of the Order was not for the most part directed at the President's basic authority to establish tribunals, but rather at the way the tribunals operate. In promulgating the Order the President relied on his constitutional authority as President and as Commander in Chief, in addition to implied statutory authority under the Uniform Code of Military Justice. Military tribunals applying the law of war were convened during the American Revolution, the War of 1812, the Spanish–American War, the Mexican War, the Civil War and World War II. Defendants included U.S. citizens as well as foreigners who were engaged in military action or conduct (like spying) related thereto. The Administration has characterized the detainees so far as unlawful combatants, presumably not only to avoid having to treat them as "prisoners of war" under the Geneva Convention, but also to fall within the Supreme Court decision in *Ex parte Quirin*.[3] In that case the Court permitted the military trial of captured German soldiers who had buried their uniforms (and thereby forfeited coverage of the Geneva Convention) and attempted sabotage in New York and Florida during World War II. They were hanged. The current situation is distinguishable in that Congress has not declared war (but it did adopt a functionally equivalent Joint Resolution), and the conflict with the Taliban and Al Qaeda is not clearly a war in the inter-state sense (the United States was at peace with the recognized, albeit rump, government of Afghanistan) or a civil war within the United States. The principal case denying presidential authority to use a military tribunal, *Ex parte Milligan*,[4] is also distinguishable from the current

3. 317 U.S. 1 (1942).
4. 71 U.S. 2 (1866).

situation because it involved the trial of a citizen for acts in the United States not connected with military service.

Given the congressional support for President Bush's exercise of his constitutional Commander in Chief power, both generally in the UCMJ and specifically with respect to the September 11 attacks, and given the precedents dating back over 200 years, it seems clear that the President has basic authority to establish military tribunals to apply the laws of war to combatants who oppose the United States. It is also seems doubtful that nonresident alien combatants in a foreign war against the United States would be entitled to constitutional protections in a military trial conducted outside the United States. The Supreme Court recently held in a non-wartime case that foreigners searched abroad are not protected by the Fourth Amendment.[5] *Reid v. Covert*[6] applied the Constitution extraterritorially in the case of a court-martialed civilian facing the death penalty, but Justice Harlan in his concurrence opined that the Bill of Rights would apply differently abroad than in the United States, with an eye to context and practicality. Accordingly, the final procedures of the military tribunals, and the situations of actual defendants brought before them, will determine whether the due process/constitutional issues raised turn out to be substantial.

Some international law scholars have also argued that the military tribunals would violate the Third

5. U.S. v. Verdugo–Urquidez, 494 U.S. 259 (1990).

6. 354 U.S. 1 (1957).

Geneva Convention of 1949[7] or, less plausibly, international human rights law generally. Assuming that the Convention applies, whether the military tribunals comply with international law will also depend on the final regulations adopted for their creation and on the actual combatants tried. In any event, the President has constitutional authority to take effective action in violation of international law, so the issue seems to be moot, at least as a matter of domestic law, and no international tribunal would appear likely to hold otherwise.

A separate issue concerns what substantive law the tribunals will apply. The President's Order declares that the attacks created "a state of armed conflict that requires the use of the United States armed forces," and that detainees may be tried for "violations of the laws of war and other applicable laws...." The final regulations will presumably clarify the specific content of the "laws of war" to be applied, but it is interesting to examine whether the September 11 attacks amount to war crimes or crimes against humanity, as those crimes have been defined in the Nuremberg Charter, the U.N. Security Council mandates for the international criminal tribunals established for the former Yugoslavia (ICTY) and for Rwanda (ICTR), and the statute of the proposed International Criminal Court.

The Nuremberg Charter defined war crimes to include murder of a civilian population, wanton

7. Done at Geneva, Aug. 12, 1949, entered into force Oct. 21, 1950, 75 U.N.T.S. 135, T.I.A.S. 3364, 15 I.L.M. 1236 (1976). Also available at http://www.unhchr.ch/html/menu3/b/91.htm.

destruction of cities, and devastation not justified by military necessity. It also defined crimes against humanity to include "inhumane acts committed against any civilian population" in connection with a war crime. The ICTY added "attack, or bombardment ... of undefended towns ... or buildings" to "wanton destruction of cities ... or devastation not justified by military necessity" as violations of the laws of war. Murder was defined as a crime against humanity if committed in the course of an "armed conflict, whether international or internal in character." The ICTR criminalized murder as a crime against humanity when part of a widespread or systematic attack against, inter alia, any civilian population. The ICC counts murder as a crime against humanity if "part of a widespread or systematic attack directed against any civilian population, with knowledge of the attack." However, the ICC definitions of war crimes appear not to cover the September 11 attacks because they exclude "isolated or sporadic acts of violence or other acts of a similar nature." Although the substantive standards to be applied by the President's military tribunals have not yet been established, it nevertheless seems likely that the September 11 attacks constituted crimes against humanity which form part of international humanitarian law or the laws of war.

As noted earlier the Bush Administration has made much of its preference for unilaterally determined action over multilateral cooperative approaches. In that regard, the President decided not to ratify the Rome Statute creating an International Criminal Court, thereby exercising a generally uncontroversial constitutional foreign affairs prerogative to decide not to ratify treaties, even those approved by the Senate. President Clinton had signed the ICC statute shortly before leaving office, after negotiating changes in the final text that were designed to alleviate American concerns about its armed forces being subject to the ICC for acts taken on U.N. peacekeeping missions or other military forays abroad. The treaty was crafted to assure that the ICC would not have jurisdiction if the defendant's state had a proper, functioning system of military justice that dealt with the crimes covered by the statute. This "principle of complementarity" would also seem to preclude ICC jurisdiction over those terrorists from Pakistan and Saudi Arabia responsible for the September 11 attacks even if they were within the statute's definition of "crimes against humanities," because those governments have some semblance of a military justice system.

The Bush Administration's rejection of multilateralism is perhaps most prominent in the field of arms control. The President gave notice to Russia that the United States would withdraw from the ABM Treaty. The President also indicated that he would not seek Senate approval of the Comprehensive Nuclear Test Ban Treaty (which it had earlier rejected) or sign the Land Mines Treaty. Secretary of State Powell stated that the United States and Russia would commit to a legally binding treaty for strategic nuclear arms reduction, but he indicated that the executive had not decided the constitutional form it would take (Article II treaty or executive agreement). The Administration effectively terminated negotiation of a Protocol to the Biological Weapons Convention, stating a preference for domestic legislation over international law. All these decisions were taken by the President in the exercise of the executive foreign affairs powers of the Constitution, and they graphically illustrate the power of the President to make and to change U.S. foreign policy.

The role of Congress in responding to the immediate crisis has been for the most part to follow the President's lead, although it has exercised some oversight functions and has provided a forum for effective criticism of the proposed military tribunals and other aspects of the President's law enforcement strategies. In general, however, Congress has been generously responsive to the President's foreign policy initiatives. It quickly approved military interventions, and dropped opposition to the National Missile Defense System and the President's withdrawal without congressional or Senate participation from the ABM Treaty. Congress passed legislation (the USA PATRIOT Act) that gave the executive branch most of its wish list regarding expanded wiretap authority, detention of immigrants, nation-wide search warrants, and access to e-mail. In the negotiation of the terms of the legislation between the executive branch and the concerned congressional committees, and in a series of public hearings, Congress nevertheless provided a check against some of the most far-reaching Administration requests. Its hearings provided a forum for criticism to which the Administration in fact responded, for example the retrenchment described above regarding the proposed military tribunals.

The executive also launched an aggressive domestic law-enforcement campaign, including "voluntary" interviews aimed at young Arab males, detentions of persons for immigration violations and minor crimes which normally would not entail imprisonment, unprecedented use of the procedures for detention of material witnesses, and monitoring a few prisoners' conversations with their lawyers in cases where such communication might facilitate terrorism. Congressional committees kept a close watch on these activities and thus performed a significant oversight role. Nevertheless, with respect to the most glaring executive shortcomings—the intelligence failures in advance of September 11, the failure to capture or kill Osama bin Laden and Mullah Omar, and the failure to solve the mystery of the anthrax attacks—Congress has been slow to investigate the failures involved.

The September 11 crisis thus brought out the functional advantages of the two political branches, speed and unity of purpose by the executive, and retrospective deliberation by the legislature. The crisis also demonstrated the dependence of foreign relations law on the political strengths of the two branches of government as precedents are set. Most conspicuously, the September 11 crisis demonstrated the preeminence of executive power in foreign relations.

The continuing threats from global terrorism, as well as the demands for government to respond to the consequences of globalism generally, will buttress the continued preeminence of presidential power over foreign relations. The functional advantages of the executive, notably speed and secrecy, confirm the wisdom of a broad interpretation of the Vesting Clause of the Constitution. Future developments will require more negotiation and more participation in international institutions, if only to provide a modicum of regulation of globalism. The challenge for United States foreign relations law will be to assure that the exercise of presidential prerogative is adequately "democratized" through the representation of all affected elements in the development and implementation of executive negotiating positions. Moreover, as the subjects of international negotiation increasingly involve matters that hitherto were domestic in nature, it will be important to develop innovative approaches to assure the involvement of Congress in the decision-making processes.

Bibliographic Note

The most controversial issues growing out of the September 11 attacks concerned the military tribunals. Contrast Joan Fitzpatrick, The Constitutional and International Invalidity of Military Commissions under the November 13, 2001 "Military Order," [email distribution]; and Curtis A. Bradley and Jack L. Goldsmith, The Constitutional Validity of Military Commissions, 5 Greenbag 2d (forthcoming Spring 2002).

A comprehensive analysis of domestic surveillance issues is William C. Banks and M.E. Bowman, Executive Authority for National Security Surveillance, 50 Am. Univ. L. Rev. 1 (2001).

Discussions of the implications of globalization on international and foreign relations law include Note, Discretion and Legitimacy in International Regulation, 107 Harv. L. Rev. 1099 (1994); and Claude E. Barfield, Free Trade, Sovereignty and Democracy (AEI Press 2001).

TABLE OF CASES

References are to Pages.

Alvarez–Machain, United States v., 184
American Tel. & Tel. Co., United States v., 567 F.2d 121 (D.C.Cir.1977), 74
American Tel. & Tel. Co., United States v., 551 F.2d 384 (D.C.Cir.1976), 74
Asakura v. City of Seattle, 153

B. Altman & Co. v. United States, 123
Belmont, United States v., 136
Bowsher v. Synar, 49
Buckley v. Valeo, 49

Chinese Exclusion Case, 26
Clinton v. New York, 100
Clinton v. Jones, 78
Consumers Union of United States v. Kissinger, 139
Crockett v. Reagan, 238
Cunningham v. Neagle, 211
Curtiss–Wright Export Corporation, United States v., 26, 36, 64, 248

Dames & Moore v. Regan, 138
Durand v. Hollins, 213

Eastland v. United States Servicemen's Fund, 105
Edwards v. Carter, 120
Ex parte (see name of party)

Field v. Clark, 123

Filartiga v. Pena–Irala, 178
Foster v. Neilson, 154
Fourteen Diamond Rings v. United States, 143
Frolova v. U.S.S.R., 157

Garcia–Mir v. Meese, 70, 185
Goldwater v. Carter, 148, 150
Guy W. Capps, Inc., United States v., 139

Haig v. Agee, 92
Hartford Fire Ins. Co. v. California, 175
House of Representatives, United States v., 74

Immigration & Naturalization Service v. Chadha, 92, 134, 240

Little v. Barreme, 199
Lovett, United States v., 96
Lowry v. Reagan, 238

McCulloch v. Sociedad Nacional de Marineros de Honduras, 174
McGrain v. Daugherty, 105
Merryman, Ex parte, 18
Milligan, Ex parte, 276
Missouri v. Holland, 87, 90
Myers v. United States, 51, 96, 150

Nixon v. Fitzgerald, 78
Nixon, United States v., 42, 75

People of Saipan v. United States Dept. of Interior, 157
Percheman, United States v., 155
Pink, United States v., 63, 136
Postal, United States v., 157
Power Authority of N.Y. v. Federal Power Commission, 171
Public Citizen v. United States Dept. of Justice, 41, 96

Quirin, Ex parte, 276

Reid v. Covert, 91, 277
Reynolds, United States v., 77

Sale v. Haitian Centers Council, 174

State of (see name of state)
Sumitomo Shoji America, Inc. v. Avagliano, 141

The Paquete Habana, 184
The Prize Cases, 198
Trajano v. Marcos, 178

United States v. _____ (see opposing party)

Verdugo–Urquidez, United States v., 92, 277

Whitney v. Robertson, 152
Will, United States v., 95
W.S. Kirkpatrick & Co. v. Environmental Tectonics Corp., 71

Youngstown Sheet & Tube Co. v. Sawyer (The Steel Seizure Case), 12, 208

*

INDEX

References are to Pages

AGREEMENTS
Treaties, this index

ALIENS
President's foreign relations power, excluding aliens not covered
    by act of Congress, 70

ANTI-DEFICIENCY ACT
Congress's foreign relations power, 84

APPOINTMENTS
Congress's provision for appointment of officials, 81
President's foreign relations power, appointment and removal of
    officials and diplomats, 48 et seq.

APPROPRIATIONS POWER
Congress's foreign relations power, 80 et seq.

ARTICLE II OF CONSTITUTION
Treaties, this index
Vesting clause, executive power and foreign relations power of
    president, 12 et seq.

ARTICLE VI OF CONSTITUTION
Treaties, domestic effect, 152

ARTICLES OF CONFEDERATION
President's foreign relations power, 21 et seq.

BLACKSTONE'S COMMENTARIES ON LAW
President's foreign relations power, 18 et seq.

CASE-ZABLOCKI ACT
Treaties, 134

289

CENTRAL INTELLIGENCE AGENCY
Intelligence operations, 247 et seq.

COMMANDER-IN-CHIEF
President and military force and intelligence operations, 11, 197, 199

COMMERCE
Congress's power to regulate foreign commerce, 79

COMMON LAW
Customary international law as having status of federal common law, 184

CONDITIONS
Treaties, this index

CONGRESSIONAL-EXECUTIVE AGREEMENTS
Formal international law, 113, 122 et seq.

CONGRESS'S FOREIGN RELATIONS POWER
Generally, 79 et seq.
Anti-Deficiency Act, 84
Appointments, Congress's provision for appointment of officials, 81
Appropriations power, 80 et seq.
Appropriations stage of legislative process, 81
Article I of Constitution, enumerated powers, 79 et seq.
Authorization stage of legislative process, 81
Bibliographic note, 107, 108
Commerce, power of Congress to regulate foreign commerce, 79
Enumerated powers
      Limitation, enumerated powers as limitation on Congress's power, 85 et seq.
      Powers granted under Article I , section 8, of Constitution, 79 et seq.
Executive branch departments, definition and creation of by Congress, 81
Federal offices, establishment of, 81
Funds, power of Congress to expressly deny funds for specific purposes, 82
Informal influences. Investigative and oversight powers, below
Investigative and oversight powers, 84, 85, 104 et seq.
Legislation, 80 et seq.
Legislative process, authorization and appropriations stages, 81
Letters of Marque and Reprisal, powers of Congress to grant, 79
Limitations on Congressional power

CONGRESS'S FOREIGN RELATIONS POWER—Cont'd
Limitations on Congressional power—Cont'd
  Generally, 85 et seq.
 Delegation of legislative power, 102 et seq.
 Enumerated powers, 85 et seq.
 Executive power, invasion of, 95 et seq.
 Export taxes, prohibition against Congress imposing, 85
 International law, 102
 Legislative veto, structural limitation, 92 et seq.
 Tariffs, prohibition against Congress imposing non-uniform
   tariffs, 85
 Tenth Amendment to Constitution, 85 et seq.
Military powers, 79
National Guard, powers of Congress as to, 79
Necessary and Proper Clause, 79 et seq.
Non-legislative powers, 84
Officials, Congress's provision for appointment of officials, 81
Oversight powers. Investigative and oversight powers, above
Stages of legislative process, authorization and appropriations
   stages, 81
Tariffs, power of Congress to levy taxes and tariffs, 79
Taxes, power of Congress to levy taxes and tariffs, 79
Treaties, this index
War, power of Congress to declare, 79

CONSTITUTIONAL CONVENTION
Military force and intelligence operations, 204 et seq.
President's foreign relations power, 24 et seq.

CONSTITUTIONAL LAW
Article II of Constitution, this index
Article VI of Constitution, 152
Congress's Foreign Relations Power, this index
Military Force and Intelligence Operations, this index
President's Foreign Relations Power, this index

CUSTOMARY INTERNATIONAL LAW
  Generally, 177 et seq.
Bibliographic note, 189 et seq.
Common law, customary international law as having status of
   federal common law, 184
Conferences, international, 181
Court's reluctance to apply, 187
Definition, 177
Diplomatic correspondence, 179
Evidence and sources of state practice, 178 et seq.

CUSTOMARY INTERNATIONAL LAW—Cont'd
Human rights law, 188, 189
Inaction as state practice, 179
Presidential power, 180 et seq.
Psychological element, sense of legal obligation, 177, 182 et seq.
State practice, 177
Universality of state practice not required, 179

DEFINITIONS
Customary international law, 177
Foreign relations, 2
Foreign relations law, 3

DIPLOMATIC CORRESPONDENCE
Customary international law, 179

DIPLOMATIC RELATIONS
President's foreign relations power, establishment of diplomatic relations, 56 et seq.

DIPLOMATS
Military force, protection of diplomats, 211 et seq.
President's power to appoint and remove diplomats, 48 et seq.

DOMESTIC LAW
President's foreign relations power, 71
Treaties, domestic effects of treaties. Treaties, this index

ENUMERATED POWERS
Congress's Foreign Relations Power, this index

EXECUTIVE POWER
President's Foreign Relations Power, this index

EXECUTIVE PRIVILEGE
President's foreign relations power, 72 et seq.

FOREIGN RELATIONS
Communicating with foreign governments, 59 et seq.
Congress's Foreign Relations Power, this index
Customary International Law, this index
Definition, 2
Diplomatic relations, establishment of, 56 et seq.
Government, recognition of, 55 et seq.
International law as providing structures and means, 109
Law, foreign relations. Foreign Relations Law, this index
Negotiations, 64 et seq.
President's Foreign Relations Power, this index

FOREIGN RELATIONS—Cont'd
Statehood, recognition of state, 51 et seq.
Treaties, this index

FOREIGN RELATIONS LAW
Aspects, anomalous, 5 et seq.
Customary International Law, this index
Definition, 3
Treaties, this index

FORMAL INTERNATIONAL LAWMAKING
Customary International Law, this index
Treaties, this index

FREEDOM OF INFORMATION ACT
President's foreign relations power, 73, 74

FUNCTIONALISM
President's foreign relations power, 34 et seq.

GOVERNMENT RECOGNITION
President's foreign relations power, 55 et seq.

GULF WAR
Military force, 223 et seq.

HISTORICAL PRACTICE
President's foreign relations power, constitutional interpretation,
    31 et seq.

HUMAN RIGHTS LAW
Customary international law, 188, 189

INTELLIGENCE OPERATIONS
Military Force and Intelligence Operations, this index

INTERNATIONAL AGREEMENTS
President's foreign relations power, 70
Treaties, this index

INTERNATIONAL COURT OF JUSTICE
International law enforcement, 110

INVESTIGATIVE AND OVERSIGHT POWERS
Congress's foreign relations power, 84, 85, 104 et seq.

IRAQ
War against Iraq, 223 et seq.

KOREAN WAR
Military force, 224 et seq.

LETTERS OF MARQUE AND REPRISAL
Congress's foreign relations power, 79

LOCKE, JOHN
President's foreign relations power, views of John Locke, 16 et seq.

MARQUES AND REPRISAL CLAUSE
Military force, 198

MILITARY FORCE AND INTELLIGENCE OPERATIONS
Generally, 192 et seq.
Bibliographic note, 257 et seq.
Central Intelligence Agency, 247 et seq.
Commander-in-Chief, 11, 197, 199
Congress's foreign relations power, 79
Constitutional Convention, 204 et seq.
Diplomats, protection of, 211 et seq.
Gulf War, 223 et seq.
Hijackers, punishment of, 213
Historical practice, 207 et seq.
Intelligence operations
    Generally, 247 et seq.
    Agencies involved, 247
    Central Intelligence Agency, 247 et seq.
    Intelligence Oversight Act, 252 et seq.
    National Security Act of 1947, 249 et seq.
Intelligence Oversight Act, 252 et seq.
Iraq, war against, 223 et seq.
Legal issues, 195 et seq.
Major wars
    Generally, 216 et seq.
    Gulf War, 223 et seq.
    Iraq, war against, 223 et seq.
    Korea, 224 et seq.
    Vietnam war, 217 et seq.
Minor wars
    Generally, 208 et seq.
    Defense of U.S. territory, 209 et seq.
    Protection of American nationals, including diplomats, 211 et seq.
    Protection of U.S. interests, 213 et seq.

MILITARY FORCE AND INTELLIGENCE OPERATIONS—Cont'd
Minor wars—Cont'd
    Punishment of pirates, bandits, poachers, hijackers and other
        criminals, 213
National Security Act of 1947, 249 et seq.
Original intent, 200 et seq.
Pirates, punishment of, 213
President's Commander-in-Chief power, 11, 197, 199
Protection of American nationals, including diplomats, 211 et
    seq.
Protection of U.S. interests, 213 et seq.
Territory, defense of U.S. territory, 209 et seq.
Text of Constitution, 196 et seq.
U.N. peacekeeping, 243 et seq.
Vietnam war, 217 et seq.
War
    Commander-in-Chief, 197, 199
    Congress's foreign relations power, 79
    Constitutional Convention, 204 et seq.
    Historical practice, 207 et seq.
    Legal issues, 195 et seq.
    Major wars, above
    Marques and Reprisal Clause, 198
    Minor wars, above
    Original intent, 200 et seq.
    President's Commander-in-Chief power, 11
    Text of Constitution, 196 et seq.
    U.N. peacekeeping, 243 et seq.
    War Powers Resolution, below
War Powers Resolution
      Generally, 192 et seq., 231 et seq.
    Consultation, 234 et seq.
    Reporting, 235 et seq.
    Sixty-day cutoff, 236 et seq.

NATIONAL SECURITY ACT OF 1947
Intelligence operations, 249 et seq.

NECESSARY AND PROPER CLAUSE
Congress's foreign relations power, 79 et seq.

NEGOTIATIONS
    Generally, 64 et seq.
Settlement of treaty dispute by negotiation, 110

NON-SELF EXECUTING TREATIES
Formal international law, 153, 162 et seq.

OFFICIALS
Executive branch departments, definition and creation of by
    Congress, 81
President's foreign relations power, appointment and removal of
    officials, 48 et seq.

ORIGINAL INTENT
Military force, 200 et seq.
President's foreign relations power, constitutional interpretation
    theory, 27 et seq.

PREEMPTION
Treaties, constitutional allocation of treaty power to federal
    government and denial to states, 110

PRESIDENTIAL-EXECUTIVE AGREEMENTS
Formal international law, 114, 115, 131 et seq.

PRESIDENT'S FOREIGN RELATIONS POWER
Absence of specific constitutional provision as to authority to
    conduct foreign relations, 10
Aliens, excluding aliens not covered by act of Congress, 70
Appointment and removal of officials and diplomats, 48 et seq.
Article II, vesting executive power in president, 12 et seq.
Articles of Confederation, revolution and, 21 et seq.
Basis of president's power, Eighteenth Century context and
        methods of constitutional interpretation
    Generally, 10 et seq.
    Absence of specific provision as to authority to conduct for-
        eign relations, 10
    Article II, vesting executive power in president, 12 et seq.
    Articles of Confederation, revolution and, 21 et seq.
    Bibliographic note, 45 et seq.
    Blackstone's Commentaries on Law, 18 et seq.
    Constitutional Convention, 24 et seq.
    Eighteenth Century context, 13 et seq.
    Executive power, Eighteenth Century context, 13 et seq.
    Functionalism, 34 et seq.
    Historical practice, 31 et seq.
    Interpretation theories
        Functionalism, 34 et seq.
        Historical practice, 31 et seq.
        Original intent, 27 et seq.
    Locke, views of John Locke, 16 et seq.

PRESIDENT'S FOREIGN RELATIONS POWER—Cont'd
Basis of president's power—Cont'd
    Original intent, 27 et seq.
    Revolution and Articles of Confederation, 21 et seq.
    Vesting clause, Article II, 12 et seq.
Bibliographic notes, 45 et seq., 78
Blackstone's Commentaries on Law, 18 et seq.
Classification of information, 76, 77
Communicating with foreign governments, 59 et seq.
Constitution. Basis of president's power, Eighteenth Century
        context and methods of constitutional interpretation,
        above
Constitutional Convention, 24 et seq.
Customary International Law, this index
Diplomatic relations, establishment of, 56 et seq.
Diplomats, appointment and removal of, 48 et seq.
Domestic law, 71
Eighteenth Century context, 13 et seq.
Establishment of diplomatic relations, 56 et seq.
Executive power, Eighteenth Century context, 13 et seq.
Executive privilege, 72 et seq.
Foreign vessels, excluding, 70
Freedom of Information Act requests, 73, 74
Functionalism, 34 et seq.
Government, recognition of, 55 et seq.
Historical practice, 31 et seq.
International agreements, 70
Interpretation theories. Basis of president's power, Eighteenth
        Century context and methods of constitutional interpreta-
        tion, above
Locke, views of John Locke, 16 et seq.
Military, president's Commander-in-Chief power, 11
Officials, appointment and removal of, 48 et seq.
Original intent, 27 et seq.
Recognition of government, 55 et seq.
Recognition of statehood, 51 et seq.
Revolution and Articles of Confederation, 21 et seq.
Statehood recognition, 51 et seq.
Substantive content
        Generally, 47 et seq.
    Aliens, excluding aliens not covered by act of Congress, 70
    Appointment and removal of officials and diplomats, 48 et
        seq.
    Bibliographic note, 78
    Classification of information, 76, 77

PRESIDENT'S FOREIGN RELATIONS POWER—Cont'd
Substantive content—Cont'd
    Communicating with foreign governments, 59 et seq.
    Diplomatic relations, establishment of, 56 et seq.
    Diplomats, appointment and removal of, 48 et seq.
    Domestic law, 71
    Establishment of diplomatic relations, 56 et seq.
    Executive privilege, 72 et seq.
    Foreign vessels, excluding, 70
    Freedom of Information Act requests, 73, 74
    Government, recognition of, 55 et seq.
    International agreements, 70
    Officials, appointment and removal of, 48 et seq.
    Recognition of government, 55 et seq.
    Recognition of statehood, 51 et seq.
    Statehood recognition, 51 et seq.
Treaties, this index
Vesting clause, Article II, 12 et seq.

RECOGNITION
Government, president's foreign relations power, 55 et seq.
State, president's foreign relations power, 51 et seq.

SELF EXECUTING TREATIES
Formal international law, 153 et seq.

SEPTEMBER 11 ATTACKS
    Generally, 260 et seq.
Bibliographic note, 278 et seq.
Captured prisoners, status, 269 et seq.
Executive order banning assassinations, 266
Joint resolution of Congress, 264 et seq.
Justification for unilateral response, 263 et seq.
Tribunals, 272 et seq.
War crimes, 278 et seq.

SHIPS AND SHIPPING
President's foreign relations power to exclude foreign vessels, 70

STATE PRACTICE
Customary International Law, above

STATES
Estrada doctrine, government recognition, 52 et seq.
Requirements under international law to qualify as state, 52 et
    seq.
Tibet, state recognition, 52 et seq.

STATUTORY CONSTRUCTION
Treaties, this index

TARIFFS
Congress's foreign relations power, 79

TAXES
Congress's foreign relations power, 79

TERRORISM
September 11 Attacks, this index

TREATIES
Generally, 109 et seq.
Article II of Constitution
    Derivative authority from earlier Article II treaty, 114
    Treaties submitted to Senate for ratification, 111, 113, 115 et
        seq.
Article VI of Constitution, 152
Case-Zablocki Act, 134
Conditions
    Article II ratification subject to conditions, 111, 117 et seq.
    Domestic effect of Senate conditions to treaty ratifications,
        166 et seq.
Congressional-executive agreements, 113, 122 et seq.
Customary International Law, this index
Derivative authority from earlier Article II treaty, 114
Domestic effects of treaties
    Generally, 109, 152 et seq.
    Article VI of Constitution, 152
    Indirect impacts of treaties, 176 et seq.
    Non-self executing treaties, 153, 162 et seq.
    Presumptions. Statutory construction, below
    Restatement (Third) of Foreign Relations Law, 157 et seq.
    Self executing treaties, 153 et seq.
    Statutory construction
        Congress presumed not to violate international law, 174
        Congressional acts presumed to apply on within United
            States, 175
Federal preemption, constitutional allocation of treaty power to
        federal government and denial to states, 110
Indirect impacts of treaties, 176 et seq.
International Court of Justice, 110
Interpretation of treaties, 140 et seq.
Negotiation, settlement of treaty dispute by, 110
Non-self executing treaties, 153, 162 et seq.

TREATIES—Cont'd
Presidential procedures to obtain domestic law to bring treaty
into force
Generally, 111, 113 et seq.
Article II treaties submitted to Senate for ratification, 111,
113, 115 et seq.
Congressional-executive agreements, 113, 122 et seq.
Derivative authority from earlier Article II treaty, 114
Presidential-executive agreements, 114, 115, 131 et seq.
Presidential-executive agreements, 114, 115, 131 et seq.
Presumptions. Domestic effects of treaties, above
Restatement (Third) of Foreign Relations Law, 157 et seq.
Self executing treaties, 153 et seq.
States, constitutional allocation of treaty power to federal gov-
ernment and denial to states, 110
Statutory construction. Domestic effects of treaties, above
Termination of treaties, 148 et seq.

U.N. PEACEKEEPING
Military force, 243 et seq.

VESTING CLAUSE
Article II of Constitution, this index

VIETNAM WAR
Military force, 217 et seq.

WAR
Military Force And Intelligence Operations, this index

WAR POWERS RESOLUTION
Military Force and Intelligence Operations, this index

†